Oregon 1859

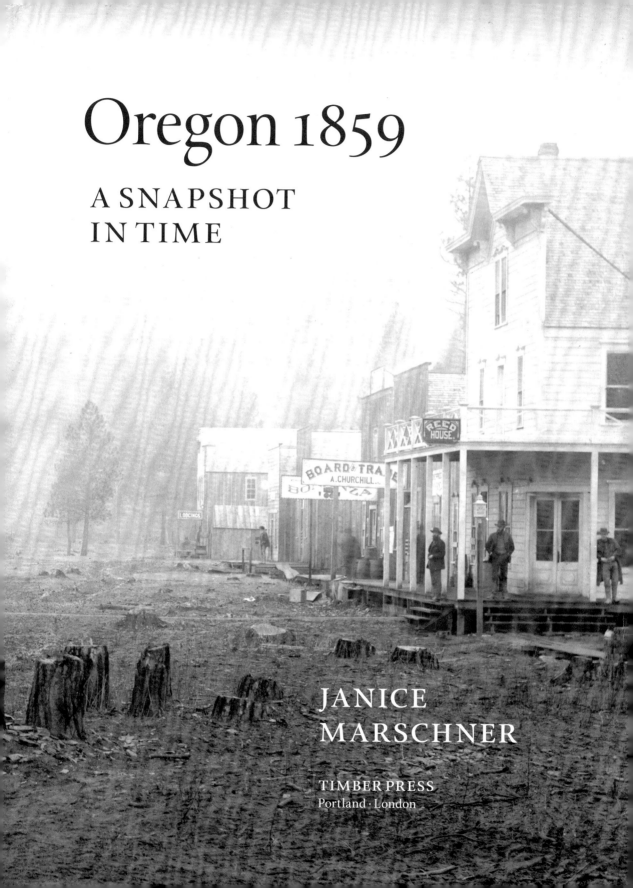

Oregon 1859

A SNAPSHOT
IN TIME

JANICE
MARSCHNER

TIMBER PRESS
Portland · London

To my late parents, Arnold and Marie Nelson,
who were born and raised in Eugene, Oregon.
I am grateful that they introduced me
at a young age to the beauty of Oregon.

Frontispiece: "Little Stumptown," ca. 1858, was the derisive nick-
name pinned on Portland by proprietors of rival townsites referring to the tree stumps that remained at the edge of town even
after development was underway. At one point the stumps were
whitewashed to prevent tripping accidents after dark. Courtesy
of Fritz and Denise von Tagen.

Maps by Allan Cartography, Medford, Oregon

Published in 2008 by Timber Press, Inc.

The Haseltine Building
133 S.W. Second Avenue, Suite 450
Portland, Oregon 97204-3527
www.timberpress.com

2 The Quadrant
135 Salusbury Road
London NW6 6RJ
www.timberpress.co.uk

Designed by Susan Applegate
Printed in China

Library of Congress Cataloging-in-Publication Data

Marschner, Janice.
  Oregon 1859: a snapshot in time/Janice Marschner.
    p. cm.
  Includes bibliographical references and index.
  ISBN-13: 978-0-88192-873-0
  1. Oregon—History—To 1859. I. Title.
  F880.M34 2008
  979.4′04—dc22   2007036182

Contents

Oregon, 1859

Oregon, present day

Oregon Counties Then and Now

1859 COUNTIES	PRESENT-DAY COUNTIES
Benton	Benton
	Lincoln (southern portion)
Clackamas	Clackamas
Clatsop	Clatsop
Columbia	Columbia
Coos	Coos
Curry	Curry
Douglas	Douglas
Jackson	Jackson
Josephine	Josephine
Lane	Lane
Linn	Linn
Marion	Marion
Multnomah	Multnomah
Polk	Polk
Tillamook	Tillamook
	Lincoln (northern portion)
Umpqua	Douglas
Wasco	Wasco
	Baker
	Crook
	Deschutes
	Gilliam
	Grant
	Harney
	Hood River
	Jefferson
	Klamath
	Lake
	Malheur
	Morrow
	Sherman
	Umatilla
	Union
	Wallowa
	Wheeler
Washington	Washington
Yamhill	Yamhill

Preface

Tall fir trees swayed in stiff breezes as a fresh March storm rolled in off the Pacific. A lone rider on horseback galloped up the muddy road from the harbor, waving his hat furiously in a celebratory gesture, hollering to anyone and everyone: "Oregon statehood! The state of Oregon!"

A small crowd gathered around the excited messenger. Merchants and customers abandoned the stores. The brawny blacksmith held a still-sizzling horseshoe with smoking tongs. Children ran toward the commotion, laughing and chattering.

"Hurrah! Hurrah!" Cheers resounded. The townsfolk eagerly slapped each other on the back and thrust their fists skyward.

The celebration was beginning. As one Oregonian noted in his diary that day: "The 'Brass Band' played Hail Columbia, Yankee Doodle, a quantity of powder and whiskey was consumed on the occasion."

It had taken over a month for the official word to arrive from Washington, D.C.: Oregon was the 33rd state in the Union. The news would spread rapidly along trails, roads, and rivers and through meadows and forest-covered mountains. A new chapter in Oregon history was unfolding. The year was 1859.

As Oregonians commemorate 150 years of statehood, it is an opportunity to explore state history—its first inhabitants, the early pioneers, and the major events that occurred before 1860. This book is a concise overview of that era—for history buffs and casual readers alike. Countless Oregon history books precede this one—comprehensive volumes that deal with the entire state over a period of time exceeding 100 years and regional titles that focus on local history in great detail. I hope many topics touched upon in this book will encourage readers to refer to a few of these books and to the many interesting Web sites available online. Others may want to conduct their own research on a particular subject. An abundance of information is available that could not be included in *Oregon 1859* without going beyond the intended scope of the book.

The book's introduction is essential to understanding each of the individual chapters, which correspond to the state's original 19 counties. These county chapters also build upon one another. The maps detail the county boundaries approximately as they existed in 1859 and the towns that had been established. Some communities established after 1859 are noted in a contrasting color to provide present-day reference points.

The lists of sites to visit in each county make this book a useful travel companion. Many of the museums are closed during the winter months, but most are willing to open by appointment. Some sites listed are private residences; please respect the privacy of the homeowners and tenants.

The order of the towns discussed in each chapter corresponds to a geographical movement through the county, but the discussion always starts with the 1859 county seat. For example, in the Benton County chapter I first discuss Corvallis and then move south to discuss Monroe, Bellfountain, and Alpine; move west to discuss the Alsea and Lobster valleys; move north to discuss Philomath, Fort Hoskins, and Kings Valley; and, finally, east to include the Adair Village area.

Tables list a sampling of family surnames of pioneers living in the various regions. They are the source of many of Oregon's place names and may be a useful tool for genealogists. The surnames selected are families and individuals who remained in the area, according to the 1860 U.S. Census. People believed to still have been residing in a particular town but who could not be located in the census have a "(?)" after their names. The 1860 census also included hundreds of names not mentioned in the accounts about the earliest pioneers, because there were many new settlers arriving in Oregon after it became a state in 1859.

The many differing accounts of people and events often made conducting the research for this book challenging. Because my intent in writing this book was not to unearth new information but merely to present an overview of the period, I have arrived at reasoned conclusions when conflicting dates and facts were encountered. I do not wish to perpetuate any erroneous information that future researchers will have to decipher. I take full responsibility for any inaccuracies that may still exist despite my best efforts.

Several books were especially helpful in my research: *Atlas of Oregon* published by the University of Oregon Press; *Dictionary of Oregon History* edited by Howard McKinley Corning; *Uncertain Encounters: Indians and Whites at*

Peace and War in Southern Oregon: 1820s to 1860s by Nathan Douthit; *That Balance So Rare: The Story of Oregon* by Terence O'Donnell; *Oregon's Promise: An Interpretive History* by David Peterson Del Mar; and several of Stephen Dow Beckham's works. The numerous regional history books, many written by local residents, added the perspective necessary to appreciate the uniqueness or similarities of the various pioneer communities.

I am extremely grateful to the historical societies and libraries that assisted me in acquiring the photographs that help tell the story of Oregon in the early days—its personalities and structures. Among those who helped with this process were Timothy Backer (Oregon State Archives); Merrialyce Blanchard (Oregon State Library); Gerald Brenneman (Albany Regional Museum); Charlene Buckley (Clackamas County Historical Society); Marian Charriere (Baker Cabin Historical Society); Larry Cole (Clatskanie Historical Society); Hannah Contino (Coos Historical & Maritime Museum); Linda Ellsworth (Monteith Historical Society); Ruby Fry-Matson (Tillamook County Pioneer Museum); Camila Gabaldon (Western Oregon University Archives); Mary Gallagher (Benton County Historical Society & Museum); Elizabeth Hughes, Cynthia Thiessen, and Kari Rolston (Salem Public Library); Claire Kellogg (Lake Oswego Library); Utahna Kerr (Gresham Historical Society); Jennifer Kozik and Winn Herrschaft (Washington County Historical Society); Virginie Laflamme (Library and Archives Canada); Lawrence Landis (Oregon State University Archives); Lesli Larson (University of Oregon); Larry McClure and Janice Kane (Tualatin Historical Society); Lucy McLean (Pittock Mansion); Elaine Miller (Washington State Historical Society); Jena Mitchell (Douglas County Museum); Connie Nice (Hood River County Historical Museum); Evaline Patt (Museum at Warm Springs); Cheryl Roffe (Lane County Historical Museum); Carol Samuelson (Southern Oregon Historical Society); Rose Scott (Josephine County Historical Society); Terry Skibby (on behalf of the Ashland Library Collection); Charles Smay (Polk County Historical Society); David Staton (Springfield Museum); Lisa Studts (Clatsop County Historical Society); Ross Sutherland (Marion County Historical Society); Gary Timms and Chenoweth Robertson (Linn County Museum); Alex Toth (Pacific University Library); Jodi Weeber (Lincoln County Historical Society); and finally, Lucy Berkley, Mikki Tint, and Evan Schneider at the Oregon Historical Society who provided the majority of the photographs following many hours of research.

Oregon Heritage Commission coordinator Kyle Jansson offered valuable advice and encouragement at the outset of this project. Richard Engeman, the former public historian for the Oregon Historical Society; Robert Kentta, the cultural resources director for the Confederated Tribes of Siletz; and Professor Stephen Dow Beckham, professor of history at Lewis & Clark College and author of numerous Oregon history books, generously took time out of their busy schedules to review my manuscript. Their suggested changes and enhancements were immensely appreciated. With his extensive research background, Professor Beckham's assistance in uncovering errors in existing historical assumptions by documenting actual data was invaluable.

Eve Goodman, editorial director at Timber Press, was a joy to work with throughout the entire process—quickly responding to my inquiries, providing encouragement and moral support, and offering superb editorial guidance. I also appreciate the skill and insight of Susan Applegate, Timber Press's art director, and the superb illustrative county maps created by Lawrence Andreas and his staff at Allan Cartography, based on their maps in *Atlas of Oregon*. Finally, applying her unique technical approach to the project, copyeditor Mary Johnson attended to the details of clarity and consistency, and accurately incorporated my numerous requested changes to the manuscript over a period of several months.

Special thanks are due to my dear friends Fritz and Denise von Tagen of West Linn for the hospitality they extended on my several visits to Oregon, and for sharing the "Little Stumptown" photograph from their collection. My cousin Anne Messenger of Beaverton provided research assistance.

Finally, I could not have completed this book without my husband, Jeff Marschner. Not only did he drive me around the entire state of Oregon, but upon our return home he provided tremendous support and assistance, allowing me to concentrate on writing. I am grateful for his superb editing skills in the final draft.

Oregon 1859

Introduction

After five years as a provisional government and eleven years as a U.S. territory, on February 14, 1859, Oregon became the 33rd state of the Union. The 1860 U.S. Census reported 52,465 residents, with only 16,564 of them native-born Oregonians. The Native American Indians were not counted in the census, but their estimated population of between 50,000 and 100,000 when Euro-Americans first arrived had been reduced by upward of 90 percent by 1850, mostly because of disease.

As Oregon commemorates its sesquicentennial—150 years of statehood—there will be much to reflect upon as citizens think about where the state has been and what lies ahead. A good place to begin is to examine the events that transpired after the arrival of Euro-Americans in the early 19th century, through and including the year of statehood. A focus on the individual residents and infrastructure that existed in each of the over 100 communities, townships, and cities established by 1859 throughout the 19 original counties will provide an appreciation of the sacrifices and accomplishments of Oregon's early pioneers.

The emigrants who endured months of hardship and suffering trudging across the plains and mountains or coming by ship around Cape Horn or the Isthmus of Panama survived because of physical health, personal faith, a desire for individual and family betterment, and occasionally, a bit of good fortune along the way. They were toughened by their journey and arrived in Oregon firmly convinced of the rewards of perseverance and hard work. After they settled in Oregon, these attributes fueled optimistic dreams that were the bedrock of the state's future. This is the uniqueness of Oregon that will be apparent in its year of statehood that is ever present today in cities, towns,

Champoeg Meeting, 1843. Oregon State Capitol Mural by Barry Faulkner. Courtesy of the Oregon State Archives.

and throughout the rural hamlets. No state in the country grew from hardier rootstock.

A Name for the State in Oregon Country

The derivation of the name "Oregon" is uncertain, but most agree that it is of Indian origin, perhaps with the Sautee or Chippewa branch of the Sioux, and that British Major Robert Rogers was the first to officially use a version of the name when, in 1765, he referred to the Columbia River as a "river called by the Indians Ouragon" in a petition for an exploration expedition. In 1778 Captain Jonathan Carver, an American, used the spelling of "Oregon" in referring to the same river written about by Rogers. Also, in 1817 poet William Cullen Bryant used "the Oregon" in a poem, after reading the account of Carver's travels. In 1822 U.S. Congressman John Floyd unsuccessfully urged Congress to consider creation of an "Origon Territory" and in 1829 Hall Jackson Kelley organized the American Society for Encouraging the Settlement of the Oregon Territory.

Until the Oregon Treaty of 1846 established a formal British-American border at the 49th parallel, the term Oregon Country referred to the region that today forms part of British Columbia and Alaska; all of Washington, Oregon, and Idaho; and parts of Montana and Wyoming. Since the late 18th century the region had been claimed by the United States, Great Britain, France, Rus-

Timeline of Pre-1859 Oregon History

10,000 BC First Indians inhabit Oregon

1543 Spanish explorers sight Oregon coast near Rogue River

1602–1794 Exploration of Pacific Coast by Spanish, British, and Americans

1765 First use of name Ouragon by British Major Robert Rogers

1803 Louisiana Purchase expands U.S. Territory to Rocky Mountains

1805 Overland expedition of Lewis and Clark reaches mouth of Columbia River

1811 Fort Astoria founded by American John Jacob Astor's Pacific Fur Company

1819, 1824 Treaties with Spain and Russia set southern and northern boundaries of Oregon Country

1825 Fort Vancouver established by Hudson's Bay Company on north bank of Columbia River

1834 First Oregon Methodist mission established by Reverends Jason and Daniel Lee

1843 First American government (provisional) on Pacific Coast formed in Oregon

1846 U.S. and Great Britain agree to northern boundary of Oregon Country at 49th parallel

1848 Oregon Territory established by Congress on August 14

1850 Donation Land Act; increase in numbers of settlers and hostilities with Indians

1851 Gold discovered in southern Oregon—Rogue and Illinois valleys

1853 Washington Territory created north of Columbia River; signing of Oregon's first ratified Indian treaty created temporary reservation at Table Rock in Jackson County

1857 Constitutional Convention held in Salem; Constitution ratified by popular vote in November

1859 Oregon admitted to Union as 33rd state on February 14

sia, and Spain—based on mere visitations or commercial activities conducted in the area. The latter three countries eventually relinquished their claims through separate treaties with the other two countries between 1803 and 1824, but what was referred to as the "Oregon Question" was not finally settled until the 1846 treaty. (A clarification of the line separating Vancouver Island from the mainland was agreed upon in 1872.) With the boundary issues settled, "Manifest Destiny"—a political phrase coined in 1845 to express the belief that the United States was divinely inspired to spread democracy and freedom across North America—soon became the justification for settlement of the Oregon Country.

Early Oregon History Overview

Oregon's earliest known social and cultural history began sometime around 10,000 BC and consists of the chronicles of its diverse Indian population. Oregon's climate and natural food resources—fish, game, and assorted roots, bulbs, fruits, acorns, and other plant life—provided a plentiful supply of food throughout the year for its first human inhabitants. The Indians became highly skilled at hunting, gathering, harvesting, storing, and trading with other tribes of Indians, and later with the arriving Europeans and Americans. They also excelled in basketry, both for everyday purposes and as an art form. They managed the environment by setting fires to the grasslands and forests to encourage growth of food plants and plants used for household items, even driving the game animals to a common center area by burning in a circle.

Oregon Indians were skilled at building and handling canoes on the ocean and inland waters. The Columbia River was a major trade route used for canoe travel, and the smaller tributary rivers were used as connecting passages. The Indians maintained trails through the hills and valleys.

By the early 18th century, the northeastern Oregon Indians were raising herds of horses acquired from the Spanish, which allowed them to travel great distances to gather, hunt, and trade. Celilo Falls on the Columbia River, Willamette Falls on the Willamette, and the Grande Ronde Valley in present-day Union County were the main trading centers.

Housing was similar throughout western Oregon, consisting of dwellings constructed with cedar planks or excavations beneath frame-board structures covered with earth. On the plateaus a special kind of tent—a longhouse—was built out of lodge poles and resembled a tipi. In northeast-

Winter lodge of the Umpqua Indians.
Courtesy of the Oregon Historical Society,
OrHi 45809-A.

ern Oregon where tule grew in the marshy areas, tule mat tipis were the norm. Some tribes lived in one area during the winter and moved to another during the summer.

The Oregon coast was unknown to European explorers until 1543 when Spanish explorers sighted the coast near the Rogue River. Other Spanish, British, and American explorers and navigators, including Captain James Cook, sailed along the coast during the next two centuries, searching for a water route (the imaginary Northwest Passage or the River of the West) that would shorten the journey of commerce between the Atlantic and Pacific oceans. However, it was not until 1792 that U.S. Captain Robert Gray confirmed the existence of the great river, naming it after his ship *Columbia*. His action gave the United States the first claim to the Oregon Country. Between 1792 and 1794 the British Captain George Vancouver mapped the western coast of North America, naming many of Oregon's mountains, bays, and capes.

When European trading vessels began plying the Oregon coast in the late 18th century, the peaceful and self-sufficient existence enjoyed by the Indians living in the Oregon Country began to dwindle. The first negative effect was the exposure to new diseases, which took a heavy toll on the Indian population. They lacked acquired immunities to epidemic diseases such as smallpox, malaria, influenza, dysentery, and measles. These debilitating episodes continued into the 1850s and beyond.

Between 1805 and 1806 the Lewis and Clark Corps of Discovery journeyed through the newly purchased Louisiana Territory and beyond its western border at the Continental Divide to the Pacific Ocean. President Thomas Jefferson commissioned the expedition to strengthen American claims to the Oregon Country. Throughout the journey, Captain Meriwether Lewis and Captain William Clark took measures to avoid offending the Indians and developed trade relations and agreements for safe passage with many of them.

Soon thereafter, in response to the demand for furs in the European and Chinese markets, the British and American fur traders began arriving to establish trading posts and forts. (Furs were used for men's sheared beaver hats and for fur coats and fur-trimmed clothes for the wealthy. Sea otter pelts were especially prized in China.) Initially the Indians were friendly, hospitable, and quite generous, but once the fur companies began running trap lines on tribally maintained lands, the Indians began resisting.

In 1811 the Pacific Fur Company, owned and operated by New York merchant John Jacob Astor and four other partners, established Fort Astoria—the first American settlement on the Pacific Coast. The outbreak of the War of 1812 interrupted Astor's original goal of establishing a trading empire on the

West Coast, but his expeditions, especially the overland one led by Wilson Price Hunt and known by the same name, had a profound influence upon the future of Oregon. The earliest permanent Euro-American residents of Oregon were members of the Astor party who settled in the Willamette Valley; many of them influenced the decision to make the temporary government of the Oregon Country an American government rather than one under Great Britain.

The Hudson's Bay Company (HBC) had been established in Canada in 1670 and its fur trading activities extended as far south as California at one time. The company played a significant role in the history of Oregon, especially while Dr. John McLoughlin was the Chief Factor of Fort Vancouver. (The HBC, one of the oldest companies in the world, still operates retail stores throughout Canada.)

In 1825 Peter Skene Ogden, an explorer with the HBC, became the earliest known explorer of central Oregon, and three years later, Jedediah S. Smith, the most famous of the Mountain Men—independent fur trappers and traders who explored the American West in search of pelts and adventure—entered Oregon from California. He was the first American to travel the full length of Oregon on land. Smith and several other American and British fur traders

Astoria in 1813 when it was known as Fort George and was under Great Britain's control. Courtesy of the Oregon Historical Society, OrHi 21681.

Dr. John McLoughlin (1784–1857)

Born in Quebec; practiced medicine in Montreal

Became partner in North West Company and was instrumental in negotiating merger with HBC in 1821

Chief Factor of HBC between 1824 and 1846, first at Fort Astoria and then at Fort Vancouver after it was built in 1825

Established numerous trading forts and posts and under his management his district became company's most profitable North American district

Generally had good relations with Indians and was known to them as "White Headed Eagle"

Extended credit for food, seeds, and farm tools, and directed missionaries and settlers to Willamette Valley, thus defying HBC orders to discourage settlement

Secured, intentionally or unintentionally, for Americans most of territory previously under his control

Laid out Oregon City in 1842 and sold lots for nominal sum

Retired from HBC in 1846; paid HBC for title to land he had claimed in Oregon City for HBC in 1829

Donated land for schools, churches, and other public uses

Owned a general store, a granary, a gristmill, sawmills, and a shipping business

Became U.S. citizen in 1851, in part to squelch controversy surrounding his property rights, and served as mayor in same year

Lost portion of his Oregon City property anyway, some of which was returned to his heirs after his death

Married to Marguerite Wadin McKay; five children, one from previous relationship

Dr. John McLoughlin, designated the "Father of Oregon" in 1957 by the Oregon Legislative Assembly in recognition of his contributions to the early development of the Oregon Country. Courtesy of the Oregon Historical Society, OrHi 248.

contributed significantly to the knowledge about Oregon's coastline. By 1828 a number of former fur trading company employees and Mountain Men and their families began settling in the Willamette Valley.

In 1832 Captain Benjamin Louis Eulalie Bonneville, on leave from the U.S. Army, organized an expedition from Missouri to explore fur trade opportunities. Nathaniel J. Wyeth led two expeditions, one in 1832 and one in 1834, seeking colonization and trade opportunities. Hall Jackson Kelley led a party of members of his American Society for Encouraging the Settlement of the Oregon Territory to the Oregon Country in 1835.

Between 1838 and 1842, the U.S. Exploring Expedition—often referred to as the Wilkes Expedition because it was led by naval officer Charles Wilkes—explored along the entire Pacific Coast and throughout the South Pacific. The expedition garnered a wealth of scientific material about the Oregon Country. In 1843 John C. Frémont completed the first official survey of a transcontinental route, uniting his survey with Wilkes's and adding information about the topography and natural resources of the far West. Later, throughout the territorial period, others conducted surveys for a variety of purposes.

Establishment of Missions

The Oregon Country Indians were first exposed to Christianity through their contacts with the trading posts. French-Canadian Catholic priests arrived in 1839 to minister to the HBC employees. Also, some British Protestant and Catholic French-Canadian trappers took Indian wives—something the fur companies encouraged to strengthen trade relationships with the Indians.

Between 1834 and 1842 Methodist, Presbyterian, and Congregational churches sent missionaries to "civilize and Christianize" the Indians. Reverend Jason Lee, his nephew Reverend Daniel Lee, and several assistants were the first to arrive in 1834, having traveled with New England merchant Nathaniel J. Wyeth on his second trading expedition to the Oregon Country. At the urging of Dr. McLoughlin at Fort Vancouver, the missionaries selected a site at Mission Bottom northwest of present-day Salem on which to establish a mission and the Indian Manual Training School.

Two small groups of missionaries joined the original party in May and September of 1837. In 1838 Jason Lee returned to the East for two years to assist the Methodist Episcopal Missionary Society in recruiting additional ministers, doctors, teachers, tradesmen, and farmers from New England and Peoria, Illinois. Many of these missionaries and professionals—the group of pioneers historians have termed the Great Reinforcement—became permanent settlers and some became leaders in the formation of the provisional government.

Other branch missions were established by the Methodists at Wascopam, Clatsop, and Willamette Falls near the present-day sites of The Dalles, Astoria, and Oregon City, respectively.

Unfortunately, by 1842 most of the Indians living in the Willamette Valley had died from disease. With very few conversions, Reverend George Gary was appointed to replace Reverend Jason Lee in 1843, and soon thereafter the Methodist missions in western Oregon were closed. Two other missions had been founded in the Willamette Valley in 1840 and 1841 by the Congregationalists and Presbyterians, but these also failed.

Reverend Jason Lee, one of Oregon's first missionaries. Courtesy of the Oregon Historical Society, OrHi 8342-A.

One Jesuit mission was established by Father Francois Norbert Blanchet and Father Modeste Demers at St. Paul in Marion County in 1839. The Catholics were interested in ministering to the French-Canadian fur trappers, their Indian wives and children, and the other Indians. Saint Anne Mission was established by Father John B. Brouillett in 1847 along the Umatilla River near the foothills of the Blue Mountains in present-day Umatilla County.

Although all of the missions failed in their primary goal of converting the Indians to Christianity, they were instrumental in the settlement of Oregon and its journey to statehood—establishing the first settlements and churches; organizing the first schools (originally to instruct the Indians in religion and industrial arts, and later to educate their own children); sparking the Oregon emigration through their written and spoken descriptions of the Oregon Country disseminated in their recruitment efforts; welcoming and assisting the settlers making the great migration along the Oregon Trail; participating significantly in the creation of a provisional government; and incessantly urging the U.S. Congress to acquire authority over the Oregon Country for their own property protection and personal safety, as well as that of the other early pioneers.

Between 1836 and 1839 the American Board of Commissioners for Foreign Missions (ABCFM), which was jointly supported by Congregationalists, Presbyterians, and the Dutch Reformed Church, established four missions in the Oregon Country, but outside of present-day Oregon. One of the ABCFM missions—the Whitman Mission established by the New York Presbyterian physician Dr. Marcus Whitman on the Walla Walla River at Waiilatpu in Washington—deserves a place in Oregon history for these reasons: (1) thousands of settlers on their way to the Willamette Valley stopped there between 1843 and 1847 to obtain medical and repair services, as well as supplies for the final leg of their long journey to the Willamette Valley; and (2) the Whitman Mission was the site of the infamous Whitman Massacre of 1847, which was triggered by the Indians' distrust of Dr. Whitman, who saved American children during a measles epidemic, but was unable to cure the Indians because they lacked a natural immunity to the disease. The incident led to the Indian War of 1848–55, the first major Indian war in the Oregon Country, and also prompted the U.S. Congress to make Oregon a U.S. territory.

"Oregon Fever" and its Impact on the Indians

"Oregon Fever" erupted during the 1840s. In addition to the incidental actions of the missionaries that promoted Oregon settlement, other factors contributed to the surge of settlers, including the following:

The journals of the Lewis and Clark Expedition and other journals and newspaper articles, scientific reports, and books published by fur traders, explorers, government agents, and eminent authors stimulated interest in the Oregon Country. New York author Washington Irving's 1837 publication of *Adventures of Captain Bonneville, U.S.A., in the Rocky Mountains and the Far West* was widely read. Guidebooks such as Lansford W. Hastings's *The Emigrants' Guide to Oregon and California,* first published in 1845, provided practical advice. Letters written home by the earliest pioneers describing the agricultural and economic potential of the Willamette Valley were also persuasive. Some settlers returned home to persuade their families and friends to emigrate.

Emigration societies such as the American Society for Encouraging the Settlement of the Oregon Territory and the Oregon Provisional Emigrating Society were established throughout the United States to encourage and organize emigration. Public lectures were held and eastern newspapers published articles about the meetings.

The lure of the Oregon Country was the hope of a better life. The notion that Oregon was a sort of Eden probably originated with a journal entry of Gabriel Franchère, one of John Jacob Astor's men sent to Astoria in 1811, who wrote: "We imagined ourselves in the Garden of Eden."

The reasons people came to Oregon depended on where they were from or the nature of their personal circumstances. Those from the Mississippi, Missouri, and Ohio river valleys were escaping the economic downturn and the prevalence of disease and infections caused by years of periodic flooding in the bottomlands. Disease was also a concern on the East Coast, and the economic Panic of 1837 resulted in the failure of banks and record unemployment for five years. The collapse of the international fur trade in 1839 and falling crop prices produced further economic suffering.

People from parts of the Midwest were motivated for different reasons. Rapid settlement of this region had occurred, triggering a virtual real estate boom. Many decided to sell their farms for a profit and use their equity to move up because the land in Oregon would be free under the Donation Land Act.

Before the Oregon Country boundary issues were settled with the British in 1846, some were encouraged to come for patriotic reasons. There was concern that if Americans did not claim the valuable farmland and vast forests, the British would. Settlements in the Oregon Country would help justify America's claim to the land.

After the discovery of gold in southern Oregon in the 1850s, fortune hunters chose the Oregon Territory as a new place to seek adventure; few of the miners intended to stay. Some families tended to move westward every five or ten years in search of a better life. And a few came to Oregon for less honorable reasons—trying to evade debt or escape the law.

Other circumstances brought people to Oregon. A few blacks accompanied their southern owners to Oregon. Slavery had been declared illegal in Oregon in 1848, but some blacks chose to remain with their families to work as servants or farm laborers. Others lived independently, working as common laborers, barbers, cooks, blacksmiths, or washerwomen. The 1860 U.S. Census counted 128 blacks in Oregon.

Hundreds of Chinese immigrants arrived in California following the discovery of gold in 1848. They were escaping the opium wars and Taiping Rebellion, as well as droughts, floods, and inflation in China. Most intended to return to China after they made their fortunes and conditions improved in their homeland. After gold was discovered in southern Oregon, some Chinese miners ventured across the California-Oregon border to avoid the Foreign Miners Tax imposed on them in 1850 by the California Legislature. The 1860

The west side of Front Street, south of Morrison, in Portland. In 1851 the first Chinese immigrants arrived by ship, many establishing wash houses such as the Hop Wo Laundry on Front Street. Courtesy of the Oregon Historical Society, OrHi 51930.

U.S. Census counted 425 Chinese living in Oregon. Kanakas from the Sandwich Islands (Hawaii) came to Oregon under similar circumstances, first having come to California during the gold rush. Others may have migrated south from Fort Vancouver in Washington, where they had been working for the HBC since the 1830s.

Many Europeans immigrated to the United States and to California after 1848 to escape undesirable conditions in their homelands—especially revolutions throughout the European continent and the potato famine in Ireland. Some of these immigrants eventually made their way to Oregon.

All of these groups contributed to Oregon's early development, but were not always readily accepted. Common perils and the travails of life faced by all often served to bridge differences.

The contagion of "Oregon Fever" and the arrival of the large wagon trains of settlers from 1843 on led to strained Indian-settler relations. Although the U.S. Congress had passed the Northwest Ordinance in 1787—the Utmost Good Faith Law designed to protect the rights of Native American Indians—

this law was not extended to Oregon until 1848 when the Organic Act created the territory.

The earliest Oregon settlers acquired their land by squatting upon the Indians' land, sometimes offering items in trade, but never filing legal claims for the land. In 1843 the provisional government passed the Law of Land Claims, an act allowing land claims of 640 acres. Amendments and a second land law were passed in 1844 changing certain requirements and benefits. The first federal law applying to the Oregon Territory was the Federal Territorial Act of 1848, which declared the land provisions of the provisional government to be null and void. Consequently, for two years no land laws were in effect until U.S. senators Thomas Hart Benton and Lewis F. Linn of Missouri wrote the Donation Land Act of 1850, which became the greatest inducement for emigration to Oregon, including many from California who had come west for the gold rush the year before.

The Organic Act of 1848 had confirmed all Indian land titles in the territory, pending their resolution by treaty, but since no treaties were in effect when the U.S. Congress passed the Donation Land Act in 1850, settlers were granted free land with no provision for its purchase from the Indians. By 1855 a total of 15 treaties were negotiated, establishing compacts with every tribe in western Oregon and the people of the northern tribes of central and eastern Oregon. However, six of the earliest treaties were never ratified by the U.S. Senate, primarily because there was no provision requiring that the Indians be moved east of the Cascade Range.

Further confusion about Indian land rights arose later when advertisements in Oregon newspapers stated erroneously that any land not included in an Indian reservation was open for settlement. Settlers often unwittingly moved onto Indian lands and began staking claims to land even as Indians were living on it. Many Indians were ruthlessly and viciously driven off their ancestral property. Increasingly, localized Indian uprisings erupted in different areas of the Oregon Territory in response to the continuing settler intrusion, which inevitably resulted in the depletion of natural resources, the disruption of the Indians' tribal hunting and gathering grounds, exposure to fatal diseases, and frequent physical abuse by lawless settlers.

The discovery of gold in southern Oregon was the final event that pushed the Rogue Indians in southern Oregon into war. The miners left the streams so muddy that the Indians could not fish. Many miners mistreated and took advantage of the Indian women in the area. The Rogue River Indian War was fought intermittently between 1850 and 1856, at which time the tribes agreed to stop fighting and move to the Coast Reservation, which, through an act of

Congress in 1875, became the Siletz Reservation on the significantly reduced reservation lands remaining at the time. (The Yakima Indian War of 1855–58 was fought partially on Oregon soil, and other Indian wars were fought in the West after 1859—two in Oregon and one just south of the Oregon-California border.)

The reservation system was initiated in 1853 by Superintendent of Indian Affairs General Joel Palmer, purportedly to protect the Indians from the settlers, and by 1858, under the terms of the various treaties, nearly all of the surviving Indians in western and parts of central Oregon were removed to reservations. The tribes east of the Cascades retained their rights to fish, hunt, and gather other natural foods off the reservations, but the tribes west of the Cascades did not. The self-sufficient economies and traditional customs of all of the Indians suffered irreparable harm.

The Indians entered into the treaties being assured that the reservation boundaries were permanent and that reservation life would provide for their sustenance. Some of the treaties were never ratified and the Superintendent of Indian Affairs was unable to provide the promised goods and services and those that were provided were of poor quality. The Indians suffered from starvation, disease, and cruel treatment by the military guards.

After 1860 the settlers started becoming interested in portions of the reservation lands for fisheries, wheat production, and livestock grazing. Subsequent treaties, federal legislation, and executive orders incrementally reduced the size of most of the reservations, usually with little or no compensation.

Oregon's Indians have persevered in their efforts to retain their culture over the past 150 years, despite disparate federal policies. Between the 1870s and 1960 the U.S. Congress instituted policies designed to encourage the Indians to move from the reservations and assimilate into nearby communities. In 1961 the policy changed to one of self-determination and empowering them to become sovereign nations governing their own lands, resources, and members. (To learn more about the events that transpired after 1859, view the Web sites of the individual confederated tribes or obtain a copy of "A Travel Guide to Indian Country" available at most visitor centers in Oregon.)

Oregon's Indian heritage is ever present today in its place names. However, few of the names are spelled exactly the way the Indians pronounced them, and over the years the English spelling of many of the proper names has varied. For example, variations of "Kalapuya" include "Calapooya," as in Calapooya Creek, and "Calapooia," as in Calapooia River.

The Oregon Trail and Other Routes to Oregon

The majority of Oregon's pioneers arrived by way of the Oregon Trail, which stretched 2000 miles between Independence, Missouri, and the Willamette Valley, requiring four to five months to traverse. The official starting point was Independence, but for each family making the journey it really began from their hometown or last place of residence. The overland trail ended at The Dalles, but it was still another 100 miles to the Willamette Valley. At The Dalles the emigrants built rafts to transport their wagons down the Columbia and Willamette rivers. Navigation through swirling rapids was dangerous, so some hired skilled Indians or commercial ferrymen.

The pioneers' covered wagons were mere farm wagons with canvas stretched over a framework of hoop slats to shelter their tools, food, and a few family heirlooms. Often it became necessary to discard the heavier items along the trail in order to lighten the load. People rarely rode inside the wagons for lack of room, unless they were deathly ill. The term prairie schooner referred to the similarity of the canvas coverings (bonnets) to the sails of ships.

The first non-missionary settlers to travel the Oregon Trail were a portion of the 1841 Bidwell-Bartelson party headed for California, who opted at Fort

Some Oregon Trail emigrants rode by sailing scows down the Columbia River. Courtesy of the Oregon Historical Society, OrHi 3080.

Hall (in present-day Idaho) to instead head for Oregon. The next year the newly appointed Indian sub-agent to Oregon, Dr. Elijah White, led over 100 emigrants to Oregon. The Burnett-Nesmith-Applegate party, a party of over 800, arrived in the Willamette Valley in 1843, becoming known as the Great Migration. Other early parties included those of Samuel K. Barlow, Stephen H. L. Meek, and Joel Palmer. Each part of the trail had its challenges and one out of ten people did not survive, typically succumbing to disease, injury, or snake bites. Cholera, the cause of which was not scientifically known until 1854, killed more travelers than anything else.

The earliest pioneers generally found the Indians they met along the way to be friendly and generous, helping them herd cattle and horses across the rivers and trading salmon, vegetables, and fruit for stock and manufactured goods from the pioneers. Many more lives would have been lost without the assistance of the Indians. Following the Whitman Massacre in 1847, travel along the Oregon Trail subsided until soldiers were enlisted to provide protection in 1850. The two Indian wars between 1855 and 1858, although fought north and south of the Oregon Trail, caused another lull in emigration until most of the Indians were forced to move onto reservations.

By 1859 the travails experienced by the earliest pioneers were lessened by the advent of trading posts, government forts, and new and improved guide books, like *The Prairie Traveler: A Handbook of Overland Expedition* written by Randolph B. Marcy and published in New York.

In 1846 Samuel K. Barlow and several partners built a toll road—the Barlow Road—around the south side of Mount Hood, providing an overland route to the Willamette Valley and avoiding the treacherous rapids on the Columbia River. Seventy-five percent of the pioneers used this route, which was called a road even though it was only a narrow rock and dirt trail, much of it based on Indian trails. Those without the toll of $5.00 per wagon and $0.10 per each head of livestock signed IOUs, but many never fulfilled their promise to pay.

In response to a tragic family drowning that occurred on the Columbia River in 1843, two members of the Applegate family, Lindsay and Jesse, along with Levi Scott and ten others, established a southern route for the Oregon Trail in 1846. Near Fort Hall, Idaho, the Southern Emigrant Route, today known as the Applegate Trail, proceeded south on the California Trail until it intersected the Humboldt River in present-day Nevada. It then headed northwest through northeastern California and north through the southwestern valleys of Oregon to the Willamette Valley. The Applegate Trail was slow to gain acceptance, especially since initially the trail had not been cleared for

Camp scene, crossing the Great Plains from 1843 to 1859.
Courtesy of the Oregon Historical Society, OrHi 6536.

Samuel K. Barlow, pioneer road builder
and resident of Oregon City. Courtesy of
the Oregon Historical Society, OrHi 3445.

wagons, but it spared the settlers from the dangers of the Columbia River and
it finally made southern Oregon accessible for them.

Another branch of the Oregon Trail opened in 1854 after nine years of
unsuccessful attempts to find a middle route from the Malheur River in present-day Malheur County to Eugene in Lane County. It became known as the
Meek-Elliott-Macy route because wagon trains led by Stephen H. L. Meek in
1845, Elijah Elliott in 1853, and William Macy in 1854 blazed various portions
of the new route, also known as the Free Emigrant Road.

Each person who attempted the perilous journey on the Oregon Trail,
regardless of whether they arrived at their intended destination, deserves
utmost admiration for what they endured. Settlers continued to make the
long and arduous trip through the 1880s. However, with completion of the
transcontinental railroad in 1869, most families took the train to San Francisco and then boarded a ship for travel up the coast to Oregon. Of the estimated 315,000 emigrants who crossed the Great Plains between 1843 and
1860, approximately 65,000 settled in Oregon. (In 1978 the U.S. Congress
designated the 2000-mile trail as the National Historic Oregon Trail. Today
the trail is marked on public lands by concrete pillars and dark brown posts.
There are 50 interpretive sites along the Oregon Trail's 547 miles in the state
of Oregon, including Oregon Trail kiosks at every major rest stop along Interstate 84 between Oregon and the Idaho border.)

Finally, some settlers arrived by ship, including the missionaries in the
late 1830s and early 1840s. Skilled Chinook Indian river pilots were regularly

employed to guide ships up the Columbia from its mouth, avoiding dangerous sand spits and gravel bars.

The majority of the emigrants arriving by ship were from the Atlantic states as it made more sense to sail around Cape Horn or take the route across the Isthmus of Panama rather than travel from the coast to Missouri to begin the journey across the plains. Upon reaching the Pacific Ocean, they sailed up the coast, stopping at San Francisco. Some investigated the prospects in California first before making their way to Oregon, but most intending to settle in Oregon sailed on to Portland. If the gold in southern Oregon was the lure, they landed at Crescent City in northern California, Port Orford in Curry County, or Coos Bay in Coos County. Unlike the Oregon Trail pioneers, who mostly were farmers, the emigrants who arrived by ship were primarily New England merchants who came with money and merchandise to establish stores, many becoming Oregon's town founders by taking land claims and selling platted land to develop commercial centers.

Settling the Oregon Country

The first settlements in Oregon were located between the future sites of Oregon City and Salem in the Willamette Valley, as well as in the Tualatin Valley. Joseph L. Meek, Robert Newell, and Caleb Wilkins were among the former fur traders and Mountain Men already living in the Oregon Country when the settlers arrived by wagon train. Some had families as a result of their marriages to Indian women.

Ewing Young was an important early settler. In 1837, with the assistance of William A. Slacum, he organized the Willamette Cattle Company to import cattle from California, thus breaking the cattle monopoly of the HBC. In 1838, on his land claim in the Chehalem Valley in Yamhill County, he built and operated the first independent sawmill in the Northwest and, according to the Yamhill County Historical Society, he also built a whiskey distillery. He died three years later, at the young age of 31. Because he left no heirs, his neighbors gathered to settle his estate. It was at these meetings that the formation of the Oregon provisional government first came under discussion.

The first claims taken in the Willamette and surrounding valleys were generally on sites near a year-round water source, especially those that would be suitable for operation of a mill or ferry. It was also desirable to have good farmland and a nearby wooded area for a source of fuel and building material. When available land became scarce, settlement spread out beyond the Willamette Valley, but generally only as far as the Coast Range to the west and the Cascade Range to the east.

With passage of the Donation Land Act in 1850, single men over the age of eighteen were granted 320 acres of land or 640 acres if they were married—and if they lived on and made improvements to the property for four consecutive years. Those men over the age of 21 who emigrated and settled in the Oregon Territory after 1850 were granted 160 acres if single, or 320 acres if married. One half of the claim of married couples was held by the wife, a right rarely allowed anywhere in the world at the time. Because there were few single adult women available, many men married Indian women or teenage or pre-teen girls to qualify for the larger land grant. Often the young bride remained with her family until she was old enough to join her husband. Eventually, however, with the increase in the number of emigrants arriving, more adult women became available and the need for teenage wives diminished.

The Donation Land Act also provided that public land could be purchased at the General Land Office for $1.25 an acre, which was the standard price of public land elsewhere in the country. Some of the later arrivals purchased squatter's rights from those who had arrived before 1850. (In 1862 Congress passed the first Homestead Act, which provided for grants of 160 acres of public land after payment of a small registration fee and completion of a five-year residence requirement. This was the impetus for the later settlement of central and eastern Oregon.)

The Donation Land Act required the surveyor general to survey the Oregon Territory for formal land claims. In 1851 the first surveyor general of Oregon, John B. Preston, established the Willamette Meridian, located northwest of Portland, which is the point from which all lands in Oregon and Washington were surveyed. Settlers who completed the filing process with the General Land Office became the legal owners. The first land office west of the Rocky Mountains was established in Oregon City; in subsequent years offices were established in other locales. Land changed hands frequently and many claims were subdivided as more and more families arrived and needed land. As children became adults and needed a place to start their own households, their parents divided their property into inheritances.

After choosing their land claims and stocking up on supplies in Oregon City, the settlers traveled to their claim, built a makeshift shelter, gathered fuel for cooking and heating, and planted a vegetable garden. Before they could start their farms they had to clear the land and plow the fields for growing wheat, oats, barley, or hay, and grazing livestock. Some pioneers brought fruit grafts across the plains for orchards, but others purchased nursery stock from nurserymen like the Luelling brothers of Milwaukie in Clackamas County.

The families arriving in areas where the Indians had been wiped out by disease or removed to reservations had a more difficult time clearing their claims because, with the Indians no longer burning the valley floors, the land was thick with oaks and firs. It sometimes took years of continuous cutting, burning, and decay to clear the land well enough to develop a productive farm.

Food preservation methods included smoking, drying, packing in salt, or curing in sugar, vinegar, and spices. Some communities had small trading posts where surplus farm produce could be traded for other necessities, but settlers in the more remote locations made periodic trips to the nearest town for supplies and needed services.

Usually the farmer with a mill was the first to map a townsite and sell lots. Almost every farmer had a second occupation to support his family—building houses, clearing farmland, planting crops, shoeing horses, making wooden barrels for food preservation, butchering livestock, tanning hides, teaching the children, conducting religious services, and so on.

Isolation nagged the settlers in the early days, with mail delivery extremely slow—transported across the Great Plains, around Cape Horn after 1851, or across the Isthmus of Panama after 1852. By 1859 there were 174 post offices; many were located in the postmasters' homes. Wells Fargo's Letter Express and Stuart Express Company delivered mail on horseback or by stage to communities that did not have a post office.

Many households had extended families and friends from their hometowns living nearby, which was comforting. A schoolhouse was often the first public structure built, and it also served as a worship and community center.

The story about Oregon's pioneers would not be complete without mentioning the industrious, self-reliant women and children who helped settle the Oregon Territory. Once a land claim was chosen and a makeshift dwelling built, men often left their families in charge of the homestead while they worked in a nearby town to earn much-needed cash; traveled to the gold fields in California or southern Oregon to try their luck; or fought in the Indian wars. Many fatherless families supplemented their income by offering meals and lodging to travelers, and marketing their handmade goods and surplus farm produce.

Peter H. Burnett, the Oregon pioneer who later became the first American governor of California, summed it up this way: "I never saw so fine a population as in Oregon. They were all honest, because there was nothing to steal; they were all sober, because there was no liquor to drink; there were no misers, because there was no money to hoard; and they were all industrious, because it was work or starve."

Discovery of Gold

When gold was first discovered in California in 1848 there was great concern in Oregon because so many of the new settlers departed seeking riches. But the Donation Land Act of 1850 and the miners' demand for wheat, fruit, meat, timber, and other Oregon products quickly stopped the exodus. The early Oregonians realized that a better life could be attained through the toil of farming and sawing lumber in Oregon, than gambling to strike it rich in the California gold fields.

Gold was discovered in Oregon in 1851 near present-day Jacksonville by two pack train operators on a gold miners' supply restocking trip from California. Many subsequent discoveries were made throughout the mountain regions of Jackson, Josephine, Coos, and Curry counties, and also along the beaches of the two coastal counties, with mining activity peaking around 1858.

The gold rushes on the Fraser River in British Columbia between 1856 and 1857 and in Idaho in the early 1860s again caused a temporary departure and prosperity cycle. Gold was discovered in eastern Oregon in 1861, which resulted in a reverse migration to that part of the state.

Provisional and Territorial Government

The earliest settlers in the Oregon Country thought little about their lack of government protection. However, in early 1841 a group of ex-HBC employees, pioneer French-Canadians, Methodist missionaries, a Catholic priest, and former American fur trappers met to discuss the loss of livestock to predators, mainly wolves. When Ewing Young died a week later with no apparent heir and no system to probate his estate, as previously noted, the recognition of the need for a governmental entity to handle estate probate matters became the genesis for drafting a code of laws.

In 1843 the first Wolf Meeting began discussing civil and military protection for the settlers. During a meeting on May 2, 1843, at Champoeg—chosen because of its accessibility by both land and water—a provisional government was formed by a close vote. The elected legislative committee members met several times to draft a code of laws for the provisional government. Four districts were vaguely defined: Twality (later spelled Tuality), Yamhill, Clackamas, and Champooick (later spelled Champoeg), with Clatsop being

Artist's conception of Rose Farm and the meeting of the first territorial legislature in 1849. From a 1926 publication of the Hesperian Society. Courtesy of the Clackamas County Historical Society, B-0160-004916.

Governor George L. Curry served as the last territorial governor before Oregon became a state in 1859. He returned to his career in newspaper publishing, which began in Boston and St. Louis, and concluded in Portland. Courtesy of the Oregon State Archives.

added the following year. As the population increased, the four districts were subdivided into counties. Amendments passed in 1845 included the creation of the office of governor. George Abernethy became the first governor of Oregon—serving until the first U.S. territorial governor of Oregon assumed office in 1849.

The greatest challenge facing the provisional government was collecting taxes for operational costs. Several appeals were made to Washington for federal aid, military protection, and for the early establishment of a territorial government. With the Cayuse War severely draining the provisional government's resources, Joseph Meek personally carried a petition to Washington, D.C.

In 1848 the U.S. Congress created the Territory of Oregon, which included all of the U.S. territory west of the summit of the Rocky Mountains and north of the 42nd parallel—present-day Oregon, Washington, Idaho, and parts of western Montana. (The Washington Territory was carved out in 1853 and also included all of the area of the present-day neighboring state of Idaho.)

President James K. Polk appointed Joseph Lane to serve as the first U.S. territorial governor of Oregon; he took office on March 3, 1849. Four other men served as territorial governors, with Governor George L. Curry serving the final term.

Oregon City had been the seat of the provisional government, but in 1852 the U.S. Congress confirmed Salem as the territorial capital. The statehouse in Salem was completed in 1855, but was destroyed by fire in late December that year. During the period of construction, the capital was briefly relocated at Corvallis, but moved back to Salem when the U.S. Treasury Department ruled against expenditure of federal funds for construction of a capitol building other than at Salem. Controversy surrounded the location of the capital until 1864, when the voters finally confirmed Salem as the state capital.

Following the capitol building fire in 1855, subsequent legislative sessions were held in rented rooms in commercial buildings until a new structure was partially completed in

Oregon's territorial capitol, which burned to the ground in 1855. Courtesy of the Oregon State Archives.

1876. (This building also was destroyed by fire in 1935; the current capitol was completed in 1938.)

Soon after Oregon became a territory, statehood became a topic of discussion and a contentious issue between the wrangling political parties. Most of the general public did not support statehood, fearing heavy taxation. Measures calling for a constitutional convention were defeated by the voters in 1854 and 1855, but finally approved at a special election in April 1856.

A constitutional convention was held in Salem from August 17 to September 18, 1857. The constitutional provisions included salaries for government officials, debt limitations for the state and the counties, strict controls on banks and corporations, and the disfranchisement of blacks, mulattoes, and Chinese.

With dissension over the issue of slavery intense throughout the entire country and with a large number of the delegates to the constitutional convention being pro-slavery, it was agreed not to discuss the issue of slavery. Instead, two related referendum issues were included on the November 9, 1857, special election ballot. The people adopted the constitution, and in separate votes they rejected slavery and excluded free blacks from the state—the latter provision, though never enforced, was not repealed until 1926.

The U.S. Congress delayed admitting Oregon to the Union for two years because of the slavery issue and because Republicans wished to prevent the

Constitutional Convention Delegates

Levi Anderson, farmer
Jesse Applegate, farmer
A. D. Babcock, lawyer
Reuben P. Boise, lawyer
J. H. Brattain, farmer
Paul Brattain, farmer
William W. Bristow, farmer
Benjamin F. Burch, farmer
A. J. Campbell, mechanic
Hector Campbell, farmer
Stephen F. Chadwick, lawyer
Jesse Cox, farmer
Joseph Cox, farmer
Reuben F. Coyle, farmer
John T. Crooks, farmer
Matthew P. Deady, lawyer

Thomas J. Dryer, editor
L. J. C. Duncan, miner
Luther Elkins, farmer
William H. Farrar, lawyer
Solomon Fitzhugh, farmer
Lafayette F. Grover, lawyer
S. B. Hendershott, miner
Enoch Hoult, farmer
James K. Kelly, lawyer
John Kelsay, lawyer
Robert C. Kinney, farmer
Haman C. Lewis, farmer
David Logan, lawyer
A. L. Lovejoy, lawyer
P. B. Marple, lawyer
John R. McBride, lawyer
S. J. McCormick, printer

Charles R. Meigs, lawyer
William Metzger, mechanic
Richard Miller, farmer
Isaac R. Moore, farmer
Daniel Newcomb, farmer
H. B. Nichols, farmer
Martin Olds, farmer
Cyrus Olney, lawyer
William H. Packwood, miner
J. C. Peebles, farmer
P. P. Prim, lawyer
J. H. Reed, lawyer
Nathaniel Robbins, farmer
Nicholas Schrum, farmer

Levi Scott, farmer
Davis Shannon, farmer
Erasmus D. Shattuck, lawyer
James Shields, farmer
Robert V. Short, surveyor
Delazon Smith, lawyer
W. A. Starkweather, farmer
William H. Watkins, physician
John W. Watts, physician
Fred Waymire, mechanic
John S. White, farmer
Thomas Whitted, farmer
George H. Williams, lawyer

addition of a Democratic state to the Union. In the interim, in anticipation of statehood and in accordance with the schedule contained in the new state constitution, an election was held in June 1858 to elect the first governor of the state of Oregon—John Whiteaker. The legislature met at Salem from July 5 to July 9, but the only action taken was the election of Joseph Lane and Delazon Smith as U.S. senators. Another session was scheduled for September 13, 1858, but only two senate members attended. The territorial legislature met on December 6, 1858, and adjourned on January 22, 1859; only routine business was transacted.

On February 14, 1859, Oregon officially became the 33rd state of the Union with its current boundaries, and on March 15, 1859, the *Brother Jonathan* sailed into Portland carrying the news, which reached Salem 13 hours later.

State and County Government in 1859

In 1859 the new state legislature passed legislation to organize the state and provide for a state seal designed by Harvey Gordon of Molalla in Clackamas County, but politics distracted them from focusing on anything else of substance during the first legislative session. Although historically most Oregonians were Democrats, most did not favor slavery and were loyal to the Union. The divisions within the Democratic Party gave the three-year-old

Oregon Republican Party some encouragement, but Democrats continued to win elections. In 1859 Lafayette F. Grover was chosen to serve as Oregon's first representative in Congress, serving 17 days until the conclusion of the 35th Congress in March. Lansing Stout succeeded Grover to serve in the 36th Congress of 1859–1861.

When the legislature elected Smith and Lane as U.S. senators in 1858, the two had drawn lots for the short- and long-term seats. Since Smith drew the short term, his term ended on March 3, 1859. Governor Whiteaker convened a special session in May to elect Smith's successor. The divisions among the Democrats resulted in nobody being elected and the senate seat remained vacant throughout the 36th Congress.

At the county government level, the primary responsibilities in 1859 were road building and maintenance, law enforcement, operating a court system, care for the needy, and tax collection. County clerks kept busy recording deeds, brands, and marriage licenses. Circuit and supreme court judgeships were combined into one office until Oregon's population reached 100,000. There was minimal home rule until 101 years later, with most transactions needing authorization or a mandate from the state legislature. County commissioners were deluged with requests for improved transportation and mail facilities. The commissioners created election districts, which corresponded to the census records precincts. Businesses or homes served as polling places.

Oregon Commerce and Industry

The farms established by the early settlers were very basic, meeting family subsistence needs, but soon expanded to larger operations as the demand for crops and livestock increased with the establishment of towns. During the 1850s, the California and southern Oregon gold rushes created new markets for agricultural products, which were transported by sea to the regional market in San Francisco or hauled to southern Oregon and northern California by pack trains. On the return trips, California traders sup-

Governor John Whiteaker
(1820–1902)

Born in Indiana; self-educated and carpenter by trade

Left home at early age; held various jobs in South and Midwest

Successful gold miner in California in 1849; returned to Missouri in 1852 for his family

Captained wagon train over Oregon Trail in 1853; settled with wife and five children on farm in Spencer Butte area before moving to Pleasant Hill in 1859

Served as Lane County probate court judge and territorial legislator

Inaugurated as first state governor on July 8, 1858

Urged development of home industries

Unpopular pro-slavery position limited him to one term

Served as state legislator, U.S. congressman, and Oregon internal revenue collector

Married Nancy Jane Hargrave; six children

Governor John Whiteaker, the first governor of the state of Oregon. Courtesy of the Oregon State Archives.

plied liquor, glass, iron, tin, and tools, or staple goods like rice, sugar, and molasses.

Hogs and sheep were the first domesticated animals in Oregon, arriving by ship when the Astor party arrived in 1811. The first sheep herded across the plains arrived in 1844. Hand carding and spinning equipment was used to process wool until 1857 when Oregon's first woolen mill was established in Salem.

After the Willamette Cattle Company drove the first herd of cattle from California to Oregon in 1837, subsequent herds of cattle and horses arrived. During the California and southern Oregon gold rushes, thousands of head of cattle raised in the Willamette and Umpqua valleys were driven to the two mining regions to feed hungry miners. Stock raising was prevalent in the more remote areas where driving a herd to market was more practical and profitable than transporting grain.

The California and southern Oregon gold rushes also boosted Oregon's industrial development. Entrepreneurs returning from the gold fields used their new-found wealth to build mills and develop other industries. A few sawmills had been in operation since the late 1830s and early 1840s, but with the increased demand for lumber from California during the gold rush many more were established—over 100 by 1859. Numerous gristmills were also in operation and played an important role in the local and export economies. Mills changed owners and operators frequently, but a few were passed down through successive family generations.

Commercial logging began in the 1850s, using combinations of river floats and horse- or ox-driven wagons to transport the logs to the sawmills. By 1859 lumber was being shipped by sea from the sawmills located on the Columbia and Willamette rivers to San Francisco. Planing mills were also in operation, providing finished lumber and also functional and decorative architectural components for building construction.

Coal was discovered in the Coos Bay coast vicinity in 1853 and resulted in another industry supported by the California gold rush. Shipments of coal were made to San Francisco to power the steamships making trips up the Sacramento–San Joaquin Delta to the gold country gateways.

A number of other small industries were established during the 1850s to provide the goods and services needed by the settlers. Tanneries manufactured harnesses, bridles, new soles for shoes, and other needed leather goods. Blacksmiths shod horses, made wrought iron implements, and repaired wagons, carts, tools, and guns. Livery stables provided services for those traveling on horseback or by wagon. Coopers manufactured wooden barrels and tubs for food preservation. Several brickyards made bricks needed for buildings and chimneys. Portland boasted two breweries and the Willamette and Rogue valleys each had a winery.

With the expansion of commerce, the transportation industry developed, with Portland serving as the shipping terminus. Individuals or newly formed companies operated pack trains, sternwheelers, steamships, and stage lines to transport mail, livestock, flour, other general merchandise, and people.

The banking industry started slowly in Oregon. Prior to the California gold rush and the influx of gold, the only universal medium of exchange was bushels of wheat, beaver pelts, or in 1849, Beaver Money, which consisted of coins privately minted at Oregon City with the authorization of the provisional government. In 1854 coins from the San Francisco U.S. Mint came into use and the government purchased the Beaver Money.

Perhaps because the original state constitution placed tight controls on banks and corporations, Oregon's first bank—the Ladd & Tilton Bank established by W. S. Ladd and C. E. Tilton in Portland in 1859—was the only bank in the state for seven years. In the meantime merchants like Couch & Company of Portland and express companies like Wells Fargo acted as agencies for receiving and forwarding gold dust, money, and other valuables.

Water-powered sawmills like this mill on Eagle Creek in Hood River County were common in early Oregon.
By C. E. Watkins, ca. 1867. Courtesy of the Oregon Historical Society, OrHi 21118.

The newspaper industry had its beginning in Oregon during the territorial period when the population was growing and political partisanship and commercial competition were intense. Rival newspapers—some short-lived—sprang up in Oregon City, Portland, Salem, and Milwaukie and reflected various political perspectives. The newspapers still operating in 1859 included the *Oregon Argus, Oregon Sentinel, Oregon Statesman, Oregon Weekly Union, Pacific Christian Advocate, Portland Daily News,* and *The Oregonian.* Today *The Oregonian* is the oldest continuously published newspaper in the West, founded as a weekly newspaper by Thomas J. Dryer on December 4, 1850.

Almanacs were a valued reference used by farmers. In 1848 the Oregon Printing Association published the *Oregon Almanac* at Oregon City. The *Oregon and Washington Almanac,* later called *McCormick's Almanac,* began publication in 1855 in Portland and continued annually through 1881.

By 1859 Oregon's business and industrial economies were well developed, but a short downturn occurred as the mining in British Columbia waned and as California became more self-sufficient. Relief was on the way by 1862, however, with the economic impact of the discovery of gold in eastern Oregon and Idaho.

Oregon's Early Transportation System

Travel within Oregon in the early days was challenging. Many roads were located where Indian trails had existed for centuries along the foothills, but dense forests, steep hillsides, and muddy conditions during the rainy season made passage and attempts at improvement difficult. A loaded wagon might require an entire day to travel eight or ten miles; most winter travel was limited to horseback.

Government participation in roadwork was minimal. During the 1850s the U.S. Congress appropriated $140,000 to build and improve a military road from Oregon to California, which came to be known as the California-Oregon Trail that approximated today's Interstate 5 from the Willamette Valley to California's Central Valley. (The military road served as the main route to California until the completion of the Oregon and California Railroad in 1887.) During the Indian wars, Congress periodically granted public land and appropriated funds for the construction of other military roads.

The inadequacy of government funding resulted in state legislation requiring property owners to annually perform road construction and maintenance, with the number of days to be worked based on the value of the taxable property. If desired, two dollars could be paid in lieu of each day not worked.

When a new road was authorized, every male in the district had to contribute one day's worth of work on the new road, even if he was not a property owner.

Two 60-foot-wide territorial roads existed in 1859 and were clearly marked by stakes or blazed trees. The Eastside Territorial Road connected Coburg with Oregon City. The other territorial road approximated the Territorial Highway between today's Anlauf in Douglas County and Monroe in Benton County, where it joined the Eastside Territorial Road. By 1859 about 100 other separate roads were established, some only partially completed.

A number of toll roads were authorized by the provisional and territorial legislatures and a few were in operation in 1859, including the Valley Plank Road in Washington and Multnomah counties, known today as Canyon Road, and

The side-wheeler steamboat *Multnomah* was built in New York, shipped in pieces around Cape Horn, and assembled in Oregon City in 1851. Courtesy of the Salem Public Library, #7955.

the Barlow Road in Hood River and Clackamas counties. Toll charges failed to cover the construction and maintenance costs incurred by private contractors as intended. Also, many pioneers tendered IOUs because they did not have the cash for the toll, but these were rarely paid. Owners and operators changed frequently. Portions of a few toll roads were plank roads with poles lying crosswise on the road to permit passage through muddy areas during the winter months.

Ferries operated across streams and rivers, and several bridges existed by 1859. The ferries were regulated and the rates were fixed by the county commissioners, with competition fierce among the operators bidding on the contracts. The smaller ferries required that the wagons be dismantled and the stock animals swim alongside.

By 1859, especially during the rainy season, riverboats were the chief means of transportation. Dredging and other improvements on the Willamette and Tualatin rivers in the early 1850s eased navigation. Competition between individuals and shipping lines was fierce. (In 1860 the Oregon Steam Navigation Company was organized, which unified many, but not all of the operators. It developed into a monopoly that lasted for two decades.)

Stagecoaches began operating in the Willamette Valley in 1851. The 50-mile trip between Portland and Salem could be made in one day. In 1859 weekly stage service connected Portland and Jacksonville, and in 1860 the California Stage Company initiated a route from Sacramento to Portland.

Transportation along the coast was the most challenging of all. The major headlands created natural barriers to any north/south travel, and the Indian trails followed the east/west valleys and rivers through densely forested

First structure on the Portland townsite built by William Overton in the winter of 1844–45 at Front and Washington streets. Courtesy of the Oregon Historical Society, OrHi 954.

Captain John H. Couch House, an 1850 Greek Revival house built in Portland facing a small lake, called Couch Lake. From the 1858 Kuchel and Dresel lithograph. Courtesy of the Oregon Historical Society, OrHi 87735.

areas. Consequently, travel was by ship, canoe, raft, or flat-bottomed boats, with landings available at Port Orford, Coos Bay, Gardiner, and Astoria. Stage lines—open wagons with wide wheels—operated on the beaches between Coos Bay and the Umpqua River.

Oregon Architecture

When the early settlers first arrived at the site of their land claim, they built one-room temporary shelters of rails or round logs to provide immediate shelter and to legally secure their claim. As soon as possible, a second house was built of peeled hand-hewn logs, a stone fireplace, living room, two small bedrooms, and possibly a sleeping loft. The windows were covered with wild animal skins, commonly from panthers or deer—scraped very thin, or they were glazed sash windows. The puncheon floors were made of split boards, raising the floor above the damp or mucky soil.

A permanent log barn usually was built next, followed within a few years by the construction of a real house—a frame house of board and batten wood construction, one to one-and-a-half stories high, with a gable roof and porches on the front and back. When sawn lumber became available, some merely covered their hewn log houses with veneer. With more frame houses being built, distinct architectural styles emerged, often reflecting the style in vogue in each family's hometown or the current trend of the country. A number of American architects, including Alexander Jackson Davis and Andrew Jackson Downing, had been publishing house pattern books since the 1840s. The pattern books, trade catalogues, and architectural periodicals illustrated with engravings and woodcuts made their way to Oregon. Greek and Gothic Revival and Italianate styles became popular. Specialty frames, siding, or trim were sometimes shipped around Cape Horn, but the majority of the homes were built with readily available local materials.

Churches and public and commercial buildings were also constructed using patterns and illustrations from architectural publications. In 1852 architect Richard Upjohn published *Upjohn's Rural Architecture*, which contained church, chapel, schoolhouse, and parsonage designs. Upjohn preferred Gothic Revival, but other publications provided patterns for Greek Revival and Italianate styles.

Today over 60 structures built by 1859 remain in either an original, reconstructed, redesigned, or replicated version. Many are open to the public and are listed as sites to visit in each county chapter. Other early buildings were destroyed by fire or floods, or demolished to clear a place for modern structures.

Oregon Organizations

Most of Oregon's early settlers were church-going people, usually Christians. Once their homes were established, the communities organized a church, often meeting in one another's homes on a regular basis for Bible study and fellowship. A schoolhouse usually was built before a church, but it would be used for church services. When a church was built, it was generously shared with other denominations and often became a community center.

The churches were typically started by a core group of charter members and the leadership responsibilities were shared and rotated among them. People tended to be loyal to their former denominations and religious practices, including how they observed the Sabbath.

Circuit riders—ministers representing various denominations who traveled on horseback to carry the Gospel—ministered to the remote settlements. They preached, prayed, and performed baptisms, weddings, and funerals in schools, meeting houses, barns, or outdoors. Everyone awaited their arrival with great anticipation and appreciated the sacrifices made by the riders and their families. Most of the riders were ordained ministers and some were also trained teachers.

The Methodists, through their mission work, were the first Protestants to become organized in Oregon in the 1830s, but were followed in the early 1840s by the Congregationalists, Baptists, Methodist Episcopalians, Presbyterians,

Gothic Revival Vigilance Hook and Ladder Fire House, Portland, ca. 1857. From the 1858 Kuchel and Dresel lithograph. Courtesy of the Oregon Historical Society, OrHi 5495.

Renowned Baptist circuit rider Joab Powell and his wife, Ann Beeler. Powell reportedly saved over 3000 lost souls while his wife and their oldest sons operated the family farm in Scio. Courtesy of the Salem Public Library, #3823.

Celebration in Portland, ca. 1858. Courtesy of the Oregon Historical Society, OrHi 5488.

Episcopalians, Unitarians, and the United Brethren. Many church congregations have complex histories of disbanding and reorganizing several times, or moving to new locations.

The Catholic Church originated with its mission work in the 1830s and the dedication of its first church building in St. Paul in Marion County in 1839. The first Jewish congregation, Beth Israel, was organized in Portland in 1859, and a couple of small, informal congregations met in towns where Jewish merchants lived and worked.

In addition to maintaining past religious affiliations, political party loyalties remained after coming west. Those from the South were likely to be Democrats and those from the northern states tended to be Whigs and later Republicans. (The Republican party was formed in 1856 in opposition to slavery and the alignment of members of the U.S. Congress and voters throughout the Union was based upon that vital issue.) The pre-Civil War Democratic Party was different from the Democratic Party of today in terms of the rural versus urban concentrations of the party's members. In 1859 the Democrats lived primarily in the rural areas and the Republicans lived in the towns and cities. Political rifts were commonplace, but the bickering subsided when dealing with social issues affecting all. For example, several temperance organizations were formed during the mid-1850s to deal with the prevalence of public drunkenness.

Various vocational organizations existed by 1859, including the Typographical Society founded in 1853—becoming the first labor organization in Oregon, and the Oregon State Educational Association founded in 1858.

In 1853 Yamhill County farmers organized Oregon's first county agricultural society and that county's first fair, a one-day event, was held in 1854. Other counties held county fairs in subsequent years. In 1858 the Fruit Growers Association of Oregon was organized at Salem, which led to the establishment of the State Agricultural Society in 1860. In the late 1850s horse enthusiasts organized jockey clubs for horse racing in Washington, Yamhill, Multnomah, and Lane counties.

Numerous fraternal organizations offered aid and assistance to their members in times of need. In 1846 the first Masonic lodge was granted a charter in Oregon City, and other Ancient Free and Accepted Masons organized in other locales during the 1850s. In 1852 Oregon's first Independent Order of Odd Fellows (IOOF) lodge was established in Salem and by 1859, The Dalles and Roseburg each had an IOOF lodge.

By 1859, traveling musical troupes or one-ring circuses offered occasional entertainment in the larger communities. In a few towns, including Corvallis, Albany, Jacksonville, and Aurora, civic pride was demonstrated by their organized bands—usually brass bands.

Education and Literacy

Initially, children were schooled at home by their parents when time permitted. The 1848 Congressional act creating the Oregon territory provided that two sections of each townsite should be reserved for schools, and when Oregon became a state, the federal government set aside a grant of land for the site of a university. However, construction of educational facilities was usually delayed until funding became available.

Many of the first schoolhouses—usually one-room log cabins—were built by generous community citizens on a portion of their land claims. That person might also serve as the teacher. Some communities raised money through subscriptions to build schools and paid the teacher's salary through tuition. Often, on a rotation basis, families provided room and board for the teacher in exchange for free tuition. School sessions were confined to only two or three months out of the year because of the inclement weather that hampered travel to and from school and because students were needed to work on their family's farm. The teachers in the rural schools were usually unmarried women, with the male teachers preferring to teach in a town or at a college where the salaries were higher. Teaching credentials were not a requirement.

The territorial legislature did not provide any funding for public school education until 1854. By 1855 most of the counties were subdivided into school districts, but communities often competed to attract private schools. Towns were eager to have a college, institute, or at least an academy, and prominent citizens vied to become trustees.

Numerous denominational academies were founded during the 1850s with courses of study usually confined to the secondary level. A few also held elementary classes. These schools had to be chartered by the state legislature.

The first attempt to promote literacy outside of the schools was the incorporation of the Multnomah Circulating Library in Oregon City in 1845 by the provisional legislature. In 1848 the U.S. Congress appropriated $5000 for a library to be maintained at the seat of government, then Oregon City. The library moved to Salem in 1852 with the capital, but was destroyed by the 1855 fire that burned the unfinished capitol building. Congress granted only $500 for a new library, so the Supreme Court Library became the only state library until the early 1900s, and included a few titles of general interest.

Oregon's Natural Landscape

Oregon is known as the Beaver State because the prized fur of the American beaver was the original draw to the Oregon Country. Beaver were over-trapped by the early arrivals and nearly became extinct, but through management and partial protection, the beaver population has been re-established throughout the state. The beaver was depicted on the obverse of the coins minted by the provisional government in 1849, but it did not earn a place on the state seal designed in 1857. However, it is depicted on the reverse side of the Oregon state flag adopted in 1925—the only state flag displaying different images on each side.

Oregon has approximately 4000 native plant species. The loss of native vegetation began during the early settlement period and continues today, but there is much effort underway to implement conservation practices. Two important native plants are the camas lily (*Camassia quamash* and *Camassia leichtlinii*) and the wapato (*Sagittaria latifolia*), which both were key food sources for the Indians west of the Cascade Range. The camas plant has a dense onion-like bulb and the wapato is a tuber similar to the potato.

Oregon's physical geography includes a wide array of mountain ranges, valleys, plateaus, rivers, lakes, and 363 miles of coastline. Particular features played an integral role in the early development of Oregon.

Oregon is well known for several of its lakes—Crater Lake, the deepest lake in the United States; Klamath Lake, the largest freshwater lake in Oregon and one of the largest in the United States; and Waldo Lake, the second largest lake in Oregon and one of the purest lakes in the world. Their locations east of the Willamette Valley excluded them from Oregon's pre-1860 history of settlement.

Early settlement took place between Oregon's two major mountain ranges —the Cascade Range, which includes Oregon's highest mountain peak, Mount Hood, and the Coast Range. The Cascades presented great challenges to the travelers on the Oregon Trail, and the Coast Range deterred early settlement on much of the coast. Hells Canyon along the Snake River between Oregon and Idaho also was a perilous portion of the Oregon Trail; it is the deepest gorge in North America. The pioneers who made the entire trip down the Columbia River passed by the greatest concentration of waterfalls on the American continent. The many falls which lie along the Columbia River Gorge in Multnomah and Hood River counties probably were not appreciated by the pioneers because of the more imminent dangers facing them on their perilous voyage down the rushing river.

Major Rivers

Columbia River—originates at Columbia Lake in Canadian Rockies in British Columbia and forms a significant portion of Oregon's northern boundary

Willamette River—emerges from mountains south and southeast of Eugene in three separate forks—Coast Fork, Middle Fork, and McKenzie River—flowing primarily north 187 miles to Columbia River

Rogue River—originates at Boundary Springs near Crater Lake, flowing 215 miles to Pacific Ocean

Umpqua River—formed by confluence of North Umpqua and South Umpqua rivers, both of which rise in Cascade Range, and flows 111 miles to Pacific Ocean

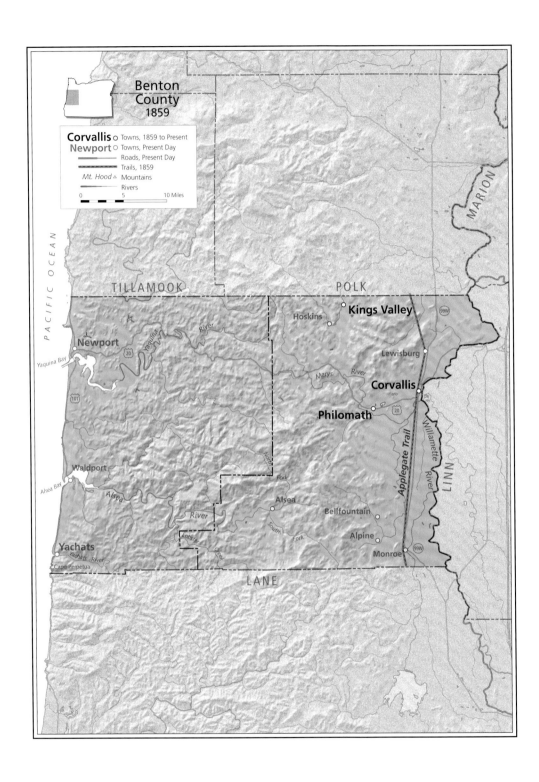

Benton
County
1859

Corvallis ○ Towns, 1859 to Present
Newport ○ Towns, Present Day
━━━ Roads, Present Day
━━━ Trails, 1859
Mt. Hood △ Mountains
━━━ Rivers
0   5   10 Miles

PACIFIC OCEAN

TILLAMOOK   POLK

MARION

Hoskins   Kings Valley

Newport

Yaquina Bay   Yaquina River

Lewisburg

Marys River

Corvallis

Philomath

Waldport

Alsea Bay

Alsea   North Fork

Applegate Trail

Willamette River

LINN

Alsea

River   Bellfountain

South Fork

Alpine

Yachats   Monroe

Yachats River

Cape Perpetua

LANE

99W
20
101

1 1859 BENTON COUNTY

Benton County was created in 1847 from all but the northern portion of the original Polk County, with Corvallis named the county seat. In 1851 it was reduced in size significantly, but retained the southern portion of present-day Lincoln County. (In 1893 the legislature created Lincoln County from portions of Benton and Tillamook counties, with Toledo designated the county seat. Newport became the county seat in 1952.) According to the 1860 U.S. Census, the county population was 3074.

In Present-Day Benton County

In 1859 the Territorial Road passed through Benton County, approximating the current route of Highway 99w. The Applegate Trail crossed the Marys River west of Corvallis. A horse trail led down the Alsea River toward the coast, and primitive wagon roads connected the Alsea and Lobster valleys to Corvallis and linked Fort Hoskins to the Siletz Agency in present-day Lincoln County.

Before bridges were built, ferries operated across the Willamette, Marys, and Long Tom rivers. The first bridge—a small plank toll bridge—was built in 1856 at the Territorial Road crossing of the Marys River. By 1859 several other bridges had been constructed.

In 1851 steamboats started operating on the Willamette River. On a weekly basis the steamboat *Canemah* traveled between Oregon City and Corvallis. The steamboat *James Clinton* began navigating the Willamette River above Corvallis in 1856, reaching as far as Eugene in the wetter months of the year.

Several stagecoach companies served the county, connecting Corvallis to Salem, Champoeg, Oregon City, Eugene, and Winchester. In 1860, the California Stage Company offered the first stagecoach service from Portland to Sacramento, passing through Corvallis.

Early History
Kalapuya Indians had lived in the Willamette Valley for many centuries. All shared a common lifestyle—living off the camas, wapato, tarweed, white oak acorns, berries, fish, and game; managing the grasslands effectively with their

Benton County Courthouse constructed in 1855 by George Wrenn, ca. 1859. By Kuchel & Dresel Lithographers, San Francisco. Courtesy of the Benton County Historical Society, Philomath, OR, 1999-060.0010H.

annual burns; and traveling the Willamette River in dugout canoes to trade—originally amongst themselves and neighboring tribes, but later with the fur traders, missionaries, and settlers. It was the Luckiamute and Marys River Kalapuyan people who occupied the area within Benton County.

A few explorers and fur trappers passed through the area as early as 1812, traveling from the Pacific Fur Company's post at Fort Astoria to the trapping and trading grounds to the south. By the time the earliest permanent settlers arrived in the mid-1840s, most of the Kalapuya had died from the diseases the explorers, traders, and fur trappers introduced. After the decline of the Kalapuya population, some Klickitat Indians, whose homeland was in the south central portion of present-day Washington, migrated south to this region; they and the Kalapuya survivors generally tolerated the arrival of the settlers.

In 1855 the Kalapuya and Confederated Bands of the Willamette Valley Treaty, sometimes referred to as the Dayton Treaty, ceded the ancestral lands of the Kalapuya and other neighboring tribes to the United States. The following year most of these Indians were removed to the Grand Ronde Reservation situated in Polk and Yamhill counties; the Klickitats were sent back to the Washington Territory, although some later returned and became members of either the Grand Ronde or the Siletz confederated tribes.

Corvallis

In 1845 Joseph C. Avery took a donation land claim on both sides of the Marys River where it enters the Willamette River. The community was first known as Avery's, then Marysville, and finally, in 1853, the name was changed to Corvallis to avoid confusion with the northern California town of Marysville. In 1851 Avery and William F. Dixon, another early settler, platted portions of their land claims and began selling lots. The following year they donated land for county seat purposes, including a site for the courthouse.

Corvallis quickly became a regional trading center after the discovery of gold in southern Oregon in 1851. Corvallis's location on a navigable portion of the Willamette River made it the ideal shipping center for steamboats carrying supplies destined for the miners in southern Oregon. As new trading centers developed closer to the mines, and eventually as the gold was depleted, Corvallis declined as a major shipping point, but it continued its growth. Corvallis served as the capital of the Oregon Territory in 1855—just long enough for the territorial legislature to pass one bill before moving back to Salem.

By 1859 Corvallis's commercial district included the typical businesses of a growing community and featured a furniture store. John and James Galbraith operated the Exchange Saloon and J. C. Avery had recently built his second general store. Today a portion of this store is integrated into the extensively remodeled hardware store located on Second Street, making it the oldest brick commercial building in the city.

Corvallis had a well-developed industrial economy with riverfront sawmills located at either end of town, a gristmill, a fanning mill for cleaning grain, a tannery that produced leather goods for both Corvallis and San Francisco customers, a wool carding mill, planing mill, sash and door factory, and several brickyards. Farms occupied the remaining land located within the current Corvallis city limits.

Asahel Bush published Corvallis's first newspaper—the *Oregon Statesman*—when the capital was temporarily located there in 1855. The *Occidental Messenger*, a pro-slavery

J. C. and Martha Avery House, ca. 1859. By Kuchel & Dresel Lithographers, San Francisco. Courtesy of the Benton County Historical Society, 1999-060.0010G.

Joseph Conant Avery (1817–1876)

Born and educated in Pennsylvania
Moved to Illinois in 1839, married in 1841; arrived in Corvallis in 1845
Opened general store stocked with goods acquired in California following success in gold fields
Postal agent for Oregon and Washington territories
Territorial legislator for two terms
Married Martha Marsh; 12 children

William F. Dixon, co-founder of Corvallis and operator of the first ferry on the Willamette River south of Salem. Harriet Moore Collection. Courtesy of the Benton County Historical Society, Philomath, 1983-019.0083.

Corvallis, meaning "heart of the valley" in Latin, ca. 1858. Courtesy of the Oregon Historical Society, OrHi 4300.

First Corvallis College building, ca. 1868. This carte-de-visite photograph of the original 1858–59 college building was taken by photographers Stryker & Dohse. It is the earliest known photograph of the predecessor of Oregon State University. Courtesy of the Oregon State University Archives, #1344.

newspaper, began publication in 1857, and in 1859 T. H. B. Ordenal published the *Democratic Crisis*, later renamed the *Oregon Union*.

The first telegraph lines reached Corvallis in 1856, but because the wire was merely strung on trees, maintenance difficulties doomed it to failure. Telegraph poles were not installed on the streets of Corvallis until 1862.

Education has been important to Corvallis since its earliest days. A log schoolhouse was built in 1848 and the Corvallis Academy was incorporated in 1856. During the 1850s the Baptists and Methodist Episcopalians established schools at various grade levels.

The predecessor of Oregon State University—Corvallis College—was established in 1858. Originally it had only elementary and secondary class levels, but by 1865 it had added college level studies.

Several denominations held their church services in the 1848 log schoolhouse. In the early 1850s the Baptists built the first church in Corvallis, and the Methodists and Methodist Episcopalians had church buildings by 1859. Since 1853 the Presbyterians had been meeting at their pastor's home; they constructed a church in 1860. The first Catholic services were held in Corvallis in 1853; they built a chapel in 1861.

Monroe, Bellfountain, and Alpine

Several small communities developed just south of Corvallis. In 1858 John and Cynthia Fiechter built a Greek Revival house that today remains within the William L. Finley National Wildlife Refuge. Following John Fiechter's accidental gunshot death in 1861, Cynthia married Archibald Johnson. The house became home to the 12 children from both marriages and remained in the family until it was sold in 1906.

In 1851 Irishman Richard Irwin took a donation land claim on Muddy Creek on the west side of the Winkle Buttes. In 1852 he established the Jennyopolis post office along with a store and saloon located on the Territorial Road. The post office closed in 1857, but the store and saloon continued to serve travelers. In 1852 Samuel F. Starr established the Starr's Point post office just north of present-day Monroe. George M. Starr operated the general store.

The area of today's Bellfountain and Alpine was originally known as Belknaps Settlement because of the many Belknaps who settled there. A schoolhouse was built about 1849; it also served as a meeting house. In 1858, the Methodists built Simpson's Chapel on a site between present-day Bellfountain and Alpine.

Alsea and Lobster Valleys

By 1850 the most desirable and accessible land along the Willamette River and its tributaries had been claimed, but those willing to venture into the harder-to-reach valleys like the Alsea and Lobster valleys discovered prime farmland. The first settlers arrived in these two valleys in 1852. By 1855—the year the Donation Land Act expired—most of the flat land was claimed, but property in the upper Alsea Valley was still available for purchase.

During the dry season, the residents of the Alsea and Lobster valleys traveled the primitive wagon road to Corvallis to stock up on staple goods they could not raise on their farms or manufacture themselves. They also had their grain ground into flour for their own use or to sell. During most of the year, these settlers depended upon one another for their survival.

Philomath

Wyman Saint Clair was one of the early Corvallis entrepreneurs, but his donation land claim was located in present-day Philomath. The community was known as Marys River Settlement until 1865 when the Church of the United Brethren in Christ chartered Philomath College. The two-story brick college building standing along Highway 20 houses the Benton County Historical Museum.

Fort Hoskins

In 1856 Captain Christopher C. Augur of the 4th U.S. Infantry established Fort Hoskins in Kings Valley to control and protect the Indians detained at the Coast Reservation and

Reuben and Mary Jane Holmes Shipley

Reuben Shipley was granted freedom from his slaveholder upon arrival in Oregon

Forced to leave his first wife and sons owned by another family behind in Missouri

First wife died and slaveholder refused to sell Shipley's sons to him

Mary Jane Holmes and her family arrived in Polk County in 1844 as slaves of Nathaniel Ford

Ford freed parents and youngest child in 1850, but Mary Jane and two siblings were not freed until 1853, following long court battle

Mary Jane remained with Ford family until 1857 when she married Reuben Shipley, who was forced to pay Ford a sum of money for the right to marry her

Shipleys settled in Philomath, raised six children, and became respected citizens—donating two of their 80 acres to county for Mount Union Cemetery, with provision permitting burial of black persons

Mary Jane Holmes Shipley Drake, ca. 1924, remarried after her first husband, Reuben Shipley, died. Harriet Moore Collection. Courtesy of the Benton County Historical Society, Philomath, OR, 1994-038.0808.

Early drawing of Fort Hoskins. Courtesy of the Salem Public Library, Ben Maxwell Collection, #4563.

to protect the settlers in the area. (There were complaints from both the Indians and the settlers about the soldiers' performance and conduct.) A sub-post blockhouse was built to the west at the Siletz Agency to further protect the reservation and prevent the tribes from leaving; a trail built under the supervision of Lieutenant Philip H. Sheridan connected the two posts.

Fort Hoskins became a regional center of economic and political activity. However, the 200 to 300 troops serving at the outpost often endured shortages of food and other supplies because of its remote location.

The onset of the Civil War in 1861 led to the eventual demise of the fort in 1865. In 1866 the buildings were auctioned off, and the land, which had been rented, was returned to the owner, Henry VanPeer. Today Fort Hoskins Historic Park offers a glimpse into the history of the fort, with interpretive displays and self-guided trails.

Kings Valley

Kings Valley was named for Nahum King, the first settler to arrive in 1845. He died in 1856, but other family members remained in the valley in 1859, including his son Solomon and his daughter Sarah and her husband, Rowland Chambers. Chambers built a gristmill around 1854, and he established the first post office in Kings Valley in 1855, serving as the postmaster.

Twenty-four pioneers accompanied the King family across the Oregon Trail and immediately began converting the area into farmland, yielding grain crops, fruits and vegetables, and also pasturage for livestock. Firewood, building lumber, and wild game were harvested from the surrounding woodlands. During the dry season, the settlers traveled to Corvallis, Oregon City, or Portland for needed goods. In addition to Chambers's gristmill, the town had a sawmill, a store, several saloons, a log schoolhouse, and a church.

The Fort Hoskins Historic Park brochure notes that farmers in Kings Valley often employed Indians from the Coast (Siletz) Reservation as farm workers. The Indians needed written permission from the Indian sub-agent to leave the reservation, and any Indian who failed to return when his work pass expired was hunted down by soldiers from Fort Hoskins, returned to the reservation, and severely punished.

Areas adjacent to Paul Dunn State Forest, Camp Adair, and Adair Village

In 1857 Green Berry Smith laid out the short-lived town of Tampico, located on the Territorial Road near Soap Creek in the vicinity of today's Paul Dunn State Forest and former Camp Adair. A post office, a school, and a number of businesses were in operation in 1859, but in 1860, Smith acquired all of the town property and cancelled the town plat.

In 1856 the Liberty post office was established northeast of present-day Adair Village. James Gingles was the first postmaster, and also one of the first elected county commissioners, serving several terms. South of Adair Village, Haman C. Lewis settled on his donation land claim in 1845. He served as a member of the state constitutional convention.

Sampling of Benton County Family Surnames in 1859

Corvallis, Philomath, and Adair Village

Abbey	Bundy	Dixon	Gingles	Johnson	Miller	Right	Swick
Alexander	Butterfield	Dohse	Graves	Kelsay	Mulkey	Roberts	Thayer
Avery	Campbell	Elliott	Hanna	Kendall	Ownby	Saint Clair	Thomas
Banks	Cardwell	Fiechter	Hartless	Kline	Piper	Scott	Vanbedder
Bell	Carter	Fisher	Hodes	Kriechbaum	Porter	Shipley	Vanderpool
Bennett	Congle	Foster	Hodges	Landerking	Reed	Slater	Williams
Blair	Conner	Friedly	Holder	Leggett	Reeves	Smith	Winkle
Brown	Currier	Fuller	Holgate	Lewis	Richardson	Stewart	Winship
Buckingham	Davis	Gaylord	Hovey	Maurer	Riggs	Stout	

Monroe Area and Alsea and Lobster Valleys

Belknap	Freel	Goodman	Hawley	Irwin	Kompp	McBee	White
Edwards	Gilbert	Hammer	Hayden	Kellum	Lloyd	Starr	Winkle

Fort Hoskins and Kings Valley

Allen	Caldwell	Galbraith	Norton	Wrenn
Auger	Chambers	King	Patterson	

In Southern Portion of Present-Day Lincoln County

Sites to Visit in South
Lincoln County

Alsea Bay Bridge Interpretive
  Center
Waldport
541·563·2002

Oregon Coast History Center
545 SW 9th St, Newport
541·265·7509

Toledo Centennial History Center
208 S Main St, Toledo
541·336·2247

Waldport Heritage Museum
320 NE Grant St, Waldport
541·563·7092

The Alsea and Yaquina coastal Indians had called the southern portion of today's Lincoln County home for thousands of years. Living primarily in the Yachats, Alsea Bay, and Yaquina Bay areas, they subsisted on mussels, clams, crab, salmon, flounder, and smelt. They smoked or dried the fish and shellfish from the ocean, and the venison and elk from the nearby hills. They also gathered many kinds of plant food. According to Robert Kentta, the Cultural Resources Director for the Confederated Tribes of Siletz, seals and sea lions were hunted near off-shore rocks, and in 1856 a reservation employee remarked that "The Yaquinas do not hesitate to go out into the open ocean to hunt whales."

In 1778 Captain James Cook sighted Yaquina Bay at present-day Newport and named Cape Perpetua, located just north of the southern Lincoln County line. In 1849 Lieutenant Theodore Talbot led a small U.S. Army expedition down the coast in search of coal, passing along the entire Lincoln County coastline.

In 1859 the U.S. government created the Alsea Sub-Agency and removed the Coos and Lower Umpqua from the reserve adjacent to the Army's Fort Umpqua in former Umpqua County to Yachats. In time, frame houses, a blacksmith shop, and storage buildings for farm equipment were built. Field crops, primarily potatoes, were planted at Yachats. Some Indians cleared land for farming along the Yachats River, but the region was not conducive to growing any types of grains. The reservation policies required all able-bodied Indians to labor in the fields and prevented them from gathering their traditional foods. The unsuited crops usually failed and as a result, many starved to death or died from disease. Unsavory Indian agents stole funds and supplies, and physically abused the Indians.

Despite the adverse conditions on the reservation, some Indians managed to eke out a meager existence. They were allowed to farm farther upriver, reaping improved crops. They also were beginning to think that there might be opportunities to pass their new homes and fishing places on to their children. However, throughout the 1860s, 1870s, and again in the 1890s, the greedy settlers encroached on the Coast (Siletz) Reservation land, lobbying for large sections to be opened to settlement through federal legislation and executive orders. The Yaquina Bay oyster, noted for its superior taste, had been discovered in the late 1850s, bringing attention to the area. In 1865 a 200,000-acre strip of land encompassing Yaquina Bay and Yaquina River was taken from the Coast Reservation and opened to settlement without compensation to the tribes. Consequently, the reservation was split in two and the approximately 525 affected Indians were forced to move again to remaining parts of the reservation.

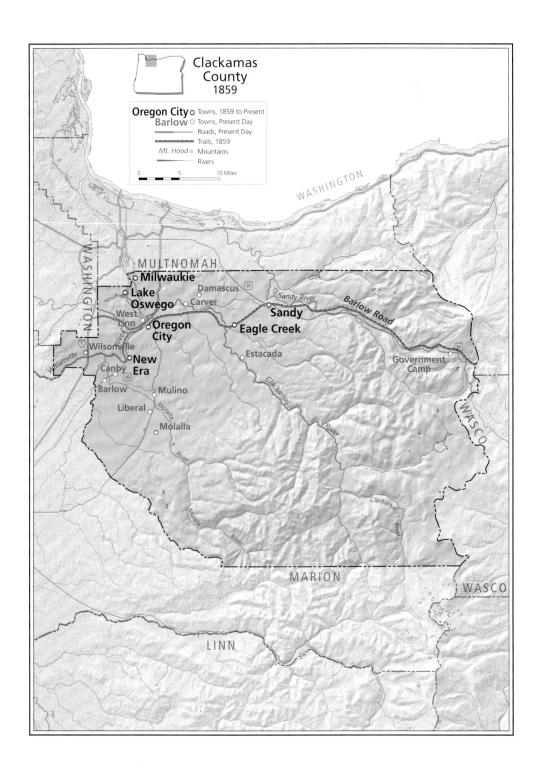

Clackamas
County
1859

Oregon City ○ Towns, 1859 to Present
Barlow ○ Towns, Present Day
——— Roads, Present Day
▬▬▬▬ Trails, 1859
Mt. Hood △ Mountains
——— Rivers

0   5   10 Miles

WASHINGTON

MULTNOMAH

Milwaukie

Damascus

Lake
Oswego

Carver

Sandy River

Barlow Road

West
Linn

Sandy

Oregon
City

Eagle Creek

Wilsonville

Estacada

Government
Camp

New
Era

Canby

Willamette River

Barlow

Mulino

Clackamas

Liberal

Molalla River

Molalla

WASCO

Clackamas River

Molalla River

MARION

WASCO

LINN

2 1859 CLACKAMAS COUNTY

Clackamas County was one of the four original districts created by the provisional legislature in 1843 and comprised a much larger area until 1854 when its current boundaries were finalized. It originally included portions of four present-day states and one Canadian province. Oregon City became the county seat in 1843, the first incorporated city west of the Rockies in 1844, the seat of the provisional government in 1845, and Oregon's territorial capital in 1848. According to the 1860 U.S. Census, the county population was 3466.

With its strategic location on the Willamette River and with the Clackamas River branching off of the Willamette to the east, much of Clackamas County's transportation in 1859 was by water. But several roads, some very primitive and impassable in the winter, had also been built by 1859: the Barlow Road, the Barlow-Foster Trail that went all the way to Portland, and Boone's Ferry Road that connected Salem to Portland as it passed through western Clackamas County. According to the *City of Lake Oswego: Cultural Resources Inventory 1989,* between 1853 and 1858, Macadam Avenue (part of today's Highway 43 and Riverside Drive as it passes through Lake Oswego) was built along the west bank of the Willamette River to connect Lake Oswego with Portland.

Several stagecoach lines were in operation connecting Oregon City and Salem, and Oregon City to Champoeg. In 1859 a bridge was constructed at the mouth of Eagle Creek near Estacada, a considerable improvement to the Barlow Road.

Early History

Prior to Euro-American settlement, Clackamas and Northern Molalla Indians inhabited the area within present-day Clackamas County. The Clackamas were Chinook Indians. Rather than a tribe, Chinooks were groups of villages that shared a similar culture and language. They lived along the Columbia River from the Pacific Ocean to present-day Wasco County. The Clackamas had occupied the area stretching from the Clackamas River north to the Columbia, and from the Willamette River east to the Cascade Range. A band of Clowewalla Indians settled around a fishing village at the site of former Linn City. The Northern Molallas made their home at Molalla Prairie. They brought horses into western Oregon around 1790, which increased their mobility and range.

Sites to Visit in Clackamas County

Baker Cabin, ca. 1856
Off Hwy 224—S Hattan & S Gron-
lund roads, Carver
503·631·8274

Barlow Road Driving Tour
Audio CD or booklet available at
many museums
1·888·622·4822

Boones Ferry Park
31240 SW Boones Ferry Rd,
Wilsonville

Canby Depot Museum
888 NE 4th Ave, Canby
503·266·6712

Captain Ainsworth House & Gardens, ca. 1851 (private business)
19130 Lot Whitcomb Dr, Oregon City
503·957·5722

Carman House, ca. 1857 (private
residence)
3811 Carman Dr, Lake Oswego

End of the Oregon Trail Interpretive
Center—Abernethy Green
1726 Washington St, Oregon City
503·657·9336

Ermatinger House, ca. 1845
(museum)
619 6th St, Oregon City
503·650·1851

Estacada Historical Museum
City Hall, 475 SE Main St, Estacada
503·630·3483

Howard's Mill/Mulino Flour Mill,
ca. 1851 (private residence)
Hwy 213, n. end of Mulino

McCarver House, ca. 1850 (Locust
Farm) (private residence)
554 Warner Parrott Rd, Oregon City

Mill Barn, ca. 1850s (private
business)
(Mill Barn Quilters & Mercantile)
26412 S Hwy 213, Mulino

McLoughlin House National Historic Site, ca. 1846
713 Center St, Oregon City
503·656·5146

Milwaukie Museum
3737 SE Adams St, Milwaukie
503·659·5780

Molalla Museum Complex
Dibble House, ca. 1859
620 S Molalla Ave, Molalla
503·651·2681 or 503·829·5521

Mt Hood Cultural Center & Museum
88900 E Hwy 26, Business Loop
Government Camp
503·272·3301

Museum of the Oregon Territory
211 Tumwater Dr, Oregon City
503·655·5574

Oaks Pioneer Church, ca. 1851
(Milwaukie's original Saint Joseph
Episcopal Church; see Mult-
nomah County sites to visit list)

Oswego Heritage House
398 10th St, Lake Oswego
503·635·6373

Philip Foster Farm, ca. 1847–83
29912 SE Hwy 211, Eagle Creek
503·637·6324

Rose Farm, ca. 1847
914 Holmes Ln, Oregon City
503·656·5146

Sandy Area Historical Museum
39345 Pioneer Blvd, Sandy
503·668·3378

Stage Stop Road Interpretive
Center
24525 E Welches Rd off Hwy 26,
Welches
503·622·4798

Willamette Falls Locks & Museum
End of Mill St, West Linn
503·656·3381

Highly prized hunting grounds were located on the Molalla Prairie that the Indians periodically burned to enhance the growth of native grasses for grazing their horses, maintaining camus patches, and attracting wild game. Seasonal encampments for hunting, fishing, berry picking, and root gathering were located along the Clackamas River. Present-day Canby was once the seasonal meeting place for tribes of local Indians; wild strawberries were abundant. For thousands of years Indians from various tribes had gathered near Willamette Falls to fish and trade. The lake the Indians called Waluga—"wild swan"—in present-day Lake Oswego may have served as a transportation route linking the Tualatin and Willamette rivers.

In the early 19th century, fur traders explored and trapped along the Willamette River in Clackamas County. Donald McKenzie of the Pacific Fur Company in Fort Astoria may have been the first fur trader to visit Willamette Falls in 1812. The earliest permanent settlers were Chief Factor Dr. John McLoughlin of the Hudson's Bay Company (HBC) and other French-Canadian employees of the company. (McLoughlin's biography appears in the Introduction.)

The Indians located in Clackamas County were a party to the 1851 unratified treaties—the Willamette Valley and Clackamas Tribe treaties—and the later 1855 Kalapuya and Confederated Bands of the Williamette Valley Treaty. By 1857 most of the few remaining Indians from this area were relocated to the Grand Ronde Reservation.

A few Indians managed to remain or return to Linn City, Lake Oswego, Oregon City, and the Molalla–Dickey Prairie area. Some had been working for the settlers transporting people and goods over the rivers, washing clothes, helping with the harvest, or working as servants. The affected settlers wanted the Indians to remain because they were willing to work for low wages if it meant being able to stay off the reservations.

Four of Clackamas County's settlements—Oregon City, Linn City, Milwaukie, and the former Multnomah City (before it was swept away by the flood of 1853)—had been contenders to become the most prosperous port in the region—the chief shipping center or head of navigation. But by 1859, Portland had secured this role.

Oregon City

In 1829 Dr. McLoughlin established Oregon City, originally known as Willamette Falls, as a lumber mill and small fur trading center for the HBC. A Methodist Mission contingent arrived in the early 1840s, followed by the first wave of Oregon Trail emigrants.

In addition to the firsts already noted, Oregon City had Oregon's first jail and library in 1845, the first newspaper and mail delivery in 1846, and the first fire department in 1854 with the formation of the volunteer Fountain Hose Company.

Oregon City grew rapidly as overland migration increased. The industrial businesses were located at the southwest end of Main Street near the falls, which provided power to operate the mills. The typical assortment of busi-

Oregon City in 1857 by Lieutenant Lorenzo Lorain. Courtesy of the Oregon Historical Society, OrHi 21079.

nesses expanded northeast on Main Street, and eventually along the cross streets, with residences, churches, and schools interspersed in between. As the commercial interests grew throughout the 1850s, residential development began on the bluff above town. Until the first stairs were built in the mid-1860s, people used Indian trails to climb the bluff.

In 1840 George and Anna Abernethy arrived by way of the Sandwich Islands with the Great Reinforcement for Jason Lee's Willamette Mission. They built a house on the north bank of Abernethy Creek at its confluence with the Willamette River. A long and narrow portion of their 640-acre land grant extended to the Willamette River; this area became known as Abernethy Green. Oregon Trail emigrants arriving on rafts from Fort Vancouver left the river at the Abernethys' house and climbed up to Abernethy Green.

Typically arriving in the late fall or early winter, most pioneers wintered over in encampments there. Their respite allowed them to locate a piece of property in the Willamette Valley, file a claim at the General Land Office, and resupply at the various stores.

Many of the Oregon Trail emigrants who chose to take the Barlow Road still finished their trek at Abernethy Green because that route essentially terminated there. During the peak years of the Oregon Trail migrations, the

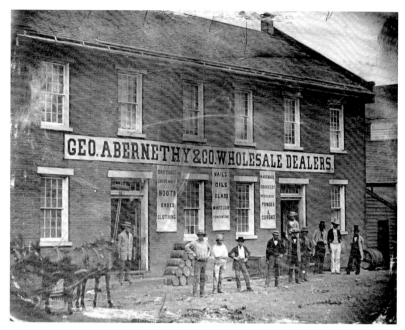

George Abernethy's 1850 store. (He may be the gentleman standing in the doorway on the left.)
Courtesy of the Oregon Historical Society, OrHi 24306.

Abernethys' neighbors Hugh Burns, Jacob Hunsaker, Hiram Straight, and Daniel Tompkins shared the overflow of covered wagons.

George Abernethy served as Oregon's first and only provisional governor from 1845 until 1849 when the first territorial governor took office. The flood of 1861–62 carried away the Abernethys' house; financially ruined, the family moved to Portland. By this time Abernethy Green was no longer used as an encampment because Oregon Trail improvements shortened the required travel time; wintering at Oregon City was no longer necessary. Today the End of the Oregon Trail Interpretive Center is located on a portion of George Abernethy's former property.

A number of other houses built in Oregon City prior to 1859 fared better than the Abernethys' house. The oldest extant house is the Ermatinger House that Dr. McLoughlin built in 1845 for his granddaughter's husband, Francis Ermatinger. Ermatinger was the chief trader for the HBC, and the manager of the company store in Oregon City. In 1846 he was transferred to Canada, where his wife and daughter joined him in 1848. (The house was built on Main Street, but was moved to Sixth Street. It is now a house museum, open to the public.)

An historic event took place in the front room of this house in 1845. Asa L.

Asa Lawrence Lovejoy, Oregon City resident and lawyer, but one of the founders of Portland. Courtesy of the Oregon Historical Society, OrHi 1432.

Asa Lawrence Lovejoy
(1808–1882)

Born in Massachusetts; educated at Cambridge and Amherst colleges; admitted to the bar in Maine

Arrived at Oregon City in 1843; opened law practice

Founded townsite of Portland in 1845 with Francis Pettygrove; sold his share to Benjamin Stark later that year

Served as judge, mayor of Oregon City, adjutant-general during Cayuse War, and provisional and territorial legislator

Major stockholder for many of Oregon's earliest businesses, including Oregon Telegraph Company

Married Elizabeth McGary; five children

Lovejoy and Francis W. Pettygrove flipped a coin to determine the name of the city they had just platted on their donation land claim. Each wanted to name the city after his own hometown—Lovejoy's was Boston, and Pettygrove's was Portland, Maine. Pettygrove won the coin toss.

Two other early extant houses in downtown Oregon City include Dr. McLoughlin's 1846 house and Dr. Forbes Barclay's 1849 house, which stand side-by-side today as part of the McLoughlin House National Historic Site operated by the National Park Service. McLoughlin and his wife Marguerite, of Cree-Swiss descent, built this house facing the Willamette Falls, and were known for their hospitality and generosity. In 1909 the house was carefully moved to its present location on Center Street.

Dr. Barclay was the chief physician for the HBC before settling in Oregon City, where he continued practicing medicine and also served as a city councilman, mayor, educator, and as Oregon's first coroner. The 1849 Barclay House, built of pine lumber brought around Cape Horn, was moved from Singer Hill to its current location and now serves as the office and gift shop for the McLoughlin House next door.

In 1843 William and Louisa Holmes settled on their land grant just south of Oregon City, especially captivated by the good spring on the property and the beautiful view of Mount Hood. The 1847 house became known as the Rose Farm because of Mrs. Holmes's beautiful rose garden.

The Holmes family hosted sessions of both the provisional and territorial legislatures, and also the 1849 gathering of 300 people when Joseph Lane, the first territorial governor, gave his first official address from their balcony overlooking the lawn below. Many other social events were held in the second floor ballroom.

Today, just south of Rose Farm, the vacant 1850 McCarver House languishes in the South End neighborhood—an area that was farm and pastureland in the 1850s. The prefabricated house was brought around Cape Horn from Maine to San Francisco, and General Morton Matthew McCarver transported it the rest of the way to Portland on his own ship. A lot reduction and subdivision is proposed for

The 1847 Rose Farm remains as a house museum open to the public.
Courtesy of the Clackamas County Historical Society, B-0160-000810.

Captain J. C. Ainsworth House, with second owner William B. Partlow standing on the porch. Courtesy of the Clackamas County Historical Society, Permanent Collection, #B-0160-000481.

the property, but the developer intends to rehabilitate the house.

McCarver was an industrious gentleman, founding towns in several different states, including Linnton in Multnomah County, which today is a Portland neighborhood. He moved to Portland in 1859, selling his house to Arthur Warner. The property became known as Locust Farm because of the locust trees lining the long driveway leading to the house.

Farther to the south, Captain John C. Ainsworth, a steamboat captain on the Willamette and Columbia rivers, built his 1851 Greek Revival mansion on a slight knoll in the Mount Pleasant section of Oregon City. The Ainsworths moved to Portland around 1859, and William B. Partlow purchased the home. Today the elegantly renovated house and gardens serve as a ceremony and reception site.

A number of Christian and private schools were established in Oregon City as early as 1849, including the Clackamas County Female Seminary founded by Reverend George H. Atkinson. In 1859 the Methodist Church operated the school as the Oregon City Seminary, and enrolled both boys and girls. Atkinson made several significant contributions to Oregon's educational system, drafting the Oregon Public School Law, opening the first public school—Barclay School

Major Thomas Charman
(1829–1907)

Emigrated from England in 1848; arrived in Oregon City in 1852

Purchased HBC store and in 1853 established Charman and Warner general merchandise business with Arthur Warner

Hosted many community events in family home he purchased in 1855

Served as major with Oregon State Militia, 1865–66

Organizer of Oregon City Woolen Mills in 1864 and Willamette Falls Electric Co. in 1888

Organizer and president of Bank of Oregon City in 1882

Active in Republican Party and served as Oregon City mayor and county treasurer

Married Sophia Diller; five children

in Oregon City; and founding, along with two other individuals, Pacific University in Washington County.

Nuns of the Holy Names of Jesus and Mary came to Oregon City from Montreal in 1859 to found a school, but they opened an orphanage instead, meeting an urgent need at the time. Tragically, many children were orphaned as their families crossed the plains.

The Methodists organized a congregation in Oregon City in 1840 and built a church in 1844. The congregation, known today as the Oregon City United Methodist Church, is the oldest continuous Protestant congregation in Oregon. Another extant congregation, Saint John the Apostle Catholic Church, completed its church in 1846. Neither of the church buildings remain, and the replacement structures were built at different locations.

West Linn, Historic Willamette District, and former Canemah

The former Linn City, located on the rocky western shore of the Willamette River below today's West Linn, was settled in the early 1840s. Robert Moore established Robin's Nest, which he renamed Linn City in 1845 in honor of his friend Lewis F. Linn, an advocate for Oregon in the 1840s and one of the U.S. senators from Missouri who later authored the Donation Land Act of 1850.

Linn City had a bustling commercial district, plus a warehouse, several wharves, and a breakwater to allow boats to load and unload cargo, making it one of the major transportation centers on the Willamette. Moore built the Linn City Works Company in 1852–53; it operated a hoist for transporting small vessels to a similar facility above the Willamette Falls. In 1859 the firm of Abernethy, Clark and Company acquired the unique company and changed the name to the Oregon Milling and Transportation Company.

Moore assumed several prominent roles during the territorial and provisional period. In the early days, he operated a ferry between Linn City and Oregon City and published the *Oregon Spectator* for a short time. He died in 1857, prior to the devastation of his town from a fire in early 1861, and the 1861–62 winter flood that caused further destruction.

Today the historic Willamette Falls Locks, built in the 1870s, are located on the former site of Linn City, along with a paper company, whose origins date back to 1889.

George Walling and his brother Albert, joined by S. M. Holderness and C. W. Savage, platted the town of Willamette in 1850. Willamette never succeeded in becoming a center of commerce; since 1916 the Historic Willamette District has been part of West Linn.

George Walling was one of Oregon's pioneer nurserymen, and Albert G.

Walling, a printer and publisher, compiled and edited several Oregon county history books. Both brothers participated in the organization of the first school district in Clackamas County, and George Walling served as the superintendent of schools for the county for 15 years.

The former community of Canemah ("the Canoe Place"), located southwest of Oregon City and today included within its city limits, was a flourishing shipping town throughout the 1850s because of its natural harbor and suitability for dockside riverboat construction on the Willamette River. The partnership of Captain Charles Bennett, Alanson Beers, Hamilton Campbell, and John McClosky built a number of steamboats there. Their *Canemah* was the first steamship to operate on the upper river and served as the first floating post office in Oregon in 1852–53. It also transported much of the valley grain crop, traveling upriver as far as Corvallis.

Absalom Hedges founded Canemah in 1845. The town had a vibrant business district, featuring the Canemah Hotel—the social center for the community. In the early 1850s Oregon's first railroad was built along a portage road adjacent to the Willamette shoreline to circumvent the Willamette Falls, connecting Canemah to Oregon City. David P. Thompson, Asa L. Lovejoy, and the Dement brothers, John and William, laid about a mile of iron track on which small open cars were drawn by mules. The train carried freight and sometimes passengers. In 1854 Peter Hatch was awarded the contract to build a new portage road around the falls to accommodate wagons.

Canemah was prospering when the 1861–62 flood struck, and it was among the few towns that survived. However, in the 1870s, when river commerce declined, the town ceased to exist as a commercial center.

Lake Oswego

On the site of the city of Lake Oswego there was once a dense forest with thick undergrowth. Albert and Miranda Durham were the first settlers to arrive in 1847, settling north of Sucker Creek, now known as Oswego Creek. In 1851 they built a house on a bluff overlooking the Willamette River in the vicinity of present-day Church and Furnace streets. In 1850, others filed claims along the river, including Jesse Bullock, F. A. Collard, Josiah Franklin, William Torrence, and Socrates H. Tryon. Most of the western portion of today's Lake Oswego remained undeveloped for many years because of its inaccessibility.

Durham operated a sawmill and acquired three schooners to transport his lumber. In 1851 he platted the town of Oswego in the area known as Old Town today, but he never registered it. Town growth was stunted in the mid- to late 1850s because of the diminishing California gold rush, the expiration

Albert Alonzo Durham, first Lake Oswego settler. His wife, Miranda White, served as Oswego's postmistress for a time. Courtesy of the Lake Oswego Public Library.

of the Donation Land Act, and the increased dominance of Portland and Linn City on the western side of the Willamette, and Oregon City on the eastern side. Transportation was the key to the commercial and industrial success of the early towns, and Lake Oswego could not compete with the larger towns.

In the late 1850s, Matthew Patton purchased Collard's claim near Sucker Lake (today's Lake Oswego); the property had very high iron content. At first Patton merely strip mined, but in 1865, with the proceeds from his success in the California gold fields, he established a mine on Iron Mountain. His Oregon Iron Company continued in operation until 1876.

A number of Lake Oswego's early pioneer families were Methodists. They organized the Oswego Methodist Church in 1854.

In her *Iron, Wood & Water: An Illustrated History of Lake Oswego*, Ann Fulton recounts the history of Lake Oswego's early educational system. In 1855 Episcopal Missionary Bishop Thomas Fielding Scott purchased Durham's townsite, along with a schoolhouse that had been built in 1850. He established the Diocesan School for Boys, later called Trinity School. The school provided both religious and secular education. Scott's goal was to provide an education for all children, and he hoped to prepare some young men for the ministry, as there was a shortage of ministers. The boarding school allowed students to pay for their tuition by working in the school's garden. In 1858 Scott bought more of Durham's property and expanded the school, but enrollment dropped after 1860 and the school closed in 1866. Until 1868, students wishing to attend a public school had to row across the river to attend Riverside School in present-day Concord.

Milwaukie

In 1848 Joseph Kellogg, Henderson Luelling, and Lot Whitcomb settled Milwaukie. All three men and several others made significant contributions to the development of the town.

Milwaukie in the late 1850s, seen from the ferry landing on the west bank of the Willamette River. Courtesy of the Oregon Historical Society, OrHi 4816.

In 1850 Whitcomb and Kellogg, and William Torrence of Lake Oswego employed Captain John C. Ainsworth and engineer Jacob Kramm to build the first steamship manufactured in Oregon—the *Lot Whitcomb*. The side-wheeler continued to operate on the Willamette and Columbia rivers until 1854 when it was sold to a firm in California. The three partners also built and operated a gristmill and several sawmills. They were large exporters of lumber to California during the gold rush. Kellogg and Torrence were involved in several other shipbuilding ventures, and Kellogg, a ship captain, remained prominent in the transportation industry throughout the rest of his long life, dying in 1903 at the age of 91.

The Veranda Hotel in Milwaukie, an imposing structure in the 1850s, was the social center for the community. Courtesy of the Oregon Historical Society, OrHi 46761.

Whitcomb donated the land and a partially completed structure for Saint John's Episcopal Church. The original 1851 church stood on today's SE 27th Street. A renovated version of the original church, known today as Oaks Pioneer Church, has survived two relocations and is located at the edge of Sellwood Park in Southeast Portland. Unlike the church facility where weddings and funeral services are held today, the original church did not have stained glass windows or a steeple. A small belfry on the roof above the entry was the only identifier of the structure's function.

Whitcomb served as a territorial legislator and also as the Milwaukie postmaster until his sudden death from malaria in 1857.

In 1847 Henderson Luelling transported 700 fruit grafts across the plains and started the Pacific Northwest nursery industry. In 1848 he and one of his son-in-laws, William Meek, who also brought fruit trees from Iowa, formed a partnership to plant orchards and operate a gristmill and sawmill. Luelling's brother Seth Lewelling, who used another of many versions of the family surname, joined the partnership in 1850. In 1853 they expanded their orchard planting into other parts of the Willamette Valley.

With the changes in the California market, Henderson Luelling and Meek eventually moved to California and settled in the San Francisco Bay Area—Luelling in 1854 and Meek by 1859. Seth Lewelling remained in Milwaukie and became one of the founders of the Oregon Horticultural Society in 1856 and the Oregon State Fair in 1861. He also propagated a variety of cherries and introduced Italian prune trees to Oregon in 1858.

Government Camp, Sandy, Eagle Creek, Currinsville, Estacada, Carver, and Damascus

The Barlow Road, the alternate route to the Willamette Valley, passed along today's Highway 26 through present-day Government Camp, which takes its name from an 1849 event. The first U.S. regiment of Mounted Riflemen crossed the plains into Oregon that year. Most of the troops traveled down the Columbia River to Fort Vancouver on flat-bottomed boats, but a small contingent, unable to fit on the bateaux, was ordered to proceed to Oregon City by way of the Barlow Road. Hampered by an unexpected October snowstorm, the troops had to make camp near Government Camp and, after a short time, abandoned over 40 cavalry wagons and much of their livestock before starting down Laurel Hill. They returned the following spring to retrieve their wagons and supplies that they had stowed away in cache pits in the ground.

The challenging Laurel Hill descent was known by all to be one of the most troublesome parts of the Barlow Road. Emigrants had to lower their wagons by ropes down steep rocky slopes. (This historic site, among others noted in *The Barlow Road Driving Tour* guidebook and CD available at most museums in the area, is worth visiting.)

In 1859 the Barlow Road tollgate was located in the area of present-day Sandy. In 1852 Francis Revenue had bought the rights to collect tolls here from Philip Foster of Eagle Creek. The following year the Revenue family became the first settlers of what would be known as Revenue until the 1870s.

Revenue opened a trading post and built the first bridge across the Sandy River. His property was the first inkling of civilization seen by the pioneers coming off the perilous Barlow Road around Mount Hood. Revenue operated the tollgate from 1853 to 1865.

After leaving Sandy, the Barlow Road travelers passed through rolling hills interspersed with meadows and timber. The Philip Foster farm in Eagle Creek became a resting place for an estimated 10,000 pioneers. Fresh produce, meat, hay, and covered shelter were available for the first time in months. Foster's wife, Mary Charlotte, served as hostess to the thousands who stopped. She also took charge of raising the ten Foster children and tending the orchards and gardens. Today the Foster homestead is open to the public, and includes the 1883 frame house Foster built, as well as the oldest lilac in Oregon, planted by Mary Charlotte using a lilac cutting she brought from Maine.

Several other families took claims in the area, including the Endersbys, John Fosters (no relation), the Glovers, McBrides, Reeds, and Richeys. These settlers and also the pioneers passing through on their way to Oregon City appreciated the general store Philip Foster operated at Eagle Creek.

The area south of Eagle Creek in Estacada and the community of Currinsville was not on the Barlow Road, but a few hardy souls ventured south and took donation land claims on the more level areas along the Clackamas River. Before the settlers could establish their farms, they had to clear the land of the dense virgin fir forests. In 1845 George and Hugh Currin settled in Zion; many years later—in 1884—the town's name was changed to Currinsville.

In 1846 Horace and Jane Baker chose an area just off the Barlow Road for their donation land claim, attracted by a basalt rock formation located on the property. He was a

Philip Foster, a shrewd entrepreneur who provided much needed goods and services to the emigrants passing through his property, while profiting handsomely at the same time. Courtesy of the Oregon Historical Society, OrHi 3448.

Philip Foster (1805–1884)

Arrived by ship from Maine with his family in 1843

Settled in Oregon City and operated Foster's Willamette Falls store, stocked with goods brought around Cape Horn

Served as first treasurer of provisional government

Helped fund, build, and regulate Barlow Road off and on until 1870s when he sold it

Moved to Eagle Creek in 1847; built cabin, blacksmith shop, gristmill, and later a frame house

Planted fruit seeds brought from Maine for creation of a nursery

In partnership with Egbert Olcott, operated Eagle Milling Company—a sawmill

Established first school in Eagle Creek in 1850 and served as Eagle Creek's first postmaster in 1867

Pioneers traversing the Barlow Road stopped in front of the tollgate, ca. 1880.
Courtesy of the Clackamas County Historical Society, C-0250-003098.

The 1856 Baker Cabin, ca. 1986—partially reconstructed by the Old Timers' Association of Oregon in 1939 for public enjoyment. Photo by Gary G. Hattan, descendant of Jane Baker. Courtesy of the Baker Cabin Historical Society.

stone mason by trade and immediately began quarrying rock and developing a successful business. Horace loaded the quarried rock onto barges and during the spring floods the barges were floated down the Clackamas River to Oregon City where the rock was off-loaded.

The Bakers' cabin is said to have been built by neighbors who took pity on Jane, who had endured life in the family's covered wagon for ten long years. Horace was too busy with his business to build a family house. He did, however, build the cabin's stone fireplace. Baker descendants lived in the cabin intermittently until 1901.

The area that later became known as Damascus had only a handful of land claims taken by 1855. Edward Pedigo is credited with selecting the name for the Damascus Church when it was organized in 1856. He was a potter who was attracted by the red soil that was ideal for the bean pots and jars he crafted. John Fisher and Chevalier Richardson were two other early land claimants in the area.

Dickey Prairie and Molalla

The most southern settlement in Clackamas County was located on Dickey Prairie east of the Molalla River. John Kilgore Dickey and his wife, Martha Ann, took a donation land claim there in 1850 and built a spacious home within a few years. They obtained the sawed lumber from John Cutting's nearby sawmill. Dickey felt guilty about acquiring his property from the government at no cost; he insisted on compensating the Molalla Indians and, as a result, he remained on friendly terms with them.

William Russell and William H. Vaughn were the first pioneers to file land claims in the Molalla area in the early 1840s; others soon followed. A school was built by 1856, and the first general store opened in 1857. The town quickly became a prosperous agricultural and trade center. In 1858 Rock Creek Church was established two miles south of Molalla.

In 1859 Horace Dibble moved into his newly built home. The New England saltbox design house that also served as a stage stop between Oregon City and Molalla remains today as a house museum located in the Molalla Museum Complex.

Needy, Macksburg, Liberal, and Mulino

A post office was established in Needy in 1855, but little is known about the early history of the town. It is believed that it was named for the unfortunate condition of its early settlers and that it had previously been known as Hardscrabble.

In 1852 William and Louisa Mack founded Macksburg northeast of Needy and built a house and school. Gribbles Prairie was located west of Macksburg; the Offield and Cross families settled there around 1852.

To the east, at least two families—the Officers and the Jacksons—settled near the future Liberal. Francis Jackson took advantage of the high quality oak and maple trees in the area and established a profitable furniture manufacturing company.

North of Liberal on Milk Creek, Charles T. Howard built a gristmill in 1851 known as Howard's Mill, and later the Mulino Flour Mill. The enlarged and renovated mill building remains standing along Highway 213 at the north end of Mulino. A restored barn believed to be more than 150 years old is situated across the road from the mill and houses a gift shop.

Barlow, Canby, and New Era

In 1852 William Barlow, son of the Mount Hood trail-blazer Samuel, bought his father's land claim in the area of the present-day community of Barlow. A

Christian Church was organized, which later merged with the nearby Canby Christian Church.

James Baker was the first to settle just north of Canby in 1838. He arrived with a cattle drive from California and married an Indian woman. The area became known as Baker Prairie and in the 1840s other settlers began arriving, including Philander and Anna Lee. The Lees established an 80-acre apple orchard on their donation land claim.

In 1855 the Joseph Parrott family settled northeast of Baker Prairie. They named their settlement New Era after the name of a religious tract published by the New Era Spiritualist Society. Parrott built a gristmill on Parrott Creek and opened a store.

Wilsonville

The western-most area of settlement in Clackamas County was today's Wilsonville along the Willamette River. Colonel Alphonso Boone, the grandson of Kentucky frontiersman Daniel Boone, arrived with his large family in 1846. The family established homesteads on the Willamette River between Oregon City and Butteville in Marion County.

In 1847 Boone and his son Jesse began operating the Boones Ferry across the Willamette just west of today's Interstate 5. One of the first ferry operations across the Willamette, it became a critical link for trade and commerce between Portland and the Willamette Valley.

With two of his other sons, the elder Boone ventured to the California gold fields in 1849 where he died. Jesse continued to operate the ferry until 1872 when he was shot to death in a dispute with a neighbor. Other ferry operators continued to provide ferry service at this location until construction of the Boone Bridge in 1954.

Jesse also began clearing a path for Boones Ferry Road in 1847, which connected Portland with Salem, passing through Marion, Clackamas, Washington, and Multnomah counties. A trading center sprang up called Boones Landing. It included a post office, several stores, a blacksmith shop, and a tavern. The town became a busy port where steamers and sternwheelers picked up and delivered passengers, mail, merchandise, and farm crops for local residents who did not own a private landing.

Today's Wilsonville was a transportation center from its earliest beginnings, but its fertile soil also attracted farmers. Several pre-1860 extant structures are located on designated Century Farms—those which have received statewide recognition for having been in operation for at least 100 years. (The state program began in 1958.)

Sampling of Clackamas County Family Surnames in 1859

Oregon City and West Linn

Abernethy	Bowman	Dement	Holmes	McCarver	Partlow	Thompson
Athey	Boyland	Dierdorff	Hunsaker	Miller	Pease	Tompkins
Atkinson	Burnett	Fisher	Jacobs	Moore	Rinearson	Waite
Barclay	Burns	Gordon	Johnson	Moss	Risley	Wilson
Barlow	Charman	Hamilton	Kelly	Murphy	Stewart	Wright
Blanchett	Curry	Hedges	Lovejoy	Parrott	Straight	Wygant

Lake Oswego

Brown	Bullock	Collard	Davidson	Kruse	Tryon
Bryant	Carman	Confer	Durham	Saffarans	Walling

Milwaukie

Bradbury	Eddy	Lambert	Miller	Waterbury
Campbell	Kellogg	Lewelling	Starkweather	Whitcomb

Eagle Creek, Estacada, Carver, and Damascus

Baker	Foster	Kandle	Miller	Revenue	Stricklin	Wehrheim
Currin	Glover	Lacy	Olcott	Smith	Tucker	Weston
Fisher	Hatch	Llewellen	Palmateer	Stephenson	Wade	Young
Folscum	Helms	Markwood	Pedigo	Stewart	Warnock	

Molalla, Mulino, and Canby

Cross	Dickey	Joslyn	Mack	Offield	Trullinger
Dart	Howard	Killin	Moreland	Russell	Vaughn
Dibble	Jackson	Lee	Officer		

Wilsonville

Boone

Hughes

Clatsop
County
1859

Astoria ○ Towns, 1859 to Present
Seaside ○ Towns, Present Day
━━━━ Roads, Present Day
━━━━ Trails, 1859
Mt. Hood △ Mountains
━━━━ Rivers

0   5   10 Miles

WASHINGTON

COLUMBIA   RIVER
Tongue Pt

Astoria

Warrenton

Fort
Clatsop

OCEAN

Lewis and Clark

Youngs

River

River

30

Westport

PACIFIC

101
26

Gearhart

Seaside

Tillamook Head

26

COLUMBIA

Cannon Beach

26

TILLAMOOK

WASHINGTON

3 1859 CLATSOP COUNTY

Clatsop District was created in 1844 out of the western half of Tuality District. Other boundary adjustments were made in 1845 (when all districts became counties) and also in 1853. Lexington (present-day Warrenton) served as the county seat until 1854 when county electors voted to transfer the seat to Astoria. A two-story frame courthouse was built in 1855, and the first meeting of the county government in Astoria took place in 1856. According to the 1860 U.S. Census, the county population was 498.

The primary obstacle to Clatsop County's early development was its lack of adequate transportation. Astoria and the north end of Clatsop Plains were connected by the Columbia River to the world and to other inland communities along the river, but the settlers farther south along the coast remained fairly isolated.

In 1845, the settlers built a public wagon road from the landing on the Skipanon River in the vicinity of present-day Warrenton south through Clatsop Plains. Families needing to reach their land claims farther to the south usually traveled by ox or horse-driven carts along the beach.

In 1858 Thomas R. Cornelius, W. W. Parker, John Adair, and others made an attempt to connect Astoria with other parts of Oregon by rail, but their efforts advanced only as far as the incorporation of a railroad company.

Early History

The Clatsop Indians lived along the present-day Clatsop County coast from the Columbia River to Tillamook Head for an estimated 10,000 years before the first explorers arrived. The Northern Tillamook (Nehalem Indians) had villages between present-day Seaside and Tillamook Bay in present-day Tillamook County. The tribes shared the abundance of native berries, salmon, clams, mussels, whales, sea lions, elk, and venison. The tribes traded and socialized together, holding ceremonies at Tansy Point and in a village near Seaside.

During the 18th century, British, Spanish, and American trading ships frequented the region in search of sea otter pelts, and explorers arrived in search of a shortened water route between the Atlantic and Pacific oceans. Prior to Captain Gray's confirmation and naming of the Columbia River in 1792,

Spanish explorer Bruno Heceta sighted the area of Clatsop Plains in 1775.

In 1805 Captain Meriwether Lewis and Captain William Clark entered the Lower Columbia River near present-day Astoria. Several Lewis and Clark historic sites are located in Clatsop County, including the replica of Fort Clatsop in Astoria where the Corps of Discovery wintered in 1805–06.

Fort Astoria, established in 1811 by American John Jacob Astor's Pacific Fur Company, was abandoned in 1825, but today a small park and a replica of the fort's blockhouse stand on the site of the original fort in downtown Astoria.

Probably fewer than ten American families remained in the area after the fort closed, until 1841 when the Methodists arrived to establish a mission on Clatsop Plains. The mission only remained in operation until 1844, but in the meantime a few members of the 1843 wave of emigrants continued west past the Willamette Valley to make their homes near the site of the former fort or on Clatsop Plains, which stretched between the Columbia and Tillamook Head.

The Clatsop Indians were cordial to the Euro-Americans ever since the first explorer set foot on their lands, and provided generous assistance to the new arrivals, offering food, working as farm hands, rafting lumber and supplies to and from ships on the Columbia, and canoeing family members and belongings to their land claims.

In 1851 the Clatsop and the Nehalem band of Tillamook Indians negotiated the Tansy Point Treaty, but the U.S. Senate never ratified it. In 1855 all of the Oregon coast tribes were supposed to be confederated under one treaty upon the Coast Reservation, but removal of the northern Oregon coast tribes to the reservation never occurred; the Clatsop and Tillamook tribes were allowed to remain on their homeland. However, they often traveled to both the Coast and the Grand Ronde reservations nearby to trade with other Indians, and a few eventually relocated to the Grand Ronde Reservation.

After the arrival of explorers and traders, hundreds of Indians perished from a recurring fever, probably a form of malaria, and most of the 600 surviving Clatsops died after

Michel (Jennie) Martineau, ca. 1895, was better known as Jennie Michel or Princess Tsin-is-tum. Census takers frequently recorded names as they sounded, so there were various spellings of all parts of her name—Meschelle, Machell, and Merchino. *Courtesy of the Clatsop County Historical Society, Astoria, Oregon. Photo #4299-005b.*

Jennie Michel (1815 or 1820–1905)

Her father, a Snake River Indian chief, and her uncle knew explorers Lewis and Clark

About 1835, Tsin-is-tum married a chief of the Tillamook tribe, who died around 1860

Married Michel Martineau, a French-Canadian and half Chippewa Indian, several years after her first husband died

Assisted an Oregon Historical Society committee in identifying the site of Lewis and Clark's salt cairn in Seaside

Celiast (Hellen) Smith (1804–1891)

Daughter of Clatsop Chief Coboway

Wife of first white pioneer on Clatsop Plains, Solomon H. Smith; raised four children of their own (three died) and several foster children

With her husband, established first school in Oregon in their home

Mediated many conflicts between Indians and settlers

Sent eldest son, Silas, to study law in New Hampshire; he became successful lawyer in Astoria

a later smallpox outbreak in 1852. The handful of remaining survivors lived primarily in the area of Tongue Point and the present-day communities of Warrenton and Miles Crossing.

Astoria

Astoria, named after John Jacob Astor, did not officially become part of the United States until 1846 when the U.S. and Great Britain settled their protracted boundary dispute by dividing the Oregon Country along the 49th parallel. The following year, James Shively opened the first post office west of the Rockies. In 1849 Customs Collector John Adair established a U.S. Customs House in Astoria to collect duties, and the customs house built in 1852 was the first federal building built west of the Rocky Mountains.

In his memoirs published in 1992 in the Clatsop County Historical Society's journal, *Cumtux*, Samuel T. McKean relates the story about Adair laying out another town on

John Adair, first collector of customs for Oregon. Courtesy of the Oregon Historical Society, OrHi 9241.

John Adair (1808–1888)

Educated in Kentucky, and at West Point and Harvard

Established law practice in Columbus, Mississippi

Appointed collector of U.S. Customs in Astoria in 1848 by President Polk; reappointed by subsequent presidents, serving through 1861

Arrived in Astoria in 1849 with his wife, Mary Ann, and seven children

Contributed to agricultural development of Clatsop County

Adairs entertained visitors often and Mrs. Adair started a Sunday school, gave piano lessons, and supervised Adair children's education

his land claim just east of the original Astoria townsite. He also moved the customs house and the post office there. The rivalry and inconvenience that resulted affected both towns. Eventually Adair's Upper Astoria collapsed, the customs house and post office were moved back to Astoria, and both areas grew into one city.

Even though Euro-Americans have lived in Astoria longer than in any other part of Oregon, its growth by 1859 was far outpaced by many other communities in the Willamette and Rogue valleys. However, several sawmills were established during the California gold rush, including two on the Lewis and Clark River. The mills provided employment and stimulated the growth of other businesses nearby. Land claims were taken along the river and a community of settlers developed. Other mills were located at Tongue Point and on the Youngs River. In time, the port boosted Astoria's prominence, second only to Portland.

In the early 1850s, Adam Van Dusen established the first general store in Astoria, and schools, churches, and other mercantile businesses followed. Commercial salmon fishing started during the 1850s, with barrels of salted salmon being shipped out routinely to Portland and California. (The first cannery was not established until the mid-1860s.)

A few permanent homes were built, including the west portion of the extant Brown House on Franklin Street, originally located in Adair's Upper Astoria. River pilot Captain Hiram Brown built the house in 1852 and later moved it to its current location. Another 1850s house is part of a bed and breakfast located on Exchange Street.

People settled at the edges of Astoria, including Samuel C. Smith who took a claim on land still known as Smith Point, and Robert Shortess who chose the area now known as the Alderbrook neighborhood of Astoria, just north of Emerald Heights.

Prior to 1860 a thick forest of hemlock and spruce timber covered much of the peninsula on which Astoria is located. In 1860, Judge Cyrus Olney, the new owner of Astoria, cut down 40 acres of the forest.

Captain George Flavel (1823–1893)

Arrived in Portland in 1849 from Virginia by way of California gold fields

Before marrying Mary Christina L. Boelling in 1854, he boarded at her father's hotel and boarding-house in Astoria

Held a virtual monopoly of tug and pilotage business on Columbia River until 1864

Owned wharf and operated successful coal business—selling ballast coal he bought from arriving international ships

Landholder and bank president

Purchased full city block in 1859 on which the Queen Anne-style Flavel House, a house museum today, was built in 1885

Left an estate of $1,900,000 upon his death

Mary Christina was socialite and philanthropist who enhanced Astoria's cultural development; couple had three children

Cyrus Olney, territorial supreme court justice, delegate to the constitutional convention, and state legislator. Courtesy of the Oregon Historical Society, OrHi 3540.

Captain George Flavel, ca. 1854, at the beginning of his long and prosperous career. Courtesy of the Clatsop County Historical Society, Astoria, Oregon. Photo #530-00Flavel.

Mary Christina Flavel, ca. 1854, married Captain Flavel when she was only 14. Courtesy of the Clatsop County Historical Society, Astoria, Oregon. Photo #532-00Flavel.

Astoria Waterfront, ca. 1855. Courtesy of the Clatsop County Historical Society, Astoria, Oregon. Photo #4471-906.

In the early 1850s Astoria began its steady ascent as a vacation destination for Portlanders seeking recreation and avoiding the hot weather in the summer. Visitors traveled by steamer down the Columbia River. Vacationers eventually ventured farther south along the Oregon coast, traveling by stagecoach on wagon roads and along the beaches.

Clatsop Plains, including Warrenton, Gearhart, Seaside, and Cannon Beach

According to Inez Stafford Hanson in her *Life on "Clatsop"*, Clatsop Plains was called Clatsop City at one time; when people referred to "on Clatsop," they meant anywhere from Tillamook Head to the Columbia. The earliest settlers on

Clatsop Plains selected various locales, with the northern-most at Tansy Point. William W. Raymond, arriving in 1842 with the intention of working at the Methodist mission, built the first frame dwelling there. He took up full-time farming when the mission disbanded two years later. (In 1859 Raymond was an Indian sub-agent and dairyman in Tillamook County.)

To the south, the former town of Lexington developed in the area of Warrenton. W. Hall platted the town in 1848, and it served as the first county seat. A mail route was established between Clatsop Plains and Oregon City in 1849. This area was also known as Skipanon because of the Skipanon River running through it.

Solomon H. Smith, who arrived in 1840 and married the daughter of Chief Coboway, built a warehouse and operated a mercantile business in Warrenton. (Several other early arrivals also had Indian wives.) Smith brought the first two horses to the area from the Willamette Valley. Calvin Tibbets herded cattle from the Willamette Valley, and John Hobson, the teenage son of William Hobson, drove herds of cattle across the mountains from California. Robert S. MacEwan arrived at Clatsop Plains with sheep, cattle, and horses he brought across the plains.

Unfortunately, wolves were a constant threat to the settlers' livestock; hunting parties were planned at Wolf Meetings. These meetings held at Smith's farm developed into venues where other issues of interest to the community were discussed, election boards formed, and petitions prepared for needed road improvements.

Most Clatsop Plains settlers farmed, but a few worked in the mills. The farmers tried various crops, finding that vegetables fared well in the coastal climate and sandy soil, but that grains did not. P. W. Gillette introduced the first cane berries to Oregon when he planted rootings his father sent him from Ohio in 1853. These were planted near the site of Fort Clatsop and were later disseminated to many parts of western Oregon.

The earliest school on Clatsop Plains was a log cabin built

Philip Gearhart took a donation land claim in 1850 where the beach resort of Gearhart is located today. With additional claims he acquired in 1859 and 1863, his total land parcel included a portion of Seaside. (Gearhart Golf Links opened in 1902, but local lore insists that a small group of Scots laid out four holes in the 1880s, making the golf course the oldest in the Western United States.) Courtesy of the Clatsop County Historical Society. Photo #9139-00G.

in 1847 near the Morrison family's house. The Presbyterians were the first to build a church in 1850; in 1859 it was also being used as the school.

By 1846 settlers had taken land claims as far south as Seaside. According to William Berg in his *Gearhart Remembered: An Informal History*, Henry Marlan built a gristmill on Mill Creek northeast of the Necanicum estuary—before he realized that Clatsop Plains was not a good place to grow wheat. Not wanting to abandon the ideal water power Mill Creek provided, he converted the mill into one for cutting lumber. Since it was difficult transporting the lumber to the Columbia River for shipment, most of it was used locally.

During the early 1850s, settlement moved farther south near the foot of Tillamook Head. Alexander Lattie's widow, Catherine Elizabeth, an Indian woman, took a land claim located on the southern half of Seaside. Her son William took a claim adjoining hers, at the base of Tillamook Head. The Lattie family established a boardinghouse in 1852 and eventually accommodated vacationers during the summer months. A married daughter, Helen Cloutrie, had developed her culinary skills while living with the Adam Van Dusen family in Astoria. Her sumptuous dinners gained widespread fame. First known as Lattie's and Bill Lattie's, the establishment was later named Summer House in 1859.

In 1850 Robert Howell was the first to settle near Ecola Creek in present-day Cannon Beach, but because the only access was along an Indian trail, further settlement did not occur until railroad service began in the late 1800s. Cannon Beach was originally known as Elk Creek and later, Ecola. The current name commemorates the cannon that washed ashore from a shipwrecked schooner in 1846.

Seaside's 1987 survey of historic resources reported that William Hobson introduced Scotch broom to Oregon in 1840 by requesting his family in the British Isles to send him seed to plant for beautification of his farm. However, he did not know that Scotch broom, when planted outside of its native habitat, over time poses a threat to native plant species and wildlife. For many years the prolific plant was welcomed by the public and even the government for its erosion control qualities. Its deep yellow bloom that filled the landscape in the spring throughout Clatsop County, came to be known as the Golden Trail. Today, however, throughout much of Oregon, Scotch and other brooms, and the related but even more destructive gorse, invade and degrade coastal and mountain ecosystems, create a dangerous source of fuel for wildfire, and inhibit forest regeneration in logged timberlands.

The only settlement east of Astoria was in present-day Clifton and Westport. Richard H. Engeman, the former public historian for the Oregon Historical Society, advises that in 1844 Henry H. Hunt built the first sawmill in Clatsop County on Hunt Creek in the present-day Clifton area. John West settled in the Westport area around 1850–51. West operated a sawmill, and much later, a salmon cannery.

Some logging began in Clatsop County during the 1840s, but because much of the area remained inaccessible, logging was not done on a large scale until the arrival of the railroad in the late 1800s.

Sampling of Clatsop County Family Surnames in 1859

Astoria, Clatsop Plains, and Westport

Adair	Callender	Crow	Hobson	Lattie	Olney	Summers
Anderson	Carnahan	Davidson	Hubbard	Louk	Pease	Tallman
Beirman	Cloutrie	Eberman	Ingalls	MacEwan	Powers	Taylor
Blodgett	Coffenberry	Elder	Jeffers	Moffit	Ramey	Thomas
Bowling	Condit	Flavel	Jewett	Montgom-	Shively	Thompson
Brown	Cook	Gearhart	Johnson	ery	Shortess	Welch
Burnside	Crosby	Gillette	Kindred	Morrison	Smith	West

Columbia
County
1859

Rainier ○ Towns, 1859 to Present
Clatskanie ○ Towns, Present Day
━━━━━━ Roads, Present Day
┅┅┅┅┅┅ Trails, 1859
Mt. Hood △ Mountains
━━━━━━ Rivers

0   5   10 Miles

WASHINGTON

Columbia River

Woodson
Clatskanie
Rainier

Goble

CLATSOP

Deer
Island
Columbia
City
St Helens

Vernonia

TILLAMOOK
WASHINGTON
Scappoose

Sauvie
Island

MULTNOMAH

4 1859 COLUMBIA COUNTY

Columbia County was created in 1854 from the northern half of Washington County. The former town of Milton served as the first county seat, until the seat was moved to St. Helens in 1857. The area held promise in its earliest days, but the 1855–58 Yakima Indian War being fought across the river in the Washington Territory and up the river in the Oregon Territory prompted many of the original settlers to depart, fearing for their safety. According to the 1860 U.S. Census, the county population was 532. Growth continued at a slow pace for another decade.

Transportation for Columbia County residents in 1859 was by boat, horseback, or wagon. The few roads in existence followed Indian trails, like the one that led from St. Helens, through Scappoose, and on to Hillsboro in Washington County.

Early History

For centuries two groups of Indians lived in present-day Columbia County—Chinook (Cathlamet and Skilloot) and Clatskanie. The Chinook lived along the Columbia River and the Clatskanie lived primarily in the hills south of the Clatskanie River in the upper Nehalem Valley. Village sites moved according to the season and location of their sources of food—elk, deer, salmon, berries, and wapato.

The Lewis and Clark Corps of Discovery explored the Columbia riverfront within Columbia County in 1805–06 and fur traders subsequently frequented the Beaver Valley. As early as 1810, Captain Nathan Winship established the first settlement along the river, but the group soon departed—discouraged by flooding and the constant threat of unfriendly Indians.

The first permanent American settlers arrived in the mid-1840s, many attracted to the extensive stands of timber located throughout the county. The few Indians who survived the smallpox and malaria outbreaks in the early 19th century were relatively peaceable.

In her *The Story of Rainier 1805 to 1925,* Anna Zerzyke reported that a chief known as Indian Tom lived in Rainier. He lived as a contributing member of the community until his death in 1865. Zerzyke also reported that there was an Indian village in Rainier in the late 1850s with about 150 residents.

St. Helens and Columbia City

Milton was once located one-half mile above St. Helens on the Scappoose Bay. Several speculators, including Captain Nathaniel Crosby Jr. (the great grandfather of Bing Crosby) and Thomas H. Smith, founded Milton in 1850–51.

Milton started out as a thriving town, and even competed with Portland for supremacy on the Columbia at one time. Crosby and Smith operated a successful sawmill during the California gold rush, shipping lumber to that state on their bark named the *Louisiana*. After Portland became the chief shipping center on the Columbia in the mid-1850s, the townsite began to fail commercially and when the county seat was transferred to St. Helens in 1857, the town was dissolved. Two separate floods between 1861 and 1862 washed away what remained of the community.

Bartholomew White built the first gristmill and sawmill in St. Helens in 1844, but it was Captain Henry M. Knighton and William H. Tappan who platted the town in 1849–50. Before taking the name of St. Helens around 1850, the site was variously named Wyeth's Rock, Knighton, Plymouth Rock, New Plymouth, and Cassino (or Cazeno or Casenou or Kasenau), in honor of the well-known Indian chief who had lived nearby until his death in 1850.

After the demise of Milton, Knighton and Tappan promoted St. Helens to become the chief shipping center. By 1852 the Pacific Mail Steamship Company had chosen St. Helens as its northern terminus and built a wharf and several warehouses. Knighton built an additional wharf and more warehouses in 1853, making St. Helens a serious contender until both of the wharves burned. Consequently, Pacific Mail and other companies chose Portland as their terminal, delivering a serious blow to St. Helens's economy and prompting some to leave. (Knighton was working in Wasco County in 1859, but apparently retained ownership of his St. Helens house. His name appears in the 1860 Columbia County census and he died in St. Helens.)

Many early settlers were determined to stay in St. Helens, including Captain Seth Pope who became the first county judge in 1859; Dean Blanchard who served as the first county clerk; and William Pope who was the post office clerk. Since there were no county buildings, official business was performed in the county clerk's home. With only a few of the original community businesses still in operation, St. Helens remained a small riverfront village for several more decades.

There were a number of beautiful 1850s houses in the town, including the one that the Knightons built in 1851 with rough lumber from the mill at Milton and finished lumber brought around Cape Horn from Maine by Captain Francis LeMont. The Knighton house remains as a private residence today, having been moved from its original location in the 1930s.

Knighton also built a church on Nob Hill in 1852–53. The material used was brought around the Horn. Dr. Thomas Condon, who later became Oregon's foremost geologist and a professor at the University of Oregon, came to St. Helens

Captain Henry M. Knighton
(1818–1863)

Born in New Jersey
Arrived in Oregon with his family in 1845, first settling in Oregon City, where he opened City Hotel and served in several government positions
Took donation land claim and established St. Helens in 1849–50
One of main contenders in competition for head of navigation designation on Columbia River
After losing competition and destruction of wharves by fire, became ship's captain on Columbia River between Portland and The Dalles
Married Elizabeth J. Martin; six children

1852 church built by Captain Henry M. Knighton on Nob Hill in St. Helens.
Courtesy of the Oregon Historical Society, OrHi 5297.

Dr. Charles G. Caples (1832–1906)

Came across Oregon Trail as teenager with widowed father, Joseph, and siblings

Success in California gold mines paid his and his sister's tuition at Tualatin Academy (now Pacific University in Forest Grove)

Married Lucinda McBride in 1855

Studied medicine in Portland and practiced in Columbia City for many years

as a Congregational missionary in 1853 and served as the first minister of the church. Condon also taught school in the church building.

In 1846 Joseph Caples built a cabin north of St. Helens. He divided his property among his three sons in 1867 and officially platted the town of Columbia City. His son Charles built the 1870 two-story home on the former site of his father's cabin which remains as a house museum in Columbia City today.

Scappoose and Sauvie Island

In 1829 Thomas McKay, stepson of Dr. John McLoughlin, chose the Scappoose plains as a place to establish a horse ranch and farm for the Hudson's Bay Company (HBC). It had been an area where the Indians gathered because it was free of the dense forests common to other areas along the Columbia River.

After the few Indians who survived the 1829–30 malaria epidemic disappeared from the Scappoose plains, the area was soon settled by sailors who had jumped ship, along with former HBC employees, including George Rowland and Malcolm McKay (no relation to Thomas McKay). Malcolm McKay and his father-in-law, Timothy Lambertson, built the first sawmill in Scappoose in 1852. Oregon Trail pioneers soon began arriving, including the Cloninger family and the extended Watts family. The settlers established farms for raising produce, dairy cows, and chickens. In 1856 two of William Watts's sons, Ben and Frank, built a mill on Scappoose Creek. A Watts descendant, James Grant Watts, built the 1902 Victorian home that houses the Watts Pioneer Museum today.

The area was known by several different names before it became Scappoose in 1872, the Chinook Indian word for "gravelly plains." Scappoose experienced a period of slow growth between 1855 and 1870, initially because of the Indian hostilities in the area, but a few typical pioneer businesses were operating. Samuel T. Gosa had a small dock on his land claim on the Multnomah Channel, selling cord wood to river steamers. Two brick kilns were also in operation on Scappoose Bay near present-day Warren.

The first school was started in a private home around 1853, and a public school was soon built on the Watts farm. It was the only school between Portland and St. Helens. Circuit riders conducted the first religious services on the Watts's property; other religious meetings were held in the schoolhouse.

The northern portion of Sauvie Island directly opposite Scappoose is part of Columbia County. The southern boundary of John Bonser's land claim coincided with that of the county's. Bonser established a dairy farm and eventually built a race track. The frequent social gatherings, horse races, and generous housing of relatives and orphaned children made the Bonser homestead the center of activity. Bonser served as the first county commissioner.

Rainier, Goble, and Deer Island

By 1859 three settlements were located alongside the Columbia River in the northeastern portion of Columbia County. Charles E. Fox platted the town of Rainier in 1855 and various business establishments were operating, including a cooperage shop where F. C. Winchester made barrels for packing the salted fish the settlers caught and shipped to world ports. Jason Fry and his brother John were in the business of supplying beef to the Oak Point Mill located across the Columbia in the Washington Territory. Francis M. Warren began operating a steam sawmill in 1854.

The site where Rainier developed had long been a stopping place for boats and canoes because of its location on the Columbia near the mouth of the Cowlitz River in Washington. After Fox arrived in 1850, he and several others built wharves. Hotels flourished as Rainier was approximately halfway between Portland and Astoria. Boats had no lights to allow for night travel and usually arrived at Rainier from either direction around nightfall.

There were no school buildings in Rainier until about 1870, but occasional schooling took place wherever a room

Mr. and Mrs. Sidney Wood, founders of Wood's Landing, now called Woodson. Courtesy of the Clatskanie Historical Society.

could be found, usually in homes. There were no church buildings, but if a missionary or circuit rider was passing through, well-attended services were held in homes.

To the south, settlement in the area of present-day Goble began around 1850. Francis A. Fowler took a donation land claim, built a house in which he provided lodging to travelers, and sold cordwood to wood-burning river boats. In 1852 Simon Neer settled just north of Goble. Just south of Goble, the Joseph Merrill family took a donation land claim in the Deer Island area.

Clatskanie and Woodson

In 1852–53 a small number of families settled on a grassland area that extended to the Columbia River in the northwestern part of Columbia County. E. G. Bryant built the first building on the Clatskanie River.

Enoch Conyers's home became a temporary haven for many of the early settlers arriving in the region, and a private school operated upstairs. A schoolhouse had been built in 1854, but it only functioned for three months because many of the families departed the following year. Most of the settlers who stayed behind were bachelors.

Around 1855, the Sidney Wood family settled a little farther west alongside the south bank of Westport Slough where they raised cattle. Their homestead became known as Wood's Landing. The Wood family developed a good relationship with the Indians still living in the area, especially since Mrs. Wood frequently offered medical assistance to them. To show their gratitude, the Indians kept the Wood family well supplied with fresh venison, salmon, wild game, and berries.

Sampling of Columbia County Family Surnames in 1859

St. Helens and Columbia City

Bennett	Cunningham	Gray	Laffer	Miller	Post
Blanchard	Fowler	Harris	LeMont	Nessley	Reed
Broyles	Fullerton	Hoyt	McNulty	Perry	Smith
Caples	Goerig	Knighton	Meeker	Pope	Stevens

Scappoose and Sauvie Island

Armstrong	Gosa	McKay	Poppleton	Watts
Bonser	Johnson	McPherson	Smith	Wetherby
Cloninger	Lamberson	Miles		

Rainier, Goble, and Deer Island

Bacon	Fowler	Gilbreath	Minear	Poland
Clark	Fox	Harris	North	Warren
Dobbins	Fry	Hunter	Peacher	Wood
Foster	Galloway	Merrill	Plympton	

Clatskanie and Woodson

Barr	Bradbury	Conyers	Pieper	Williams
Bohnhart	Bryant	McClane	Ross	Wood

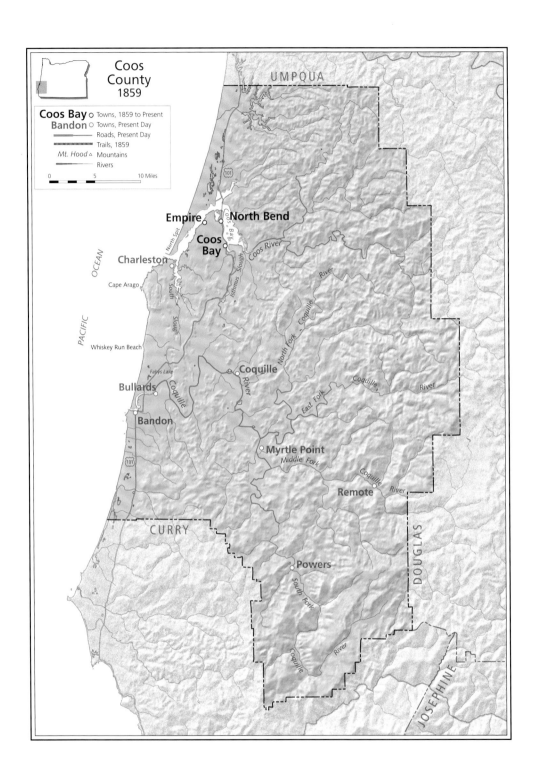

Coos County 1859

Coos Bay ○ Towns, 1859 to Present
Bandon ○ Towns, Present Day
───── Roads, Present Day
═════ Trails, 1859
Mt. Hood △ Mountains
───── Rivers

0   5   10 Miles

UMPQUA

Empire

North Bend

Coos Bay

Charleston

Cape Arago

Coos River

Coos Bay

Isthmus Slough

North Spit

OCEAN

PACIFIC

South Slough

Whiskey Run Beach

Fahys Lake

Coquille

Coquille River

Bullards

Bandon

101

North Fork – Coquille

River

East Fork

Coquille   River

Myrtle Point

Middle Fork

Coquille River

Remote

CURRY

DOUGLAS

Powers

South Fork

Coquille   River

JOSEPHINE

5 1859 COOS COUNTY

Coos County was created in 1853 from parts of former Umpqua (now Douglas) and Jackson counties. Various boundary adjustments were made with Curry and Douglas counties between 1855 and 1983. Empire City (a district of the present-day city of Coos Bay) was the county seat until 1896, when it was moved to Coquille City. Growth was slow-paced due to the lack of overland routes into the county. According to the U.S. Census, the 1860 county population was 445.

Indian trails were followed within the county to connect Empire City with other settlements and the Coquille River. The Indian trail west of South Slough—known as Seven Devils Road–Randolph Trail—was heavily used during the brief gold rush in Randolph.

Travel to the Willamette Valley for Coos County residents was by boat across Coos Bay; then by stage up the beach to present-day Winchester Bay; then by steamer to Scottsburg on the Umpqua River in Umpqua County; and finally by horse or stage to the inland valleys. In 1857 the territorial legislature granted permission for construction of a wagon road from Coos Bay to Roseburg, but it was not until 1872 that the Coos Bay and Roseburg Wagon Road—today called the Coos Bay Wagon Road—finally crossed the mountains. Those traveling to or from Portland or San Francisco boarded coastal schooners or steamers at Coos Bay or on the Coquille River.

Henry "Hank" Hudson Barrett was one of the first operators of a stage line along the shoreline of the Oregon dunes. Arriving in Coos Bay in the 1850s after trying his luck in the California gold rush, he started a stage line between Coos Bay and the Umpqua River, later adding a line from the Umpqua River to Florence. He died in 1905, but his four sons continued the service for many years.

Early History

For thousands of years before Euro-Americans arrived, the Hanis and Miluk Coos Indians and the Upper Coquille lived, hunted, fished, and gathered food along Coos Bay and its estuaries, and also on the lower Coquille River and in the adjacent forests and meadows. The many different species of fish were consumed or dried for trade.

Marshfield-Drain stage in breakers on the beach. Courtesy of the Coos Historical & Maritime Museum, 992-8-0024 (Slattery).

Villages were located near the confluence of the two forks of the Coquille River where Myrtle Point is located today, and also at the current sites of Coquille, Bandon, and Charleston. Indians also inhabited the Tenmile Lakes region north of Coos Bay, which was visited by all of the Indians in the region for harvesting a variety of roots.

British and Spanish sea captains sailed along the southern Oregon coast during the 16th century, and British Captain James Cook sighted Cape Arago in 1778. Hudson's Bay Company (HBC) fur traders led by Alexander Roderick McLeod first reached Coos Bay by land in the 1820s.

In 1828 American Jedediah Smith led an expedition north from California along the southern coast of Oregon, camping at various sites between Bandon and the Coos/current-Douglas county line. Many of the camps were less than two miles apart because the heavy brush and bogs they had to traverse slowed their progress.

However, little was known about the Coos Bay area until 1852 when the U.S. transport schooner *Captain Lincoln* was stranded on the North Spit near the mouth of Coos Bay. During their four-month encampment at "camp castaway" in the dunes, and before being rescued by settlers from Umpqua City, the surviving soldiers and crew explored the area. Word spread of their discovery of gold on nearby beaches and the abundance of natural resources. Gold prospectors and settlers soon flocked to the area.

When Euro-American settlement began in Coos County, peaceful relations with the Indians developed, except in present-day Bandon, where the local Indian village was attacked in 1854 by gold miners, resulting in the death of 16 Indians. Even during the Rogue River Indian War, a relative peace endured. With the exception of some of the Upper Coquille, the Indians living within Coos County stayed out of the war.

Fear among the settlers prompted them to build a fort at Empire City, but there never were any hostilities at Coos Bay. In 1856 the fort was used to hold the Coos Indians under guard before they were forced to move north to Fort Umpqua.

In his *Uncertain Encounters: Indians and Whites at Peace and War in Southern Oregon: 1820s to 1860s*, Nathan Douthit writes about Indian women, especially in Coos County, marrying Euro-Americans and hoping to avoid being relocated to reservations. In *South Slough Adventures: Life on a Southern Oregon Estuary*, The Friends of South Slough recount the story of Mary Ann Hodgkiss, a Coquille Indian, who remained with her American husband, Charles Hodgkiss, after most of the other Coquilles were sent to the Coast Reservation in 1856. (She later married George Wasson in 1862, becoming Susan Wasson; they raised a large family at the head of South Slough.)

Douthit also notes that personal journals show that Indians, both male and female, were living in the Coos Bay area eight years after the end of the Rogue River Indian War. Some of the men were working in the mills. However, soldiers from the reservation periodically made sweeps and marched the Indians back to the reservation.

Coos Bay and North Bend

In 1853 the Coos Bay Commercial Company was formed to promote settlement in the Coos Bay area. The partners staked out timber and coal mining claims, and laid out the town of Empire City, six miles above the Coos Bay Bar.

There were 19 original members of the Coos Bay Commercial Company. Donation land claims were taken for the Empire City site and locations where other towns were eventually founded: Captain W. H. Harris took a claim at Empire City; Freeman G. Lockhart at North Bend; and J. C. Tolman at Marshfield. Other company members settled adjacent to those claims and along the Coos River. Indian villages were still located in the area, and many of the company members married Indian women. Other members and their already established families relocated there.

Commercial enterprises grew in Empire City to meet the needs of residents and visitors alike, including a sawmill owned and operated by Henry Luse. Initial logging operations utilized teams of oxen to haul the logs from the forests to the mill, where a two-man whipsaw was used. However,

Lottie Evanoff and her father Chief Daloose Jackson, one of the last Coos chiefs, were survivors of the march to Fort Umpqua in 1856 and the relocation to Yachats in 1859, ca. 1905. Courtesy Coos Historical & Maritime Museum, 992-8-3153 (Slattery).

Reverend Thomas F. Royal was one of the first circuit riders in Coos County. Religious meetings were held in homes, businesses, or the schoolhouse until the Methodist Episcopal Church was established in 1857. Courtesy of the Oregon Historical Society, OrHi 35595.

Empire City, the western district of Coos Bay, in 1855.
Harper's Magazine. Courtesy of the Oregon Historical Society, CN022249.

as the nearby timber was depleted, the logs were dragged to the river or bay, then floated to the mill.

In 1859 Empire City was the port of delivery for the U.S. Customs District of Port Orford in Curry County, which served southern Oregon between Coos Bay and the California border. One of the most frequently imported products arriving from San Francisco was flour, as Coos County did not have its own gristmill until John Schroeder built one on his land claim near Myrtle Point in 1860.

In 1855 Captain Asa Mead Simpson bought a claim held by Glen Aiken and established the mill and shipbuilding town of North Bend the following year. The cargo ships he built were used to carry the finished lumber from his adjacent mill, and also coal and agricultural products destined for Portland and San Francisco. He accommodated his many employees by building housing, both dormitory-style for single men and small living quarters for those men with families. He also kept a store stocked with food and merchandise delivered by his returning ships.

Where J. C. Tolman settled became known as Marshfield sometime between 1853 and 1855. Tolman moved to Jacksonville in 1854; later claimants to portions of his property were

Simpson Shipyard in North Bend, with partially completed ship on the right. *Courtesy of the Coos Historical & Maritime Museum, 988-P539 (H29, S1).*

Captain Asa Mead Simpson (1826–1915)

Born in Maine; learned shipbuilding trade from father as young man

Emigrated to California in 1849; opened lumberyards in Stockton, Sacramento, and San Francisco

Founded North Bend in 1856 and later several towns in California and Washington

Partner of Captain George Flavel of Astoria for period of time, providing bar pilot service on Columbia River

Purchased steam tug to pilot his ships in and out of Coos Bay harbor following loss of relatives and ships passing over hazardous Coos Bay Bar

Acquired many more sawmills after 1860, first at Port Orford

By 1880s, was building four-masted ships; over a 64-year period his crews built over 50 ships at North Bend

His commercial seagoing businesses stretched from Monterey Bay to Puget Sound

Maintained his permanent residence in San Francisco; four children

A. J. Davis, retired Captain George Hamilton, and Wilkins Warwick. A boat landing, store, and trading post were built at Marshfield around 1854. Little growth took place until after 1867 when a shipbuilding business was established. (Marshfield was not renamed Coos Bay until 1944, when it was changed by voter referendum.)

Coal mining began in the Coos Bay region with the first settlers who arrived in 1853. Coal veins were discovered in the vicinity of the present-day cities of North Bend and Charleston on South Slough, in the former Bunker Hill and Libby areas, as well as east of Isthmus Slough. Towns developed near the larger mines, typically providing housing, a hotel, saloon, and blacksmith shop. The coal miners loaded the coal on sailing ships primarily for shipment to San Francisco.

Myrtle Point

Establishment of farms in the upper Coquille Valley, near the south and middle forks of the Coquille River, began in the mid-1850s. Abraham Hoffman established ferry services across both forks. Ephraim Catching settled on a donation land claim with his Indian wife, Frances. After the second

Patrick Flanagan (1824–1896)

Born in Bainbridge, Ireland

Came to America in 1843; California gold fields in 1849; Oregon in 1850

One of founders of Umpqua City in former Umpqua County in 1850

Began coal mining south of Marshfield in 1854, eventually owning and operating Libby Mine

Had contract to remove Indians from lower Rogue River to Grand Ronde and Coast reservations

Founded Flanagan & Bennett Bank in 1889 with J. W. Bennett

Married Ellen Jane Winchester in 1859; seven children

change of ownership of Catching's property in 1866, Christian Lehnherr platted present-day Myrtle Point.

In 1858 and 1859 members of the Baltimore Colony, led by Dr. Henry Hermann, settled along the Coquille River between the present-day communities of Broadbent and Arago. They were a group of about 40 settlers primarily from Baltimore, Maryland, seeking relief from the economic reversals of the 1857 depression. The men represented various trades and professions. They arrived by way of the Isthmus of Panama, San Francisco, and Port Orford, traveling by land to the Coquille River, where boats transported them to the valley. A few members of the colony incurred very high freight bills for the shipment of a piano, a portable sawmill, millstones for use in a gristmill, and a steam boiler and engine.

In 1859 Captain William R. Rackleff sailed his schooner *Twin Sisters*, that he built on the Umpqua River at Scottsburg in former Umpqua County, into the mouth of the Coquille River, reaching the north fork of the river at Myrtle Point in three days. He sold goods directly from the schooner to the Baltimore Colony settlers who were in dire need of supplies. Soon after, he bought a claim at the forks of the North and South Coquille rivers and established The Forks trading post. He traded groceries and dry goods brought from San Francisco by his son William E., in exchange for gold dust and the produce and lumber from the Coquille Valley.

Several earlier arrivals settled south of Myrtle Point, including Sam Dement. In 1854 Bovine Johnson, known as "Coarse Gold Johnson," discovered gold nuggets on the creek at the foot of Johnson Mountain north of present-day Powers. Placer gold mines remain in operation in this region today. To the east, a few pioneers settled where Remote later became a stopping place on the Coos Bay Wagon Road.

Bandon and Bullards Beach

In 1853, south of the Coquille River, Thompson Lowe and Christopher Long took the first donation land claims where Bandon later developed. Long brought the first cattle to the area, driving them from Illinois. After the Rackleffs' *Twin Sisters* schooner began making trips up the Coquille River, ferry and commercial enterprises developed.

Gold was discovered on Whiskey Run Beach north of Bandon in the early 1850s. A town of tents and shacks sprang up at the town of Randolph; by 1853 more than a thousand men had arrived. In 1854 a storm washed the gold-bearing sands away and most of the miners left for the newly discovered gold strikes to the south. Randolph existed for a couple of years afterwards and a post office was established in 1859 on the Edward Fahy farm located on Fahy Lake.

In 1853 George Wasson and two partners built the first sawmill in Coos County near present-day Bullards Beach. Five years later, Fahy and John Hamblock established a small lumber mill in the vicinity of today's Bullards Beach State Park.

Sampling of Coos County Family Surnames in 1859

Coos Bay and North Bend

Aiken or Akin	Catching	Hall	Jackson	Northrop	Pershbaker	Wasson
Barrett	Davis	Hayward or	Jordan	Packwood	Rogers	Winchester
Cammann or	Flanagan	Haywood	Lockhart	Parker	Ross	Woodard
Cannann	Foley	Hodgkiss	Luse			

Myrtle Point

Culver	Gant or Gaunt	Hermann	Hull	Roland	Volkmar
Dement	Getty	Hoffman	Pohl	Schroeder	Yoakam
Dully	Hanson	Holland	Rackleff		

Bandon

Baldwin	Fahy	Harris	Kenyon	Lewis	Vitneer
Carpenter	Hall	Johnson	Lapp	Thrift	

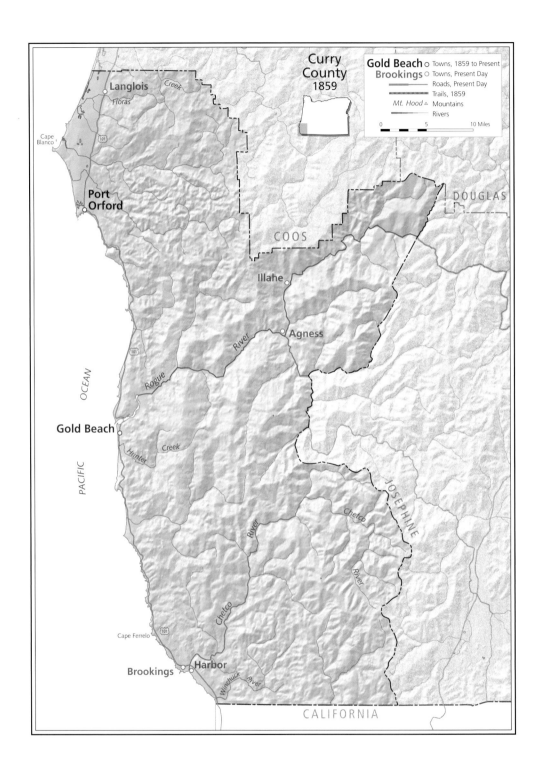

Curry
County
1859

Gold Beach ○ Towns, 1859 to Present
Brookings ○ Towns, Present Day
Roads, Present Day
Trails, 1859
Mt. Hood △ Mountains
Rivers

0   5   10 Miles

Langlois
Floras   Creek

Cape
Blanco
101

Port
Orford

COOS   DOUGLAS

Illahe

River   Agness

Rogue

Gold Beach

Hunter   Creek

PACIFIC   River   Chetco   JOSEPHINE

River

Chetco

Cape Ferrelo
101

Harbor
Brookings

Winchuck   River

CALIFORNIA

OCEAN

6 1859 CURRY COUNTY

Curry County was created in 1855 from the southern part of Coos County. Further boundary adjustments were made with Coos County in 1872 and 1951, and with Josephine County in 1880 and 1927. Port Orford was the temporary county seat until 1859 when an informal vote of county citizens made Ellensburg the permanent site. (The names of Ellensburg and Gold Beach were used interchangeably by the locals; in 1891 Ellensburg was officially renamed Gold Beach.) According to the 1860 U.S. Census, the county population was only 393.

In 1859 water transportation by sea or on the Rogue River was the only form of transportation in Curry County except for a few Indian trails. Pack trains carried goods over the 100-mile path that ran along the ocean bluffs during the 1850s until the 1890s from Bandon in Coos County to Crescent City, California. Michael Riley owned the first wagon in the area, but from his home in Port Orford the furthest he could travel was Hunter Creek south of Gold Beach, about 30 miles away.

Early History
The Tututni Indians lived in villages along the lower Rogue River and on the coast north and south of its mouth. The closely-related Chetco lived along the Chetco River, the Winchuck River, and regions to the north as far as Cape Ferrelo. The Tolowa lived in the southeast portion of the present-day county. For thousands of years before Euro-Americans arrived these Indians had derived their sustenance from the plant foods that grew in the fertile soil, the abundance of fish in the sea and rivers, and the sea mammals, elk, deer, and other wild game.

British Captain George Vancouver anchored his ships just south of Cape Blanco in 1792. Alexander Roderick McLeod and his Hudson's Bay Company (HBC) expedition of 1826–27 explored along the coast as far south as the Rogue River. Jedediah Smith's 1828 expedition made its first Oregon campsite on the north bank of the Winchuck River; their second campsite was on the south side of the Chetco River. Curry County's first settlers arrived in the early 1850s.

Chief Tecumtom ("John") was a major Rogue Indian chief during the 1855–56 war. Chief John's famous charge was: "It is not your war but your peace [placing Indians on reservations] which has killed my people." Courtesy of the Oregon Historical Society, OrHi 4355.

The Indians maintained friendly relations with the earliest arriving settlers until 1854 when hostilities erupted in the Chetco Valley. In 1855 the various coastal bands signed treaties—ceding their lands to the United States. (The Chetco were one of the bands of Indians that received no compensation because the U.S. Senate never ratified their treaty. In 1950 the Chetco were the first band to recover damages from the U.S. government in the amount of $489,085.20.) In 1856 the Indians who survived the war of 1855–56 were marched with Chief John and other Rogue Indians to the Coast Reservation.

In his *Uncertain Encounters*, Nathan Douthit notes that along the Rogue River, with the death of so many Indian men during the war, Indian women more readily developed relationships with the male settlers in order to avoid removal to the Coast Reservation. Particularly in the Agness and Illahe areas of today, small communities of mixed Indian-white families developed. Over 150 Indian families remained in the coastal mountains east of Gold Beach through 1857, but most were eventually tracked down by bounty hunters and taken to Fort Umpqua and later removed to the Coast Reservation. Some were killed.

Gold Beach

In 1853 gold was discovered in the beach sand near the mouth of the Rogue River at Gold Beach. A mining town immediately sprang up to meet the needs of the hundreds of arriving miners, and eventually several small communities developed on both sides of the Rogue River, including Elizabethtown, Gold Beach, Sebastopol, Wedderburn, and Whalesburg. The beach mines never were very productive, but several successful mines were established along the Rogue River in the area of Marial and Illahe, in the northeastern portion of the county. The Gold Bar Mine was established near Illahe in 1856.

During the Rogue River Indian War, battles were waged in the vicinity of Gold Beach. Most of the original houses burned to the ground.

By 1857 the first ferry service was operating across the Rogue River, and A. F. Myers was engaged in a commercial fishery business in which he salted and barreled salmon. John H. Gauntlett established the Gauntlett Hotel in 1859. The county purchased land from him for the site of the first courthouse.

Some settlers engaged in farming in the early days, finding a ready market in the mining community for any surplus commodities. A few arrived with cattle, hogs, and horses. Wheat did not grow well in Curry County, so until 1860 when a gristmill was built in Coos County, flour came by ship from San Francisco to Port Orford. The Geisel family raised some of the first livestock north of Gold Beach. In 1856 Indians killed Mr. Geisel and his three sons, and they captured his wife, Christina, and two daughters, but later released them. Christina became Mrs. Frank Buggey in 1858.

Brookings and Harbor

Pre-1880 history for the southern portion of Curry County is sketchy. Sometime between 1851 and 1853 about a dozen men settled in the Chetco Valley between the Winchuck and Chetco rivers. Among the earliest arrivals were James Jones, Augustus F. Miller, James W. Taggart, Hiram and Christian Tuttle, and Thomas Van Pelt. As in other areas, some of the first settlers married Indian women.

Over 300 Chetco Indians lived in the area and did not initially demonstrate much opposition to the emigrants settled in the midst of their villages. But in 1854 at least three elderly Indians—or maybe as many as fifteen—died when the settlers set fire to their dwellings. Various versions of the incident exist, but the end result was the same. The Chetco retaliated by burning a number of the settlers' houses. A tenuous peace followed, but the Indians realized they were about to lose their land. When the Rogue River Indian War broke out, the Indians, both Rogue and Chetco, proceeded to burn the settlers' homes to the ground. All but four or five of the pioneers fled.

After the Chetco were sent to the Coast Reservation, the settlers who had fled returned and new ones arrived. However, for many years there was no town—only individual farms. Augustus Miller was the primary business operator, running a ferry service, a store, a hotel, and a commercial fishery.

The 1857 Harrison G. Blake house is the oldest extant structure in the Chetco Valley. It houses the Chetco Valley Historical Museum today. Blake planted the huge Monterey cypress standing in front of the house.

In 1857 John Cresswell settled south of Cape Ferrelo near the mouth of Lone Ranch Creek. In his Curry County Historical Society article about the

Captain William V. Tichenor, town founder and sea captain. Courtesy of the Oregon Historical Society, CN 018029.

Lone Ranch Borax Mine, John McWade noted that Cresswell began raising sheep and cattle, but soon noticed a white chalky substance along the creek. Soon he established the Lone Ranch Borax Mine, selling what turned out to be borate of lime for use as silver polish or a substitute for chalk for boat builders and carpenters.

Port Orford and Langlois

Port Orford, a natural deep-water port, required only a few man-made improvements, including a wharf. It was the port of entry between the Oregon-California border and Coos Bay; Benjamin Brattain was the collector of customs for the Port Orford District in 1859.

The first Euro-Americans to arrive at Port Orford were Captain William V. Tichenor and the small party of men who became embroiled in a skirmish with Indians at nearby Battle Rock in 1851. Versions differ as to exactly what happened during that two-week siege. Later that year, Tichenor established Fort Point, a civilian blockhouse fort.

The discovery of gold on the black sand of the beaches and on the river bars and tributaries drew miners to the area—some with families. Stores, hotels, and saloons opened, and a post office was established in 1855. The first county courthouse was located in the home of Judge Frederick Smith. Port Orford's inability to finance construction of a conventional courthouse was a factor in the vote to move the county seat to Gold Beach in 1859.

There was a heavy reliance on imported goods, and the local economy depended on the exportation of goods. Some early settlers established farms.

Success in any commercial business was a challenge, and by 1859 many families had departed for greener pastures. The Tichenor family remained, as did the Knapp family, which consisted of Rachel Knapp and her son Louis. Louis worked at the Peter Ruffner Hotel in 1859 and later became the owner of his own hotel—the extant Knapp Hotel—built in 1867.

The 1856 discovery of the fabled Port Orford Meteorite 30 to 35 miles from Port Orford by a geologist for the U.S. Department of the Interior remains an enigma to this day. Dr. John Evans died in 1860 before arrangements were finalized for further exploration, so its location was lost and never rediscovered. Some are of the opinion that the meteorite is bogus.

William V. Langlois and his family settled on Floras Creek in 1854. Jonathan Scott settled nearby in 1859, and the Isham Cox family settled on Floras Lake in the same year.

Sampling of Curry County Family Surnames in 1859

Gold Beach

Buggey	Cuniff	Gauntlett	Miller	Myers
Colebrook	Dickenson	Hazard	Moore	Riley
Colvin	Foster	Lundry	Morrison	

Brookings and Harbor

Blake	Johnson	Tuttle
Cresswell	McVay	Van Pelt

Port Orford and Langlois

Brattain	Knapp	Ruffner	Tichenor
Dyer	Langlois	Scott	Wilson

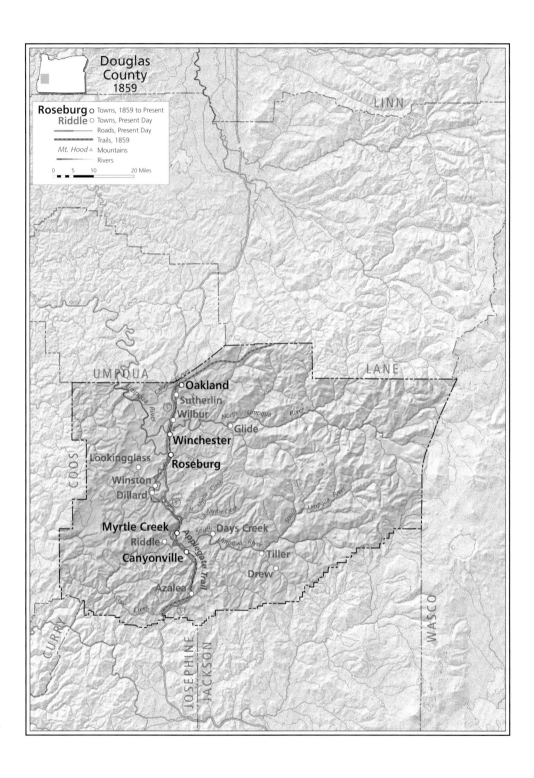

Douglas
County
1859

Roseburg ○ Towns, 1859 to Present
Riddle ○ Towns, Present Day
—— Roads, Present Day
·─·─· Trails, 1859
Mt. Hood △ Mountains
—— Rivers

0   5   10   20 Miles

LINN

UMPQUA

LANE

Oakland
Sutherlin
Wilbur
Glide
Winchester
Lookingglass
Roseburg
Winston
Dillard
Myrtle Creek
Days Creek
Riddle
Tiller
Canyonville
Drew
Azalea

Umpqua River
Calapooia Creek
North Umpqua River
Myrtle Creek
South Myrtle Creek
Applegate Trail
South Umpqua River
South Umpqua River
Cow Creek

COOS

CURRY

JOSEPHINE

JACKSON

WASCO

7 1859 DOUGLAS COUNTY

Douglas County was created in 1852 out of the portion of former Umpqua County lying east of the Coast Range. In 1862 Douglas County absorbed the remainder of Umpqua County—as it had existed for the previous ten years. Other minor Douglas County boundary adjustments were made in 1856 and 1915. (See the discussion about the western portion of present-day Douglas County—the former Umpqua County—in the Umpqua County chapter.)

Winchester was the initial county seat, but by popular election in 1854 Deer Creek (present-day Roseburg) was chosen as the seat. The following year the first courthouse was built. According to the 1860 U.S. Census, the county population was 3203.

The Applegate Trail passed through the north-south center of Douglas County. The most difficult stretch through the county was the 1300-foot descent from the pass at the head of Canyon Creek to Canyonville. In pioneer times, the canyon was known as Umpqua Canyon.

Between 1852 and 1857 the U.S. Congress made several appropriations for the construction of a military wagon road between Scottsburg in Umpqua County and California. The Southern Oregon Military Road portion passing through Douglas County was completed in 1858. By 1859 a weekly stage was running from Corvallis to Oakland.

Several ferries were operating in the county and a wooden bridge was built across Myrtle Creek. In 1859 the only way to reach the coast from Douglas County was by way of Scottsburg and the Umpqua River until the Coos Bay Wagon Road was constructed across the Coast Range in 1872.

Early History

Four distinct groups of Indians had lived for thousands of years within the boundaries of the 1859 portion of Douglas County. The Yoncalla band of the Kalapuya Indians lived along the Calapooya Creek, the dividing line between Douglas and Umpqua counties. They are discussed more fully in the chapter on Umpqua County, where most of them lived before they were removed to the Grand Ronde Reservation in 1856.

The Upper Umpqua lived on the abundant fish, game, roots, nuts, and berries of the Umpqua Valley. In all of the low valleys of the Umpqua region

Sites to Visit in Douglas County

Applegate Trail Interpretive Kiosk
Canyonville Pioneer Park
Historic Downtown Canyonville

Colliding Rivers Information Center
& Wayside
18782 N Umpqua Hwy (Hwy 138),
Glide

Deardorff House, ca. 1850s (private
residence)
Front & Ash streets, Oakland

Dearling House, ca. 1855 (private
residence)
Maple & Second streets, Oakland

Douglas County Museum of History
& Natural History
123 Museum Dr, Roseburg
541·957·7007

Floed-Lane House, ca. 1860s, pioneer's home
544 SE Douglas St, Roseburg
541·459·1393

Oakland City Hall
(historic walking tour map
available)
637 Locust St, Oakland
541·459·4531

Oakland Museum
130 Locust St, Oakland

Pioneer-Indian Museum
421 W 5th St, Canyonville
541·839·4845

Roseburg Visitor's Center
410 SE Spruce, Roseburg
1·800·444·9584

they annually set fires to maintain food gathering areas and game habitat. Specific known locations where they harvested their sustenance were the Camas Valley and Camas Swale where they gathered the camas bulbs; the groves of myrtle trees along Myrtle Creek where they collected the seeds of the trees; the South Umpqua Falls northeast of present-day Tiller where they gathered and fished; and the portion of the North Umpqua River known today as the Colliding Rivers near present-day Glide, where they speared salmon and steelhead from pole platforms. The Colliding Rivers Viewpoint includes several interpretive panels about the area.

The Southern Molalla lived near the South Fork of the Umpqua River. Their culture included some elements of the Molalla Indians of central Oregon, but they generally shared lifeways common to the other valley Indians.

The original Cow Creek Indians were a named band of Umpqua Indians, but they were not related to other tribes in the Umpqua region. Their territory included the Umpqua River's tributary Cow Creek in southern Douglas County, and abutted their cousins, the Takelma of the Upper Rogue Valley in Jackson County. Cow Creek Indians lived in independent villages consisting of several families led by one headman. Although they had their own distinct culture, their food gathering and resource management practices were similar to the Umpqua as described above. The Cow Creek had permanent winter villages, but foraged the rest of the year to replenish their food supply.

A Hudson's Bay Company (HBC) expedition led in 1828 by Alexander Roderick McCleod probably was the first group of fur traders to travel through the Umpqua and South Umpqua valleys on their way to California, but the Scottish botanist David Douglas had preceded them around 1826 when he was making his famous discoveries of the Douglas fir and Oregon myrtle tree. Several groups of Americans passed through the region in the 1830s and '40s, including the Ewing Young party of cattle drivers; a detachment of the Wilkes U.S. Exploring Expedition on its way to California; the Lansford W. Hastings party of emigrants led by Stephen H. L. Meek traveling from the Willamette Valley to California; and a small group of wagons coming north from California to the Willamette Valley. In 1846 Jesse and Lindsay Applegate and Levi Scott blazed the new Southern Emigrant Route to Oregon through this area—the trail that today is known as the Applegate Trail.

Douglas County's first settlers arrived in the late 1840s. There is evidence that the Umpqua Indians had friendly relations with the early settlers in their region. For example, the Umpqua had a winter village on the North Umpqua River; they often ferried settlers across the river by canoe and one Indian named "Cash Trask" was known to have saved many from drowning. He was raised by William Trask, who ran a sawmill on his donation land claim on the North Umpqua River.

General Jackson, Umpqua chief and signer of the Umpqua and Kalapuya Treaty of 1854. Sketch by Eugène de Girardin at the Grand Ronde Reservation in 1856. Courtesy of the National Archives of Canada, C114448.

The Umpqua signed the Umpqua and Kalapuya Treaty of 1854, ceding their lands and agreeing to move to a permanent reservation. They were among the tribes originally assigned to the Coast Reservation, but before the move was completed, plans for the Grand Ronde Reservation were made and most of the Umpqua tribe were instead taken to the Grand Ronde Reservation.

Like the Umpquas, the Cow Creek Indians were generally peaceful and tolerant of the many Euro-Americans passing through or settling on their lands. In his *History of Early Days in Oregon*, George W. Riddle, son of William and Maximilla Riddle, wrote about his childhood and having an Indian hunting companion and friend by the name of "Citizen John," who was the grandson of Chief Miwaleta. After the late 1850s, Citizen John lived on the Grand Ronde Reservation until his death in the early 1900s.

The population of the Cow Creeks was reduced by half following an epidemic triggered by miners and settlers in 1852–53, and by occasional fatal encounters with them. In addition, their food sources were depleted significantly. After the Rogue River Indian War, there were few surviving adult males; Citizen John was one of the oldest boys left.

In 1853 before the outbreak of the last stage of the Rogue River Indian War, the Cow Creek Indians had signed a

Aaron Rose (1813–1899)

Born in southeastern New York State

Upon arrival by way of the Applegate Trail in 1851, purchased squatter's claim from Louis Raimey for a horse and filed for donation land claim on which to establish a farm, house with rooms for boarders, store, butcher shop, and horse sales business

Platted townsite of Deer Creek and began selling plots of land to businesses and families

Instrumental in removal of county seat from Winchester to Roseburg through offer of land and funding for new courthouse; also offered hospitality to settlers who came from other parts of county to vote on county seat issue

Donated land for school and several churches

Territorial legislator; contributed to 1872 construction of Coos Bay Wagon Road

Married four times, four children

Aaron Rose, founder of Roseburg. Photo by H. D. Graves, Courtesy of the Douglas County Museum, N815.

treaty—the Cow Creek Umpqua Treaty. Chief Miwaleta advised the Cow Creeks to avoid war and seek a peaceful solution to the growing animosity between the Indians and settlers. They ceded their homeland (over 800 square miles) to the United States.

Shortly after the treaty was signed, Chief Miwaleta died. At the urging of Chief Miwaleta's successor, who had a less peaceful philosophy, the Cow Creeks sporadically participated in the Rogue River Indian War. The U.S. government later canceled its treaty obligations, which included a payment of $12,000 to cover the cost of supplies and services for survival. (Following a long, protracted legal process, a monetary settlement was awarded to the Cow Creeks in 1984.)

Once reservations outside the area began opening, attempts were made to remove the Cow Creeks, but with little success. Entire families hid out in the mountains on the South Umpqua River. They were hunted down by bounty hunters and taken to the reservations or killed.

Roseburg, Winchester, Wilbur, Sutherlin, and Oakland

The Umpqua Valley comprises many adjoining valleys surrounded by large stands of sugar pine, Douglas and white fir, hemlock, spruce, and cedar. Early settlers established farms on the level portions of the valleys bordering the Umpqua River and along the many meandering creeks. Roseburg, founded as Deer Creek in 1851 by Aaron Rose, was in such a valley. Roseburg acquired its current name in 1857, although until 1894 the spelling was slightly different—Roseburgh.

During the Rogue River Indian War, the headquarters for the Northern Battalion of Oregon Volunteers was located in Roseburg, which contributed to the town's early growth. By 1859 there was an assortment of pioneer businesses, plus two doctors, two dentists, a shoemaker, Moses Parrott; and a barber from the West Indies, Richard A. Bogle. T. P. Sheridan operated a hardware store in Roseburg's first brick building—a two-story structure.

Roseburg's first school was built on Aaron Rose's property. The first Baptist church was established in a private home in

Roseburg in 1853, with Reverend Thomas Stephens serving as the first pastor.

The daughter of Roseburg farmer Thomas Owens became the first woman doctor west of the Rockies. In 1859 Bethenia Owens and her husband, Legrand H. Hill, were living in Roseburg where she operated a millinery and dressmaking store. She divorced her husband, left Roseburg with her son the following year, attended an eastern medical school, and returned to Roseburg twenty years later with her medical degree in hand. Dr. Bethenia Owens opened her first medical practice in Portland in 1881. She became Dr. Bethenia Owens-Adair after marrying Colonel John Adair Jr., the son of John Adair of Astoria. She continued to practice medicine and participate in many social movements, including women's suffrage.

In 1850 a group of businessmen from the San Francisco trading company of Winchester, Payne & Co. founded Winchester. The group, also known as the Umpqua Exploring Expedition of San Francisco, commissioned their land surveyor Addison R. Flint to lay out the town. Flint settled in Winchester, later moving to Roseburg in 1858; in the mean-

Richard A. Bogle immigrated to New York City at the age of twelve and to Oregon four years later. He opened his barber shop in the late 1850s after apprenticing with a barber in Yreka, California, for several years. In 1863 he married America Waldo, a former slave of Daniel Waldo, an early Salem settler. Shortly after their marriage the couple moved to Walla Walla in the Washington Territory. Courtesy of the Oregon Historical Society, OrHi 12649.

Governor Joseph Lane (1801–1881)

- Born in North Carolina; grew up in Kentucky; primarily self-educated
- Moved to Indiana where he served in both houses of legislature and as Indiana volunteer in Mexican-American War
- Appointed first Territorial Governor of Oregon by President Polk; arrived in 1849 and settled his family in Winchester in 1853
- Commanded troops during Rogue River Indian War
- Served as Oregon's delegate to U.S. Congress between 1851 and 1859, when he became Oregon's first U.S. senator, serving until 1861

- After forced retirement from politics in early 1860s because of his pro-slavery stance and Southern sympathies, moved with his wife into small house southeast of Roseburg near Lane Mountain to be closer to his children and grandchildren
- Spent much time in extant 1860s Floed-Lane House in Roseburg visiting his daughter Emily Lane Floed and her family, but never lived there
- Many state and local landmarks named for him, including Lane County
- Married Polly Hart in 1820; ten children

Governor Joseph Lane, enormously popular until the issue of slavery, which he favored, entered Oregon politics. Photo by H. D. Graves, Courtesy of the Douglas County Museum, N12629.

Retired trapper Alexander Dumont, a self-described "half-breed Sauteaux from Green Bay," first farmed at French Prairie, but relocated to Douglas County on the remote Little River. Courtesy of the Douglas County Museum, N2791.

time, he assisted in establishing schools and churches and served as county clerk and Winchester's first postmaster.

During the few years that Winchester served as the county seat, it was the largest settlement in the Umpqua Valley, but when the seat was moved to Roseburg, it dwindled to a small village serving as a supply center for the surrounding farms. A number of families were raising cattle, sheep, and grain on donation land claims they took in 1853 and 1854 east of Winchester near Glide; claims were also taken on the North Umpqua River, Oak Creek, Fall Creek, Little River, French Creek, and near Scott Mountain. A few families settled west of Winchester in Garden Valley.

Fleming R. Hill built a home along the Applegate Trail in 1851 and provided bed and board to passing travelers. Known as the Wilbur Tavern today, it is one of the oldest standing buildings in Douglas County and southern Oregon.

Reverend James H. Wilbur opened the Umpqua Academy, later called the Wilbur Academy, as a feeder school for Willamette University in Salem. It started out in a log building in 1854, but in 1857 a frame structure was built, and the territorial legislature incorporated the academy. Some of southern Oregon's most noted early politicians, businessmen, doctors, and lawyers were graduates of Wilbur Academy.

James T. Cooper was the first to settle near Cooper Creek in the valley that came to be known as Sutherlin Valley. The valley was originally called Camas Swale, because of the thick blanket of deep blue blossoms of the camas plant that appeared every spring.

John Franklin Sutherlin, his wife, and their ten children and their spouses arrived around 1850. They introduced turkeys to Douglas County and planted the first fruit orchard, along with other crops. Sometime in the 1850s John Sutherlin built a gristmill and sawmill, which he leased.

In the 1940 *Oregon: End of the Trail*, the Workers of the Writers' Program of the Work Projects Administration in the state of Oregon noted an interesting fact—but one which could not be confirmed. Supposedly, Lucy Richardson, Fendal Sutherlin's wife, rode a bluegrass thoroughbred most of the way across the plains as her family emigrated to Oregon in 1849. This horse is said to have been the ancestor of many famous race horses of the Willamette Valley.

A few members of the first Applegate Trail party stopped at present-day Oakland for the winter of 1846–47, but the first actual settler did not arrive until 1851. Dr. Dorsey S. Baker built a gristmill and by 1852 the town was rapidly developing along Calapooya Creek. E. G. Young arrived that year and established a store. He and Dr. Baker formed a partnership for the operation of Baker's gristmill and Young's store, calling the store the E. G. Young and Company Store. The usual businesses of a pioneer town were in operation, and Oakland soon became a major trading center and the terminus for the main stage line south of Portland.

The vault in the E. G. Young and Company Store became a popular holding place for the residents' cash—for a small fee. Young eventually offered many of the services a bank would, including savings accounts and loans. (Dr. Baker moved to Portland in 1857.)

The first schoolhouse was not built until the 1860s, but children had been taught in log cabins since the early 1850s. They were sent to the Umpqua Academy in Wilbur or to Eugene if higher education was desired.

Oakland has a unique later history worth noting. With the arrival of the railroad in 1872, which bypassed the 1852 townsite one mile to the south, residents moved many of the wooden buildings to a new townsite next to the railroad tracks. Two 1850s houses that were moved remain today—the Dearling House, which was originally a saloon, and the Deardorff House, along with several 1860 structures.

(Note: On an 1859 map, Oakland is located within Douglas County—right on the border. However, Oakland residents are listed in the 1860 U.S. Census for Umpqua County.)

Reverend James Harvey Wilbur (1811–1887)

Born in New York; licensed as minister in 1842

Arrived in Oregon City by way of Cape Horn in 1847 to assume position of secretary of Oregon and California Methodist Conference and superintendent of Umpqua mission field

Took donation land claim with wife, Lucretia Ann Stevens, at Bunton's Gap, near Wilbur

Established several educational institutions, including Methodist Umpqua Academy in 1854

Built Wilbur Methodist Church and parsonage in 1854

Known as Father Wilbur and respected by all who knew him, he promoted spirituality and education throughout southern Oregon

Dr. Dorsey S. Baker gristmill established on Calapooya Creek in 1852.
Courtesy of the Douglas County Museum, N371.

Dillard and Lookingglass

Several donation land claims were taken in the vicinity of the present-day community of Round Prairie and the Winston-Dillard area where some of the most productive agricultural land existed. Reverend John Dillard and his wife, Jane, established the first Presbyterian church in Douglas County in 1854. Several families settled along Rice Creek south of Dillard, including the first to arrive in 1853—Harrison and Martha Ann Rice. They built a two-story house, planted an orchard, and raised cattle and hogs.

By 1859 Lookingglass—northwest of Winston—had the largest concentration of settlers. One of the donation land claimants was Reverend Abbott L. J. Todd. A potter by trade, he made pottery from clay located on his property, but he also spent time organizing Disciples of Christ (Campbellite) churches throughout the area.

Myrtle Creek, Canyonville, Riddle, and Azalea

Lazarus Wright, a successful gold miner, is generally credited with founding Myrtle Creek along the Applegate Trail in 1852. Several other families played significant roles in its early development. The donation land claim on which the town was settled, originally owned by the Weaver family, changed hands a couple of times. By 1859 there were a few stores, hotels, gristmills, and sawmills. John Hall and Susannah Weaver Hall operated a livery stable and one of the hotels. The community's businesses serviced the local farmers and the packers from the southern Oregon gold mines. The business from the packers died off when the gold rush was over, but upon completion of the military road through the area in 1858, the local merchants and farmers enjoyed new prosperity.

Almost all of the streams in southern Douglas County were explored by gold prospectors, but only a few appeared promising. Sometime during the 1850s (historians' dates range from 1849 to 1858), gold was discovered in Coffee Creek, which is a tributary of the South Umpqua River. A mining camp was established about 15 miles east of Myrtle Creek and included the usual rowdy saloons. Other productive streams were located in the vicinity of Canyonville and Riddle in 1852. Settlers and itinerant prospectors filed mining claims, but very few struck it rich.

Canyonville was known variously in its earliest days as Kenyonville and then North Canyonville, to distinguish it from South Canyonville, which eventually merged with Canyonville. Joseph Knott and Joel Perkins operated a ferry across the South Umpqua River as early as 1851 and Knott built the first store. Jesse Roberts platted the townsite in 1858 and named it Canyonville. He also built the Roberts Hotel and a gristmill in 1856. David Ransome operated a sawmill. During the gold rush period, Canyonville was a way station for the packers transporting miners' supplies from Scottsburg in neighboring Umpqua County, and it still continued to have its share of passersby traveling the Applegate Trail to the Willamette Valley.

Samuel and Susanna Briggs established the first congregation of the Church of Christ in Douglas County in Canyonville in 1852. They arrived the year before from Iowa with Sephronia and Cornelius Hills, their daughter and son-in-law.

In his 1968 article, "Pioneer Days in the South Umpqua

Jesse Roberts, founder of Canyonville. Courtesy of the Douglas County Museum, N3627.

William H. and Maximilla B. Riddle were the parents of George Washington Riddle, a prominent figure in Oregon in later years. Courtesy of the Douglas County Museum, N1622.

Valley," in the South Umpqua Historical Society's annual publication, Ira Poole noted that families lived in the area of present-day Days Creek northeast of Canyonville in the 1850s. Poole wrote that some men were former HBC employees who married Indian women. The community built a schoolhouse in 1856.

The Cow Creek Valley and present-day Riddle had a large population of settlers, with the William and Maximilla Riddle family being among the first. They called their homestead Glenbrook Farms, which was located south of the future townsite. The townsite property was originally owned by J. Q. C. VandenBosch.

The early settlers found the Cow Creek Valley's rich soil to be excellent for growing crops and grazing livestock; by 1855 almost all of the land in the valley had been claimed. Hans Weaver Jr. raised stock and farmed in the valley. It is believed that at one time he was the largest land holder in Douglas County. There were placer mining opportunities on Cow Creek, but no substantial deposits were ever found.

A number of farms were established near present-day Azalea in the early 1850s. Jennene Johns noted in her 1995 article in the South Umpqua Historical Society's annual publication that more than 14 of the farm houses were burned during the Rogue River Indian War. However, the 1860 census indicates that a number of families remained or had returned to the area by the end of the decade.

Sampling of Douglas County Family Surnames in 1859

Roseburg, Winchester, Wilbur, Sutherlin, and Oakland

Abraham	Clark	Flint	Jones	Myers	Rose	Tower
Adams	Clayton	Floed	Kelley	Oden	Sawyers	Trask
Akin	Cockeram	Fordyce	Lane	Owens	Shaw	Vail (Vale)
Anderson	Cox	Fortin	LaRaut	Parrott	Sherwood	Whitman
Archambeau	Crosby	Goodell	Lawrence	Perdue	Shrum	Whitmore
Banks	Crouch	Gordon	Lord	Phipps	Simmons	Williams
Barker	Daniels	Green	Mallory	Pinkston	Smith	Williamson
Beal	Dearborn	Grubbe	Marks	Powers	Starr	Willis
Blakely	Deardorff	Hall	Martin	Price	Stearns	Wilson
Bradley	Emmitt	Hamilton	McClendon	Ransome	Stephens	Wimberly
Brown	Engels	Hanna	McGee	Raper	Stratton	Winston
Cathcart	Everman	Harvey	Moore	Reed	Sutherlin	Woodward
Chadwick	Finch	Hinkle	Morgan	Roberts	Tibbets	Young
Chapman	Fitzhugh	Hurst	Mosher			

Dillard and Lookingglass

Davlin	Fetter	Huntley	Patterson
Dillard	Higginson	Miller	Rice

Myrtle Creek, Canyonville, Riddle, and Azalea

Bailey	Burnett	Fate	Levins	Riddle	Thomason	Weaver
Barton	Butler	Gazley	Martindale	Roberts	Thorne	Wilson
Bigham	Catching	Golden	Mynatt	Russell	Tiller	Worley
Boyle	Cowels	Hall	Nichols	Smith	Vanden-	Wright
Briggs	Dyer	Ireland	Redfield	Thomas	Bosch	Yokum
Browning	Elliff	Jones				

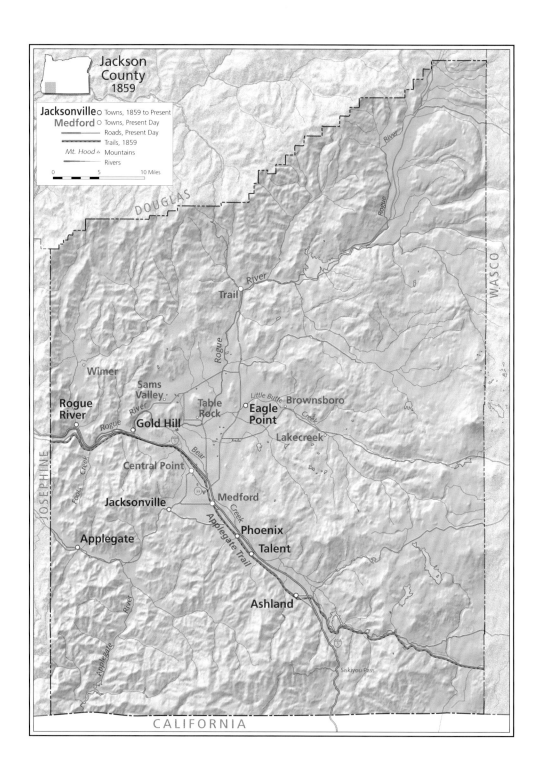

Jackson County 1859

Jacksonville ○ Towns, 1859 to Present
Medford ○ Towns, Present Day
▬▬▬ Roads, Present Day
▬▬▬ Trails, 1859
Mt. Hood △ Mountains
▬▬▬ Rivers

0   5   10 Miles

DOUGLAS

WASCO

River

River

Rogue

Trail

Rogue

Wimer

Sams
Valley

River

Rogue

Little Butte

Brownsboro

Eagle
Point

Creek

Rogue
River

Table
Rock

Gold Hill

Lakecreek

Creek

Fools

Bear

JOSEPHINE

Central Point

Jacksonville

Medford

Creek

Applegate Trail

Phoenix

Talent

Applegate

River

Ashland

Applegate

Siskiyou Pass

CALIFORNIA

8 1859 JACKSON COUNTY

Jackson County was created in 1852 from the southwestern portion of Lane County and a portion of the unorganized area to the west. Its boundaries changed several times with the formation of new counties to the west and east. Jacksonville became the first county seat in 1853, but would later lose that distinction to Medford in 1927. (Medford's growth as a city was stimulated when Medford was chosen as a depot for the Oregon and California Railroad in 1885.) According to the 1860 U.S. Census, the county population was 3736.

In 1859 the communities throughout Jackson County were linked by Indian hunting and trading trails, and by new trails blazed between the various gold mining camps. The gold discoveries in both Jackson and Josephine counties prompted the establishment of a primitive road between Jacksonville and Crescent City, California, for the transport of supplies for the mines by mule pack trains. An improved road to accommodate stage lines was completed in 1858. James Cluggage and John Drum operated a tri-weekly stage to Crescent City, leaving from Jacksonville and traveling along the Applegate River into Josephine County. By 1859 a weekly stage was operating between Jacksonville and Salem in Marion County.

What is known today as Old Military Road was completed in 1854 and became part of the military road completed between Jacksonville, Myrtle Creek in Douglas County, and Scottsburg in Umpqua County in 1858. By the same year, stage lines were operating along today's Old Stage Road heading north out of Jacksonville.

A portion of the Applegate Trail passed through the county, entering at its eastern edge along today's Greensprings Highway and proceeding north along Bear Creek and generally along today's Interstate 5 through the rest of the county. It became a popular route for gold miners heading for California.

The ancient Indian Siskiyou Trail over the Siskiyou Pass into California had been used since the 1820s by the Hudson's Bay Company (HBC) trappers and later by other trappers, cattle drivers, gold miners, and mule train packers. In 1858 a toll road authorized by the territorial legislature was built over the pass. In Jackson County it began seven miles below the summit and

Sites to Visit in Jackson County

Applegate Valley Historical Society
Museum
Hwy 238 & North Applegate Rd,
Applegate

Ashland Mountain House B & B, ca.
1852 (private business)
1148 Old Hwy 99 S, Ashland
541·482·2744

Beekman Bank, ca. 1863, pioneer
owner
California & 3rd Streets,
Jacksonville

Beekman House, ca. 1876, pioneer's home
352 E California St, Jacksonville
541·773·6536

Birdseye House, ca. 1856 (private
residence)
West side of Hwy 99, 2 miles south
of city of Rogue River

Britt Gardens
350 S 1st St, Jacksonville

Colver House, ca. 1855 (private
residence)
150 S Main St, Phoenix

Eagle Point Museum
201 N Royal Ave, Eagle Point
541·826·4166

Gold Hill Historical Society
Museum
504 1st Ave, Gold Hill
541·855·1182

Hanley Farm, ca. 1850s–1950s
1053 Hanley Rd, Central Point
541·773·6536

Jacksonville Chamber of Com-
merce/Visitors Center
(walking tour map available)
185 N Oregon St, Jacksonville
541·899·8118

Jacksonville Museum & Children's
Museum
206 N 5th St, Jacksonville
541·773·6536

Lithia Park (site of 1854 millrace)
Winburn Way, Ashland

McManus House, ca. 1855 (private
residence)
117 W 1st St, Phoenix

Phoenix Historical Society &
Museum
607 N Church St, Phoenix

Southern Oregon Historical Society
History Center (research library)
106 N Central Ave, Medford
541·858·1724

Tubb Springs State Wayside
18 miles east of Ashland off Hwy
66, east of Green Springs Inn

Upper Rogue Historical Society's
Trail Creek Tavern Museum
144 Old Hwy 62, Trail
541·890·0695

Walker House, ca. 1856 (private
residence)
1521 E Main St, Ashland

Woodville Museum
Oak & First streets, Rogue River
541·582·3088

---

ended near the present-day California town of Hilt. The route can still be followed on Old Highway 99 S and Interstate 5.

A number of ferries were operating across the Rogue River, Little Applegate
River, and a few creeks in the county. A toll bridge across the Rogue River near
Gold Hill was constructed in the late 1850s on Thomas Chavner's property.

Early History

The Takelma, Applegate, Shasta, and Upper Takelma lived in the area within
present-day Jackson County for centuries before the first Euro-Americans
arrived. The Indian hunters and traders frequented various locations along
the Rogue River and its tributaries; Sams Valley and the area surrounding
the Table Rock mesas; and Wasson Canyon east of Eagle Point. Villages were

located throughout the region. The Indians developed a trail between the Umpqua River in Douglas County and Klamath Lake. The small town of present-day Trail is located at a spot where they would stop along the way. The Indians also visited the curative springs located southeast of Ashland, where the Buckhorn Springs resort operates today.

A number of Euro-Americans passed through the Rogue Valley during the early 1800s, including HBC explorer Peter Skene Ogden in the 1820s; trapper and cattle dealer Ewing Young during the 1830s; the overland U.S. Exploring Expedition in 1841; the 1846 Applegate Trail blazers; and the 1848 prospectors on their way to California.

It was the French-Canadian fur trappers who gave all of the Indians in southern Oregon the collective name of "Les Coquins," or "Rogues" in English, because of their aggressive nature. In his *Uncertain Encounters*, Nathan Douthit argues that the term was undeserved, at least after the discovery of gold in southern Oregon in the early 1850s and the arrival of the first settlers and miners. He believes restraint and courtesy were common traits of both the Rogue Indians and the new arrivals, even though there were occasional skirmishes.

After the discovery of gold, Jackson County was at the center of activity—both positive and negative. It was also the richest economically. Business was booming and farms proliferated throughout the Rogue and Bear Creek valleys. Mining was a year-round occupation for the serious prospectors, but many of the settlers who took donation land claims were involved in both activities—mining during the winter months when the smaller streams were flowing with water, and farming during the summer. New gold strikes were made throughout the 1850s and early '60s, and although the easy-to-reach gold was depleted by 1855, the large mining companies were still in operation well into the 1870s.

During the mid-1850s there were continual hostilities with the Rogue Indians. The Table Rock Treaty of 1853 established the temporary Table Rock Reservation, which encompassed the two landmark mesas located south of present-day Sams Valley—named after Chief Sam, a signer of the treaty—and ran along the north side of the Rogue River between Upper Table Rock and Evans Creek. The reservation may have provided for a temporary peace, but within two years a full-fledged war was underway. In 1856 the Indians gave up fighting and were removed to the Coast and Grand Ronde reservations, some aboard the steamship *Columbia* and some marched overland. Those who avoided removal escaped to remote areas of the county, constantly living in fear of capture or being killed by bounty hunters. In his daily journal, Wel-

David Linn (1826–1912)

Arrived in Yreka in 1850; worked as carpenter

Moved to Jacksonville after discovery of gold; became one of founding fathers

Constructed sluice boxes, wooden water pumps, cabins, and sheds for miners

Built furniture factory and planing mill; expanded his business into construction of furniture, coffins, doors, windows, houses, and stores, as well as lumber for resale

Imported one of Rogue Valley's first steam engines in 1858 for use in his factory and mill

Constructed Fort Klamath in 1863, using his own portable sawmill

Member of 1869 James Sutton party that explored and named Crater Lake after exploring lake in boat built by Linn

Continued his furniture business until 1903 even though his factory burned to the ground in 1888

born Beeson, a pioneer of present-day Talent, mentions the existence of a few Indians in Jacksonville and other nearby locations in 1859, most of whom had probably fled from the Coast and Grand Ronde reservations.

Jacksonville, Ruch, and Applegate

Today's historic Jacksonville had its start when two packers, James Cluggage and John R. Pool, accidentally discovered gold in Rich Gulch during the winter of 1851–52 while on their way to the California gold fields. Cluggage took a donation land claim where a tent city that he named Table Rock immediately arose.

Typical mining town commerce developed—saloons and gambling halls, general stores, hotels and boardinghouses, and breweries. Once farms were established in the Bear Creek Valley and eastern Rogue Valley, they provided most of the foodstuffs for the miners, but other needed supplies were transported by mule pack trains from Scottsburg and Crescent City.

Several skilled carpenters, including Patrick Fehely and David Linn, constructed some of the historic buildings remaining today. An historic landmark walking tour map is

Jacksonville in the summer of 1858. Courtesy of the Southern Oregon Historical Society, #738.

available at the Visitor Information Center that showcases such 1850s structures as attorney B. F. Dowell's 1859 house; J. J. Holeman's 1856 Eagle Brewery Saloon; Martin & Zigler's 1859 blacksmith shop; the 1855 J. W. McCully Building that housed a general store on the ground floor and a Jewish synagogue on the upper floor; John Orth's 1854 butcher shop; and the 1856 P. J. Ryan Hotel Building; along with over 80 other pre-1900 structures. The 1855 Brunner Building was the first brick building to be built in Jacksonville.

In 1855 the Rogue Valley acquired its first newspaper when William Green T'Vault and his partners purchased and moved the printing equipment of Scottsburg's *Umpqua Gazette* to Jacksonville. First known as the *Table Rock Sentinel*, in 1858 it became *The Oregon Sentinel*.

A number of lawyers and doctors were practicing in Jacksonville in 1859 and Legrande J. C. Duncan was serving as the Jackson County sheriff, later becoming a judge. T'Vault served as the district attorney until 1858 when he became a territorial legislator for the county.

Chinese miners, tired of paying California's Foreign Miners Tax instituted in 1850, ventured over the border from Yreka as early as 1852. Some arrived independently, but most had a contract with a Chinese boss such as Jim Ling who arranged for their employment in existing mines, deducting from their pay any remaining transportation costs incurred during their trip from China. Oregon's first Chinatown soon developed in Jacksonville, which led to the same anti-Chinese sentiment they fled in California. The territorial legislature enacted a number of prohibitions against the Chinese and in 1859 Jackson County imposed mining and merchant taxes on its Chinese residents.

One Chinese miner, Gin Lin, became a successful and respected businessman after purchasing a mine in the Applegate Valley, where it is estimated he mined two million dollars in gold from his claims. The time of his arrival is unverified and the stories about him vary, but nonetheless he is a notable fixture in Oregon history. Gin Lin is memorialized on the Gin Lin Trail, a short interpretive trail south of Jacksonville. The trail passes through an 1850s mining

Peter Britt (1818–1905)

1844 Swiss immigrant; arrived in Jacksonville in 1852 from Illinois

Attempted prospecting and mule packing; hauled foodstuff and mining tools from Crescent City

By 1856 resumed his previous career as photographer; recorded southern Oregon culture and history for next 50 years

Landscape and portrait oil painter

Horticulturist, winemaker, beekeeper, meteorologist, rancher, orchardist, and financier

Raised his three children alone after his wife of ten years died in 1871

Friendly with Chinese, unlike most Jacksonville residents; rented housing and loaned money to them, and allowed them to mine gold on his property for percentage of profits

Most of his estate given to Oregon University system—minus beautiful 1860 Gothic Revival home destroyed by fire in 1960

His grounds are a county park and the site of the annual Peter Britt Festival

Peter Britt, a Jacksonville pioneer of many talents. Courtesy of the Oregon Historical Society, CN 000266.

Cornelius C. Beekman
(1828–1915)

Born in New York City; ventured to West Coast in 1850; first worked in Nevada and California as carpenter, miner, and express messenger

Opened his own express company in Jacksonville in 1856; delivered gold dust, parcels, and letters from Jacksonville and Yreka to Crescent City

Parlayed his express company into banking and assaying business by 1857; became a Wells Fargo agent in 1863

Served as school trustee, city trustee, and mayor of Jacksonville, and financially supported several educational institutions

Married Julia Elizabeth Hoffman; two children

Beekman House that family built in 1876 is living history museum during summer months

Gold mining in the Oregon Territory. Courtesy of the Oregon Historical Society, OrHi 58280.

area where the Chinese carefully scoured the area for gold. There is also evidence of the hydraulic mining that took place there in later years.

There were two other minorities in the Jacksonville area in 1859. In her *Settling the Rogue Valley: The Tough Times: The Forgotten People*, Barbara Morehouse Hegne reported that Kanakas from the Sandwich Islands lived outside Jacksonville in an area called Kanaka Flat. They were denied citizenship and could not take donation land claims, so many eventually returned home.

A number of blacks lived in Kanaka Flat or Jacksonville. A few had escaped from their masters en route to Oregon; others had been freed by their owners after their arrival in Oregon. Some were engaged in mining, but most, like Richard Conway, worked for wages. A couple of blacks like Daniel Jones and M. P. Howard operated small businesses; they were both barbers in Jacksonville.

Public school classes met in Jacksonville as early as 1853 and a single-room cabin was built in 1854. C. C. Beekman built Jacksonville's first official schoolhouse in 1856. The schoolhouse remains today as the south portion of a private residence on the Jacksonville walking tour.

The extant church, known today as Saint Andrews Methodist Episcopal Church, was built in 1854. The generous Methodist Episcopalians shared their facility with the Presbyterians and later five other denominations. The Saint Joseph's Roman Catholic Church, which is also extant, was completed in 1858, but the first church service was not held until 1860. Prospering and growing during the 1850s, Jacksonville was incorporated in 1860 and shed its former name of Table Rock City.

In the mid-1850s, several families settled at Logtown, a small mining camp near the confluence of Poormans and Forest creeks north of present-day Ruch. Melvin D. Sturgess was operating the general store and hotel in 1859.

The present-day ghost town of Buncom southeast of Ruch attracted over a thousand miners during the mid-1850s, including many Chinese. The Chinese were content to live in shanties in the nearby pastures; the buildings remaining today are from a much later era.

James Sterling's 1854 discovery of gold on Sterling Creek near Buncom led to the rapid development of Sterlingville. Mining declined significantly in the late 1850s, but in 1859 some mining was still being done and a small community of families remained. Theodoric "Tod" Cameron was operating a bakery and George Yaudes and his brother Mathias had a general store.

Rich placer deposits were discovered in the Applegate Valley west of Jacksonville along Humbug and Keeler creeks and Ferris Gulch. By 1859 the easy gold was depleted and the Applegate Valley was a community of farms. Henderson Luelling of Milwaukie in Clackamas County traveled through there in 1858 selling his fruit trees.

Conrad Slagle and Kaspar Kubli settled on Missouri Flat near Slagle Creek. Kubli had been operating a trading post and running a pack train since his arrival in 1852; he later opened a hardware store and bank; in 1859 he was serving as the Applegate postmaster.

Phoenix, Talent, and Ashland

Gasburg, renamed Phoenix in the 1880s, arose near the Samuel Colver Jr. family home located on the main wagon road through the Bear Creek Valley. Merchant Patrick F. McManus lived nearby and both of their 1855 homes remain as private residences today. Sylvester M. Waite built one of the first gristmills in the valley.

During the Rogue River Indian War, the settlers built a blockhouse west of Phoenix. Called Camp Baker, it protected local residents from the occasional Indian raids in 1855 and 1856.

Eli K. Anderson and Jacob Wagner were the first to settle in the area of Talent in 1852. They both took donation land claims on creeks named after them and established farms for growing wheat, potatoes, and vegetables, and for raising stock. It is believed that Wagner built the first irrigation ditch in Oregon on Wagner Creek in 1852.

Samuel Colver Jr. (1815–1891)

Born in Ohio; studied law in Indiana

Arrived in Bear Creek Valley in 1851 with his brother Hiram and their respective families

Served as Indian agent between 1852 and 1854; one of signers of Table Rock Treaty of 1853

Laid out Phoenix townsite on his land in 1854

His extant 1855 house served as the community center; called Colver Hall it was used for school classroom, dances, church services, and lodge

Traveled back east to handle family business and advocate for transcontinental railroad between 1858 and 1859; returned with French horses and mules from Canada

Operated saddle and pack train between Walla Walla, Washington and mines in northeastern Oregon in 1861

Instrumental in construction of county road from Rogue Valley over mountains to Klamath County in 1869

Attempted to obtain a peace agreement in early part of Modoc Indian War of 1872–73

Poet, debater, abolitionist, prohibitionist, and advocate for women's rights

Plagued by several family tragedies in his later years and either drowned or froze to death in 1891

Married Huldah Callender; two children

The 1855 Samuel Colver House, the community center called Colver Hall, remains as a private residence today. Courtesy of the Oregon Historical Society, CN 021527.

After the arrival of additional settlers in 1853, Wagner named the settlement Wagner or Wagner Creek. (A. P. Talent platted a townsite in 1889, thus its current name.) In the mid-1850s, soldiers from Fort Jones in northern California helped the pioneers build Fort Wagner on Wagner's property for protection from the Indians, both for the settlers and for the pioneers traveling through on the Applegate Trail. A log stockade surrounded the blockhouse where the Wagners lived. The fort was never needed for its intended purpose, so it was used instead as a place for worship services and social gatherings.

The John Beeson family arrived in 1853. He was an outspoken proponent of civil rights for Indians; his controversial views forced him to flee the Rogue Valley around 1856 in order to save his life. His family stayed behind and his son Welborn assumed the operation of the family farm. Welborn Beeson's daily journal kept over a 40-year period is preserved in a special collection of the University of Oregon and the Talent Historical Society, documenting pioneer life in southern Oregon.

Militiamen standing in front of the Ashland House, ca. 1860, including Abel Helman, two Applegate sons, Minus Walker, and Welborn Beeson, all of whom served at Fort Wagner during the Rogue River Indian War. Prints by Terry Skibby. Courtesy of the Ashland Library Collection.

Ashland's first settlers arrived in early 1852. Recognizing the business opportunities presented by the southern Oregon gold rush, they built a boardinghouse, gristmill, sawmill, and store. By 1859 these and other established businesses had changed ownership and several of the original pioneers had left the area; the most influential settlers remaining included James A. Cardwell, Eber and James Emery, Robert Hargadine, and Abel Helman.

In 1855 Helman donated twelve lots from his donation land claim for establishment of the townsite of Ashland Mills. (The word Mills was dropped in 1871.) In 1859 Eber Emery built the Ashland House on The Plaza, and much of the business section of town, previously located adjacent to the sawmill, moved near the hotel and The Plaza.

The Ashland Flouring Mill was located on what is now the entrance to Lithia Park in downtown Ashland. Today Shakespeare enthusiasts on their way to the theaters from the lower duck pond cross the millrace that Helman and Emery created to power the mill.

Until the first public school was built in 1860 on land donated by Robert Hargadine, school classes were held in Eber Emery's home. Church services were also held in private homes. The Jacksonville Presbyterian circuit rider Reverend Moses Williams lived in Ashland and was a pastor to his neighbors when he was not preaching at the churches he formed in Jacksonville and other communities. Priests from the Catholic Church established in Jacksonville in 1858 visited Ashland regularly to say Mass.

Two pre-1859 houses remain in Ashland today. The 1856 John Walker House was the home of rancher and public education supporter John Walker. In 1857 Walker became the director of the local school board, advocating successfully for the first school tax levy in Ashland.

The 1852 Mountain House is located southeast of Ashland just off the former Applegate Trail and along the old Siskiyou Trail. Hugh Barron, John Gibbs, and James Russell built a two-story inn called the Greensprings Mountain House on their adjoining donation land claims to provide food and accommodations to the many travelers using

Abel D. Helman (1824–1910)

Born in Ashland County, Ohio

Cabinetmaker before heading west—first to California gold mines in Yreka

Took donation land claim in Ashland in 1852, later donating lots for townsite development

Returned to Ohio to escort Emery's family and his to Oregon

With partners, built sawmill and flour mill

Served at Fort Wagner during Rogue River Indian War

After selling his interest in the mills, resumed carpentry work; built houses, barns, and cabinets

Postmaster for 27 years; also school board member

Married twice; eight children

Ashland Flouring Mill, ca. 1860. Prints by Terry Skibby. Courtesy of the Ashland Library Collection.

The Mountain House in 1870 by foremost Ashland photographer Peter Britt.
Courtesy of the Southern Oregon Historical Society, #3646.

the two intersecting trails, and for feed and rest for their animals. By 1859 the Mountain House was an established stagecoach stop and travelers' rest stop. Hugh Barron and his wife, Martha, were operating the inn by themselves, as James Russell sold his interest in 1854 and John Gibbs had died. Today the Ashland Mountain House Bed & Breakfast welcomes guests to an elegantly renovated restoration of the original house.

Rogue River and Gold Hill

In 1850 Davis "Coyote" Evans became the first settler near the present-day city of Rogue River. Rogue River has variously been known as Tailholt or Tailholt Crossing, Gold River, and Woodville in the 1870s. In 1912, when the city was incorporated, the name Rogue River was adopted.

Evans built two log cabins and a ferry at the mouth of Evans Creek. The Tailholt name for Rogue River came into use because some settlers and gold miners could not afford the ferry and instead swam across the fast-moving Rogue River, holding on to their horses' tails.

Evans built a sawmill on Evans Creek in 1852, a second ferry below the Savage Rapids in 1853, and served as the first postmaster in 1855 for Gold River. (The name Tailholt was revived for a time after this.) In 1857 Evans sold his property to Albert and Sarah Bethel, who continued to operate the ferry for several years. James and Margaret Savage settled along the Savage Rapids portion of the river in 1853.

Southwest of the city of Rogue River, David N. Birdseye settled on the south bank of the Rogue River in 1851 with his new bride, Clara Fleming. His stockaded log house served as a fort called Fort Birdseye during the Rogue River Indian War. In 1856 he built a frame house, which remains as a private residence along Highway 99.

Gold was discovered on Foots Creek just east of Birdseye Creek in 1852; O. G. Foot was one of the early prospectors. Placer discoveries were made on other nearby creeks, including Evans, Galls, Pleasant, Sam, and Sardine creeks, and were worked for many years.

In their *The Salt of the Earth: Pioneers of Evans Valley*, Gladys Boulter and Connie Weide Liles state that William P. Hillis was the first settler in the Evans Valley on Evans Creek north of Rogue River. He built a cabin near the present-day community of Wimer when many Indians were still living in the area and developed good relations with them. Similarly, when gold was discovered on Sykes Creek in 1856, he employed Chinese miners and paid them a percentage of the proceeds from their efforts.

A few families settled in the area of Rock Point. Jacob and Sara Neathamer were farming and selling their surplus food to the miners. John B. White served as Rock Point's first postmaster in 1857 and his post-1859 house on North River Road became a stage stop and remains standing today as a private residence.

Gold Hill was not founded until after lode gold was discovered in 1859. Thomas Chavner established a quartz mine there in 1860. The Dardanelles was settled in 1852 on the south bank of the Rogue River southeast of today's Gold Hill. A large gold nugget was discovered at Big Bar on the river in 1852. There was an immediate influx of over 200 miners, including many Chinese. The Dardanelles slowly disappeared as the gold mining moved across the river.

Central Point, Eagle Point, Brownsboro, and Lakecreek

Placer deposits were discovered along the creeks and gulches in the vicinity of Central Point, bringing miners and giving rise to several communities as the miners turned to farming

James and Margaret Savage are considered Josephine County pioneers today, but in 1859 their home near today's Savage Rapids Dam was located in Jackson County—before the county line was slightly adjusted in 1885. Courtesy of the Josephine County Historical Society.

Contemporary photograph of the 1856 Birdseye House, which served as a stage stop.

after the diggings dwindled. They raised vegetables, fruit, wheat, oats, poultry, hogs, cattle, and horses.

Willow Springs developed near present-day Central Point. Alonzo A. Skinner took the first donation land claim there in 1851, but had left the area by 1856. Several other farms were operating in the region, warranting a post office in 1853 and the construction of Fort Lane in the same year to maintain peace between the settlers and the Indians on the nearby temporary Table Rock Reservation. David Clinton and Archibald Welton arrived in 1852, but sold their land claims to the Michael Hanley family around 1856. The Hanleys were raising their family there in 1859, and today the Hanley Farm, with buildings ranging in age from the 1850s to the 1950s, is open to the public during the summer—the first weekend of each month. (Some descendants of Michael Hanley remain large landholders in eastern Oregon.)

Along Bear Creek east of Central Point, the community of Manzanita developed in the early 1850s. Several of the earliest donation land claimants had moved on by 1859—some having lost their houses to fires set by Indians during the war. William Merriman, a farmer, blacksmith, and wagon-maker, was among the remaining pioneers.

The Little Butte Creek area where Eagle Point, Brownsboro, and Lakecreek developed was settled immediately after gold was discovered in Jacksonville. Those prepared to farm and raise stock saw it as an ideal location with a market of hungry gold miners nearby. More than 25 men, a few with families, arrived in the early 1850s, but at least 15 of them had abandoned their claims by 1859—many during the Rogue River Indian War.

Among the original pioneers who stayed were the James J. Fryer, Joseph Swingle, and Nicholas A. Young families, along with John McDaniel. Fryer, an Englishman, is considered the "Father of Eagle Point," as he was one of the first to acquire property on Little Butte Creek in 1852. He tended his orchards on the present townsite of Eagle Point and operated a store. Young owned the first general store in Eagle Point, and McDaniel built a sawmill on Little Butte Creek and operated a blacksmith shop. Eagle Point's first school was organized in 1857, but children did not attend school on a regular basis until 1863.

Sampling of Jackson County Family Surnames in 1859

Jacksonville, Ruch, and Applegate

Allen	Brooks	Dowell	Higenbotham	Long	Miller	Schutz
Anderson	Brown	Drum	Hinkle	Love	Orth	Sears
Armstrong	Brunner	Duncan	Hoffman	Lyon	Overbeck	Slagle
Badger	Buckley	Emery	Holeman	Martin	Phillips	Sturgis
Baker	Bybee	Fehely	Hopkins	Matney	Prim	Truax
Beekman	Cameron	Fisher	Howard	Maury	Ray	T'Vault
Berry	Chappell	Fowler	Irvine	McBride	Reed	Walker
Bigler	Cluggage	Glenn	Ish	McCully	Reynolds	Watkins
Bishop	Conway	Griffin	Jordan	McDonough	Ryan	Williams
Boaz	Cook	Griffith	Kerr	McKay	Sachs	Wood
Bowen	Davis	Haines	Kubli	McKee	Saltmarsh	Yaudes
Britt	Day	Head	Ling	Mensor	Schofield	Zigler
Broadwell	Dean	Helms	Linn			

Phoenix, Talent, and Ashland

Ammerman	Carlisle	Dunlap	Hargadine	Margraff	Myer	Robison	Van Dyke
Anderson	Chaffee	Dunn	Hart	Marks	Naylor	Rockfellow	Vincent
Applegate	Chapman	Emery	Helman	Martin	Neal	Rodgers	Wachter
Ball	Chase	Evans	Hess	McAtee	Oatman	Sheldon	Wagner
Barron	Chegar	Fordyce	Hiatt	McCall	Obert	Shepphard	Waite
Beebe	Clark	Foreman	Howell	McCallister	Paddock	Snyder	Walker
Beeson	Clayton	Giddings	Hoxie	McDonald	Patterson	Songer	Weathers
Bittner	Cole	Gillette	Hutchens	McManus	Payne	Stearns	Weiss
Blake	Coleman	Goldsmith	Jacobs	Mikelson	Reams	Sterling	Wells
Bowen	Colver	Gooding	Kelly	Million	Rector	Taylor	Westfall
Bozarth	Condrey	Gore	LaPorte	Minor	Redick	Thomas	Whitehurst
Brittain	Crowley	Gould	Lindley	Moon	Renshaw	Thornton	Woolen
Burch	Davenport	Graff	Lynch	Mullen	Riley	Tolman	Wright
Caldwell	Dolton	Gridley	Major	Murphy	Robertson	Toothaker	Yandel
Cardwell	Dota	Grubb					

Rogue River and Gold Hill

Abbott	Chavner (?)	Hall	Kahler	Neathamer	Ralls	Taylor
Artz	Cox	Haymond	Magruder	Parker	Ross	Wakeman
Bethel	Dawson	Hicks	Marshall	Pence	Savage	Walker
Birdseye	Fisher	Hughes	Murphy	Pyle	Swinden	White

Central Point, Eagle Point, Brownsboro, and Lakecreek

Amy	Cook	Heckathorne	McNeil	Payne	Rosencrans	Tatom
Bradley	Curry	Hendrix	Meade	Pelton	Shelton	Taylor
Brown	Fox	Hopwood	Merriman	Peterson	Shock	Thompson
Butler	Fryer	Hurst	Moon	Plymale	Simon	Turman
Cameron (?)	Hailey	Linksweiler	Neal	Rader	Stowe	Watson
Collins	Hanley	Matney	Nye	Rice	Swingle	Young
Constant	Hayes	McDaniel	Pankey	Robinson		

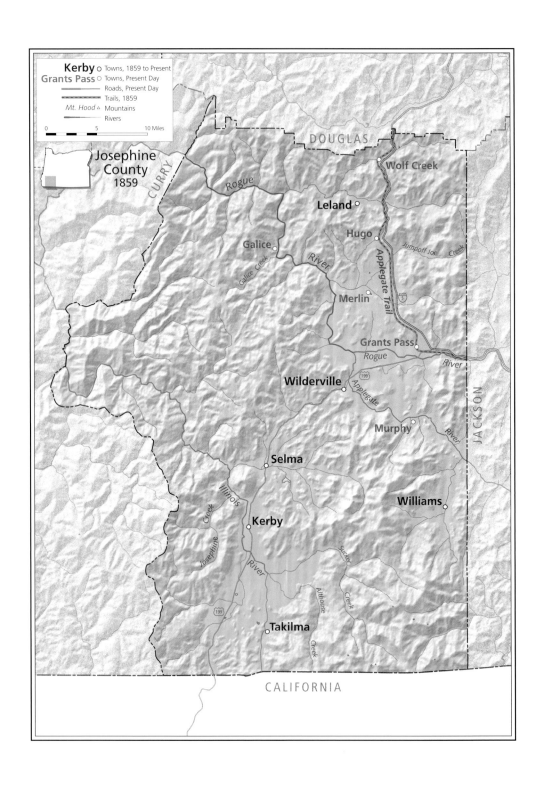

Josephine County 1859

Legend:
- Kerby ○ Towns, 1859 to Present
- Grants Pass ○ Towns, Present Day
- Roads, Present Day
- Trails, 1859
- Mt. Hood △ Mountains
- Rivers

0   5   10 Miles

DOUGLAS

CURRY

Rogue

Wolf Creek

Leland

Hugo

Jumpoff Joe Creek

Galice

Galice Creek

River

Applegate Trail

Merlin

Grants Pass

Rogue

River

Wilderville

Applegate

Murphy

River

JACKSON

Selma

Williams

Illinois

Creek

Kerby

Josephine

River

Sucker

Creek

Althouse

Creek

Takilma

Creek

CALIFORNIA

9 1859 JOSEPHINE COUNTY

Josephine County was created in 1856 from the western half of Jackson County. It was the 19th and final county to be created before Oregon became a state. Its mountainous and thickly forested terrain probably deterred settlement by the early pioneers passing through along the Applegate Trail until there was an added attraction—the gold discovered in 1851 in the Illinois Valley.

Waldo was the first county seat, but in 1857 the seat was moved to Kerbyville (Kerby today), where it remained until 1886. The third move to present-day Grants Pass was the result of the railroad arriving in Grants Pass in 1883—the train bypassed Kerby. According to the 1860 U.S. Census, the county population was 1623, plus a large number of untallied Chinese miners.

The Chinese miners in Josephine County encountered the same conditions as existed in Jackson County. They were taxed and relegated to their own living areas—a Chinatown being established in Waldo. The Chinese tended to move into the areas where the Euro-American miners had tired of the extra effort required after the surface diggings were mined; the Chinese used their skill and patience to rework these gravel bars.

For centuries Indian trails had passed through the more remote, densely forested areas of present-day Josephine County, but a party of miners led by Lloyd Rollins blazed the first trail into the Illinois Valley to be used by Euro-Americans, departing from the Applegate Trail and traveling over Hayes Hill. They were headed to California when they learned from the Indians about the gold in the valley. After taking their share of gold along Josephine Creek, they proceeded with their original plans and left for California.

By 1855 the trail along the Applegate River to Jacksonville was well traveled by pack trains. James Lowery and William Sutherland were the operators of one of the Waldo pack train companies. In 1859 the Josephine Wagon Road Company built a road between Deer Creek and Applegate, crossing Williams Creek.

The Applegate Trail passed through the northeastern portion of Josephine County, closely approximating today's Interstate 5. Exactly where pioneers crossed the Rogue River near Grants Pass depended on the height of the river at Jones and Vannoy creeks. Both of these routes then joined the main Apple-

Sites to Visit in Josephine County

Applegate Trail Interpretive Center
500 Sunny Valley Loop, Sunny
   Valley
1·888·411·1846

Illinois River Valley Visitor's Center
201 Oregon Caves Hwy, Cave
   Junction
541·592·4076

Indian Mary Park
Merlin-Galice Rd, Merlin

Kerbyville Museum
24195 Redwood Hwy, Kerby
541·592·5252

Josephine County Historical
   Society
512 SW 5th St, Grants Pass
541·479·7827

First Josephine County jail built in Kerby soon after it became the second county seat in 1857. Courtesy of the Josephine County Historical Society.

gate Trail again near Hugo. The military road coincided with this route as it passed through present-day Leland and the Louse Creek Stage Station.

For those pursuing gold mining opportunities in Galice, a trek to the west over a primitive, narrow road had to suffice. Supplies were also packed in this way by mule. An Indian called Umpqua Joe ferried the gold miners and pack team operators across the Rogue River.

The stage line between Waldo and Jacksonville was completed in 1857. The tri-weekly stage line operated by James Cluggage and John Drum, between Jacksonville and the Illinois Valley, traveled along the Applegate River, past Fort Hayes, and through Kerby. In 1858 the Crescent City Plank Road and Turnpike Company built a wagon and stage toll road connecting Waldo and Crescent City, California. The following year John W. Patrick built a toll bridge across the Illinois River. Today Highway 199 roughly parallels the original Jacksonville-Crescent City road. Several other ferries were in operation in 1859, providing transport across the county's numerous streams.

Early History

For centuries the Takelma, Applegate, and Galice Indians had been living within the area of present-day Josephine County. Prior to the discovery of gold, there had only been occasional contact with Euro-Americans. When the gold rush and its attendant lawless communities sprang up, the Indians were unable to deal with the sudden intrusions of people who often had little or no regard for the Indians' rights and who generally considered the Indians to be obstructing their mining efforts. Thus, Josephine County was the site of many hostilities between the Indians and the arriving miners.

The same Euro-Americans who passed through Jackson County before 1850 passed through northeastern Josephine County approximating the route of today's Interstate 5. After the discovery of gold, small settlements—many of them temporary mining camps—were scattered throughout the Illinois and Applegate valleys, and also in the area of the county northeast of the Rogue River. (This changed by 1860, however, when placer mining diminished and those without the funds to establish hydraulic mining operations moved on to new strikes in other parts of the Pacific Northwest.)

Because altercations between the settlers and Indians were common, four temporary forts were built for protection: Fort Briggs near Waldo, Fort Hayes in the Illinois Valley, Fort Leland in Leland, and Fort Vannoy in the vicinity of Grants Pass. Numbers of men from the Waldo area served with the military during the Rogue River Indian War—many losing their lives. An unprovoked attack on the Indians was also recorded.

The Takelma in the Illinois Valley were sent to the Table Rock Reservation in Jackson County in 1854. After the end of the Rogue River Indian War, the surviving Indians at Table Rock were sent to the Coast and Grand Ronde reservations.

The Takelma living in the northeastern portion of Josephine County stayed in the area until after the war, when they were also sent to the reservations. One Indian family living near Galice managed to avoid removal from their homeland because of the gratitude they had earned in 1855. The wife of Umpqua Joe told him about overhearing some Indians making plans to attack the settlers nearby. Umpqua Joe, in turn, warned the settlers, thus saving their lives and property. Joe, his wife, and three children were allowed to stay on their land where they planted fruit trees, grew vegetables, and operated a ferry across the Rogue River for the gold miners and settlers. After Joe's death in the mid-1880s, his oldest daughter, known as Indian Mary, remained on the family's land and continued to operate the ferry. In 1885 the U.S. government granted to her the land where Indian Mary Park lies today alongside the Rogue River. Local lore characterizes it as the "smallest Indian reservation."

Kerby and the Illinois Valley

Around 1855 Dr. Daniel Sherman Holton founded Kerbyville on donation land claim parcels he purchased from James Kerby. Since Kerby was inconsistent in the spelling of his name—even Kerbey sometimes—the town was variously known as Kerbyville or Kirbyville. On a personal whim, Holton lobbied the territorial legislature to change the name to Napoleon, but the unpopularity of that name among local residents resulted in changing the name back to Kerbyville by 1860; later it was shortened to Kerby.

Holton became a prominent citizen in the Illinois Valley. He had a medical practice and served in several territorial and county positions, including county coroner.

At the peak of the gold rush occurring on all sides of Kerby, it had the usual amenities of a mining town. There were many hotels, because Kerby was an overnight stage stop for the stage line traveling between Crescent City and Jacksonville. Kerby's first schoolhouse was built in 1856.

The first two gold discoveries in Josephine County were made in 1851, west and south of Kerby. The Lloyd Rollins party made one of the discoveries on Josephine Creek, a tributary creek of the Illinois River. Rollins's daughter Josephine was with him, thus the name of the creek and the county.

Some historians place the second gold discovery on Canyon Creek, another Illinois River tributary west of Kerby. The settlement of Canyon Creek that developed there in 1851 was called Sebastopol after 1855.

Most historians, however, prefer to recount the story about the sailors who jumped ship at Crescent City in 1852 and, while traveling to the gold fields in Jacksonville, made the second gold discovery in Josephine County along the Illinois River south of Kerby. Gold miners soon swarmed into the area, leading to the establishment of the settlement of Sailors' Diggings, later called Waldo, which encompassed a 20- to 25-square mile area that became one of the richest mining areas in Oregon. In 1859 Waldo had a thriving gold rush business district, saloons, mercantile stores, hotels, and even a bowling alley.

The Sailors' Diggings Water, Mining, and Milling Company was organized in 1852 to bring water from the East Fork of the Illinois River to the mines in the Waldo area. The company, managed by John C. Weston in 1859, used the water to operate its mines and also a sawmill. The company sold water to other mine owners. Hydraulic mining in the 1920s and '30s washed away the few early buildings remaining in Waldo. Large tailing mounds and two cemeteries, one Chinese, are all that remain on Waldo Road east of the Redwood Highway.

Other mining camps sprouted near Waldo, including Allen Gulch (also known as Allentown) southeast of Waldo; Browntown, Grass Flat, and Althouse on Althouse Creek; Democrat Gulch; an unnamed camp in the vicinity of present-day O'Brien; Sucker Creek; and French Flat northwest of Waldo and Frenchtown on Althouse Creek, two camps of exclusively French-speaking miners. Allen Gulch, Browntown, Grass Flat, Frenchtown, and Althouse were more than temporary mining camps—each having one or two well-established businesses.

In 1852 the noted Oregon historian Albert G. Walling, with two partners, established the first trading post in Althouse, later known as Holland. Charles H. Beach and Abraham W. Platter bought the business in 1854, and by 1859 Walling was living in Portland and one of the other partners had moved on. Catholic Church services were held at Allen Gulch and Methodist services along Althouse Creek.

Early days in Waldo in late 1850s. Courtesy of the Josephine County Historical Society.

The rich soil throughout the Illinois Valley attracted farmers as early as 1852. Alonzo P. Turner took the first donation land claim and many others followed, including John W. Patrick, William R. Ross, and Samuel R. Scott, who became Josephine County's first state senator.

There was a thriving market among the miners for the food the farmers and ranchers produced. J. W. Riggs was among the first to plant fruit trees that were delivered to him from Crescent City by pack train. Cattle and hogs were driven from the Willamette Valley and when they were ready for market the ranchers drove them to the mining towns and had them butchered on the spot for purchase. Wheat was grown in the valley and by 1858 there were a number of gristmills and sawmills in operation.

Selma, Wilderville, Murphy, Williams, and Grants Pass

The Ebenezer Hogue family settled in the Deer Creek Valley in 1859 and began ranching. When a stage stop was established there in 1854, it became known as Anderson, but since 1897 it has been named Selma. The William B. Hay family was settled farther north along the stage route and their log home served as a stage stop.

Slate Creek was another stage stop along the stage road to Jacksonville. A community of farmers developed in the late 1850s with fruit orchards and cattle transforming the landscape. The Slate Creek post office was established in 1858, but the name was changed to Wilderville around 1878.

Bernard Murphy took the first donation land claim along the Applegate River, but the town of Murphy was not established until the 1870s. In 1859 Calshill Caldwell was operating a hotel and saloon nearby, and Hugh Heaps operated a "noon stop" for the stage. His property was called Prospect Ranch and his services included stabling, feed supply, and hotel accommodations.

The Davidson family settled near Williams Creek in the 1850s. (Their son Elijah was the young man who discovered the Oregon Caves in 1874.) In 1859 the town of Williamsburg, now called Williams, was founded. Gold had been discovered the year before so it developed as a typical gold mining town. Daniel L. Green supplied hand-split shakes and other lumber. Several families settled there, but the majority of the population was single men. John T. Layton, with two partners from out of the area, dug a ditch to bring water to the diggings, but within a short amount of time the gold was depleted and the town disappeared.

In 1859, the eastern portion of Grants Pass was part of Jackson County. In 1885, in order to qualify Grants Pass as the new county seat, the Jackson/

Josephine county border was adjusted slightly, bringing the entire city boundaries into Josephine County. The original name was Grant's Pass, but the apostrophe was eventually dropped by local residents.

A ferry had been operating on the Rogue River west of Grants Pass since 1851. James Vannoy acquired it in 1853 and by 1856 there was a store, hotel, and post office in Vannoy—also known as Fort Vannoy during the Rogue River Indian War. The post office closed in August 1859, and by 1860, according to the census records, James Vannoy was living in Galice.

Galice and Hugo

Families took donation land claims in the area of present-day Merlin. However, several families were killed during the Rogue River Indian War and most of the survivors departed, with no new settlement occurring until the mid-1860s.

Gold was discovered on Galice Creek in 1851; mining in the area continued through the 1870s. Galice, known as Galiceburg, was established in 1852. Louis Galice, a French doctor turned miner, was one of the first prospectors on Galice Creek, thus the name, although the correct French spelling was Galleis. Galiceburg was located upstream from the mouth of Galice Creek, but when present-day Galice was founded in 1900, it was established along the Rogue River, a couple of miles north of the original site.

In 1859 there were the businesses common to a gold mining town, although several had burned during the Indian war, which was especially severe in Galice in 1855—enough to curtail gold mining activities. However, by the fall of 1856, mining resumed and new businesses were established. The population decreased again during that same year, because many miners were lured away by the gold rush on the Fraser River in British Columbia.

The Walker brothers, Augustus and Wesley, took donation land claims near Jumpoff Joe Creek Falls and built a sawmill there in 1858. Several families lived in the area of

A. M. Jess was the first merchant and the first justice of the peace in Galice, but his store was burned during the Rogue River Indian War. In 1857 he sold his property and moved to Wilderville to farm and operate a ferry across the Applegate River. Courtesy of the Josephine County Historical Society.

the present-day community of Hugo, including David and Caroline Sexton. (During the Indian war, widowed Caroline Niday bravely remained on the donation land claim she and her late husband took in 1853; in 1857 she married David Sexton.)

Leland

In 1846 the first emigrant train to travel the Applegate Trail camped on the north side of Woodpile Creek, which came to be known as Grave Creek because a 16-year-old member of the encampment, Martha Leland Crowley, died of typhoid fever and was buried nearby. James H. Twogood took a donation land claim there in 1851 and named his property the Grave Creek Ranch to commemorate the tragic event.

In 1851 Barney Simmons was operating a rest stop for Applegate Trail travelers along Grave Creek. By 1855 James Twogood and McDonough Harkness owned the business and built a hotel next to the log wayside.

During the Rogue River Indian War a stockade was built around the two structures and it was called Fort Leland. McDonough Harkness was killed during the war; his brother Sam Harkness purchased Twogood's half interest in 1866.

The 1855 Twogood and Harkness House, also called the Grave Creek House and later the Leland Creek House. It became a stage stop for the California-Oregon Stage line in 1860. Courtesy of the Josephine County Historical Society.

During the 1850s Grave Creek and Coyote Creek were productive placer gold sites. Quartz mines were established nearby and were operated throughout the rest of the century. James Twogood patented one of the largest mines in 1859.

The William Thomas family settled on Coyote Creek in 1859. Farther north, Francis M. Romane operated a stage stop in the Six-Bit House east of today's Wolf Creek Inn. (The 1883 Wolf Creek Inn, a state heritage site today, features the oldest continuous use hotel in the state of Oregon.)

Sampling of Josephine County Family Surnames in 1859

Kerby and Illinois Valley

Backus	Bull	Fisher	Kenady	Mendenhall	Riggs	Sutherland
Banks	Caldwell	Ganiard	Kerby	Messinger	Ross	Tanner
Barkwell	Cassidy	Godfrey	Koshland	Morford	Sann	Thomas
Beach	Chapman	Hall	Logan	Morris	Sawyer	Thompson
Bigelow	Charles	Hayden	Love	Newman	Scott	Waters
Bolt	Coyle	Hendershott	Lowery	Patrick	Sibley	Watkins
Briggs	Dodd	Holton	Macklin	Patterson	Smith	Wells
Broughton	Downing	Joseph	Matthews	Platter	Spear	Weston
Brown	Evans	Jourdan	McGrew	Post	Sprague	White

Selma, Wilderville, Murphy, Williams, and Grants Pass

Abbott	Davidson	Green	Howell	Murphy	Rehkopf	Taylor
Bailey	Davis	Guest	Jess	Nail	Ringold	Vining
Belknap	Dickerson	Haskins	Kent	Northcutt	Sheehan	Warner
Benedict	Doan	Hay	Layton	Pennington	Sloan	Watts
Caldwell	Elliott	Heap	Luellen	Pernoll	Sorenson	Williams
Cheney	Gilpin	Hogue	McKoin	Powell	Sparlin	Wilson
Covington	Goodwin	Holsclaw	McMullen	Reeves	Stevens	

Galice, Hugo, and Leland

Appleton	Dutcher	Jackson	Olds	Simmons	Turner	Walker
Blackledge	Evans	Martin	Romane	Simms	Twogood	Wallace
Croxton	Harkness	Miller	Sanders	Taylor	Umpqua Joe	Wills
Dimmick	Hook	Nagle	Shough	Tuffs	Vannoy	

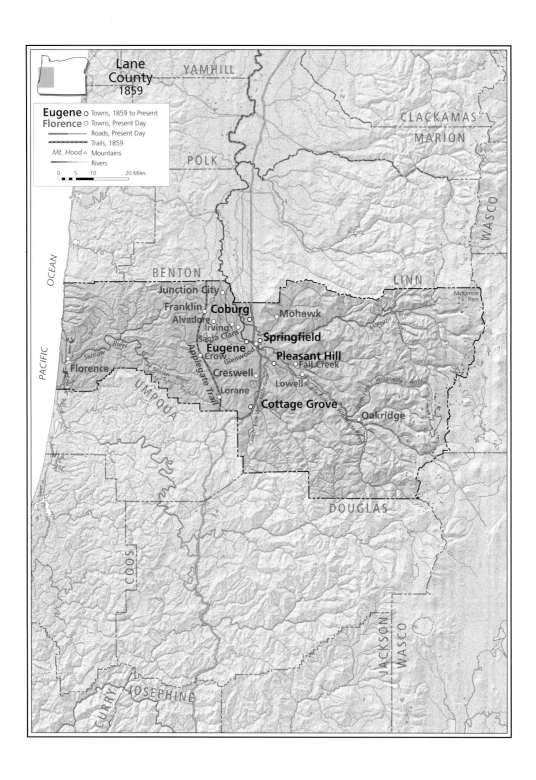

Lane
County
1859

Eugene ○ Towns, 1859 to Present
Florence ○ Towns, Present Day
━━━━ Roads, Present Day
━━━━ Trails, 1859
Mt. Hood △ Mountains
━━━━ Rivers

0   5   10   20 Miles

YAMHILL

CLACKAMAS

MARION

POLK

BENTON

LINN

McKenzie
Pass

OCEAN

PACIFIC

Junction City

Franklin

Alvadore

Coburg

Mohawk

Irving
Santa Clara

Springfield

McKenzie   River

Eugene

Crow
Glenwood

Pleasant Hill

Fall Creek

Creswell

Lowell

Lorane

Florence

Siuslaw   River

Siuslaw   River

Applegate Trail

Cottage Grove

Oakridge

Coast Fork Willamette River

South Fork   Willamette River

Middle Fork   Willamette   River

Willamette   River

UMPQUA

DOUGLAS

COOS

JACKSON

WASCO

CURRY

JOSEPHINE

10 1859 LANE COUNTY

Lane County was created in 1851 from the southern part of Linn County and a portion of Benton County. Its size and location were later changed by numerous boundary changes between 1852 and 1923. An 1853 election selected Eugene to serve as the county seat. The county clerk's building constructed in the same year was used as the courthouse until the first courthouse was built in 1855. A stone jail was constructed shortly thereafter. The clerk's office was converted into a residence and moved several times; today it stands next to the Lane County Historical Museum on the Lane County Fairgrounds. According to the 1860 U.S. Census, the county population was 4780.

In 1859 two routes of the Applegate Trail passed through Lane County. The Eastern Route went through Cottage Grove, Creswell, Eugene, and Junction City, generally following today's River Road and Highway 99. The Western Route, which followed Indian and Hudson's Bay Company (HBC) horse trails, became the most traveled Applegate Trail route, and is generally approximated by today's Territorial Highway, which passes through Lorane, Crow, and Franklin.

In 1851 Lane County was directly connected to Oregon City by the Eastside Territorial Road when it was extended to Spore's Ferry at Coburg. The Territorial Road was established in 1856 to connect Eugene to Corvallis and Portland.

Locally, the county began developing roads in the early 1850s. These roads were marked, but unimproved and muddy during the rainy months. Among the county's early roads were those connecting the Territorial Road to the ferries operating across the rivers and a number of roads connecting the farmlands to Eugene, which roughly paralleled today's Alder and Willamette streets, and Franklin and Blair boulevards.

Blair Boulevard also served as the main stagecoach road north to Corvallis and Portland. By 1859 a weekly stagecoach operated between Portland and Jacksonville, passing through Lane County.

In 1853 a crude wagon road was constructed along the Middle Fork of the Willamette River and over the Cascade Range. It was the road over which Elijah Elliott's Lost Wagon Train traveled when seeking a middle route from the Malheur River. This caravan of future Lane County settlers became lost, ran

Sites to Visit in Lane County

Applegate Pioneer Museum
Seventh & Broadway, Veneta
541·935·1836

Christian House, ca. 1855 (private
    residence)
170 E 12th, Eugene

Cottage Grove Historical Museum
Birch & H streets, Cottage Grove

Creswell Historical Museum
55 N 5th St, Creswell
541·895·5464

East Skinner Butte Historic Land-
    mark Area
High & Pearl streets, and 2nd & 3rd
    avenues, Eugene
(Replica of Skinner's cabin: west
    side of Butte on Cheshire Ave)

Henderson House, ca. 1857 (private
    residence)
260 High St, Eugene

Lane County Historical Museum
740 W 13th Ave, Eugene
541·682·4242

Masterson House, ca. 1857 (private
    residence)
2050 Madison St, Eugene

Oakridge-Westfir Pioneer Museum
76433 Pine St, Oakridge
541·782·2402

Siuslaw Pioneer Museum
278 Maple St, Florence
541·997·7884

The Springfield Depot
101 South A St, Springfield
541·746·1651

Springfield Museum
590 Main St, Springfield
541·726·2300

University of Oregon Museum of
    Natural & Cultural History
1680 E 15th Ave, Eugene
541·346·3024

out of food, and was facing certain death until rescued by settlers in the present-day Lowell area. In 1855 Army engineers explored the road as a possible railroad right-of-way. Today the Willamette Highway (Highway 58) approximates this early road.

In 1856 the first sternwheeler reached Eugene on the Willamette River, bringing the region into the 19th century—like the other communities on the lower stretches of the river. However, this was only possible five or six months out of the year when rains were sufficient to maintain an adequate water depth. During floodwaters, steamboats could make it to Springfield.

Ferries were vital to Lane County's transportation system—linking the various roads. Eugene Skinner's ferry crossed the Willamette River in Eugene and Jacob Spores's ferry crossed the McKenzie north of Eugene. Others included Isaac Briggs's ferry at Springfield.

Early History

For centuries, separate villages of the various bands of the Kalapuya Indians had been established in such areas as present-day Coburg, Cottage Grove, Creswell, Eugene, the Mohawk Valley, Oakridge, and Springfield. (For a description of their lifeways and fate during the 1850s, see chapter 1.) The Siuslaw Indians lived in the western and coastal portion of Lane County on and near the Siuslaw River, deriving their sustenance from the abundance of fish and sea mammals in the sea and rivers, and the native plants growing in the fertile soil.

Many of the same fur trappers and explorers who traveled along the Willamette River in Clackamas and Benton counties and the Umpqua Valley in Douglas County ventured into present-day Lane County along the same routes, including Donald McKenzie in 1812 and botanist David Douglas in 1826. Fur traders trapped along the rivers in the Cottage Grove area, and in the 1820s the HBC expedition led by Alexander Roderick McLeod explored the Siuslaw River near Florence.

In 1855 the Siuslaw Indians were a party to the Coast

Treaty, which proposed cession of the entire Oregon Coast to the U.S. government, but this treaty was never ratified. Instead the executive order of 1855 created the Coast Reservation. Initially this had little impact on the Siuslaw Indians because their ancestral lands were located within the southern portion of the reservation. Most of the Siuslaw families remained in their homeland and attempted to farm along the river as instructed by Jean Baptiste Gagnier, a French-Canadian retired HBC employee who settled among them with his local Indian wife. (By an act of the U.S. Congress in 1875 the southern part of the Coast Reservation, including the Siuslaw Valley, was opened to non-Indian settlement, leaving the remaining Siuslaw families surrounded by Euro-American settlers.)

In 1856 the Kalapuya Indians living within Lane County, in accordance with their treaty, were removed to the Grand Ronde Reservation. However, some of them, particularly those from the Springfield area, managed to return, and some found employment on local farms.

Eugene, Coburg, Springfield, and Pleasant Hill

In 1846 Elijah Bristow, William Dodson, Felix Scott, and Eugene F. Skinner arrived in the Eugene area. Skinner took a land claim on and around what came to be called Skinner Butte, but his companions chose sites outside of today's Eugene city limits. Skinner selected his claim for its suitability as a townsite and ferry crossing, not as a place to farm. Following the advice of some Indians he met, he built his log cabin on the west side of Skinner Butte to avoid the annual flooding of the Willamette River. Skinner and his wife operated a trading post and a post office out of their cabin until 1854, when they moved into a new frame house. Today a replica of the cabin is located in Skinner Butte Park.

Prior F. Blair, Daniel Christian, James Huddleston, and Charnel Mulligan took land claims adjacent to Skinner's in 1847 and 1848. Blair maintained his farm throughout most of his life, becoming wealthy from his commercial grain-producing business.

Flooding during the winter of 1851–52 made the townsite originally platted by Skinner and Judge David Risdon so muddy that locals began calling it "Skinner's Mud Hole." The following year a revised town plat was made on higher ground.

Skinner and Mulligan donated adjacent parcels for the construction of county buildings and a public square. Another portion of their donated land was laid out into lots to sell in order to raise funds for needed county projects.

Eugene F. Skinner (1809–1864)

Born and educated in New York

Moved to Illinois in 1845 with wife of six years, Mary Cook

Arrived in Willamette Valley in 1846 by way of California

Founded Eugene in 1852 with Judge David Risdon

Donated land for county seat purposes and for St. Mary's Episcopal Church, which his wife helped found

Practiced law, served as postmaster, clerk of first district court, and city council member and mayor

With Mary, had five children

View of Eugene from Skinner Butte, 1856–59. The region surrounding the city consisted of rich alluvial soil under cultivation in wheat, oats, and vegetables. By Kuchel & Dresel Lithographers, San Francisco. Courtesy of the Oregon Historical Society, OrHi 4861.

Eugene F. Skinner, co-founder of the city of Eugene. Courtesy of the Lane County Historical Museum, GN5297.

In 1850 Mary Skinner selected Eugene City for the name of the quickly developing townsite. (The word City was dropped from the name sometime after 1870.) By 1859 the town area had an array of pioneer businesses. Numerous professionals and trades people were offering their specialized services, including the daguerreotype photographer Philip E. Castleman.

After the 1851–52 floods, Hilyard Shaw and Avery Smith dug a millrace to serve as a source of power for Eugene's first lumber and gristmill by excavating a long ditch and connecting two natural sloughs of the Willamette River. Although a portion of the millrace was located on Shaw's claim, the remainder ran through three other claims. Shaw was granted easements from the other owners. The two mills were the first manufacturing businesses established in Eugene, and the millrace soon became the center point for future industrial enterprises. Other sawmills were later established along the banks of the Willamette River. (In the 1890s when the millrace was no longer needed for power, it became a recreational waterway used by University of Oregon students.)

Today Eugene has three 1850s extant houses. The southwest portion of Henderson House was built in 1857 as part of the Heatherly and Bailey Tavern, located at the corner of

View from the millrace of the Eugene Mill & Elevator Company, ca. 1910. The structure on the right is the original 1850s Eugene Mill Company structure. Courtesy of the Lane County Historical Museum, GN93.

8th and Pearl streets. It was moved to its present site on High Street in 1909. The Henderson name refers to a later owner, Reverend Enoch P. Henderson, who was the first president of Eugene's Columbia College.

The 1855 Daniel Christian III home remains near its original site on East 12th Avenue. Christian cut and hand-hewed the lumber for the First Methodist Church of Eugene when it was constructed in 1858, and the whole family was active in civic and cultural affairs. William A. Masterson's house that he built in 1857 still stands on Madison Street.

Eugene's first school was established in the early 1850s in Fielden McMurry's farmhouse, which was located at the site of today's University of Oregon Erb Memorial Union. McMurry was a territorial legislator and served as the first treasurer of Lane County until his death in 1860. The city's public school system was organized in 1854, and the first public school building was constructed in 1856.

Also, in 1856, the Cumberland Presbyterian Church founded Columbia College, a short-lived, but prestigious co-educational private college located on what became known as College Hill. Conflicting political views with local residents—especially on the issue of slavery—and two suspicious fires that destroyed the first and second school buildings, led to Columbia College's financial ruin. A third building was never completed, and the college was closed in 1860.

Some of Columbia College's students became prominent figures in Oregon history, including the social activist and poet Joaquin Miller, county judge and University of Oregon Board of Regents member Joshua J. Walton, circuit riding gospel preacher Rufus G. Callison, and the *People's Press* reporter and later publisher Harrison Kincaid. Sarah Rinehart, Judy Mulholland, and sisters Judy and Adelia Harlow were among the women who attended. Several alumni were involved in the founding of the University of Oregon in 1876.

Various church denominations organized in the vicinity of Eugene in the early 1850s. The Cumberland Presbyterian Church was the first to construct a church building in Eugene in 1857. The Presbyterians shared their church building with several other congregations until each built its own place of worship. In 1854 the First Methodist Church congregation formed in the log home of Solomon and Nancy Zumwalt, who lived northwest of Eugene; a church building was constructed in 1858. The Saint Mary's Episcopal congregation began meeting in the courthouse in 1854 and built a church in 1859, as did the First Presbyterian Church, which organized in 1854.

Many of Eugene's earliest arrivals stayed only briefly in the townsite area before taking permanent donation land claims in some of the outlying areas known today as Glenwood, Santa Clara, and Irving. In addition to growing crops and raising stock to feed their own families and to trade for other goods and services, these settlers, especially in the Santa Clara and Irving areas, raised wheat for commercial purposes. Settlement along the River Road area began as early as 1850 and it eventually became a significant commercial crop growing area.

To the northeast, in the late 1840s, Jacob Spores and John Diamond settled Willamette Forks—today's Coburg. The two men built a sawmill in 1855. The ferry Spores operated across the McKenzie River was used heavily by wagon trains moving north and south through the Willamette Valley.

His family continued the ferry service until a bridge was built across the river in 1878.

In 1854 the Mitchell Wilkins family built their home overlooking Centennial Butte. The Willamette Forks post office was located in a small building on their property. Like many of their neighbors, the Wilkins raised grain and cattle.

In 1853 the Hulin Miller family arrived, which included a "favorite son" of Coburg—Joaquin Miller. His brother George was not as famous, but he contributed significantly to the development of Lane County as a real estate developer. He founded several towns, including Florence on the coast in the 1890s, and he built many homes in Eugene.

Two schools were established in Coburg, and two congregations that later built churches in Eugene were organized in the homes of Coburg residents. Mahlon H. and Frances B. Harlow hosted meetings to organize the Willamette Forks Baptist Church of Jesus Christ, later changed to the First Baptist Church when a church structure was built in Eugene in 1867; and Charles W. Young held meetings to lay the foundations for the Cumberland Presbyterian Congregation.

A few early pioneers, including Spores's son James M. Spores, took donation land claims in the Mohawk Valley during the 1850s. John Templeton Craig settled in the Camp Creek area just north of Springfield. The settlers grew grain and hay, and raised cattle and horses.

In 1848 the Elias M. Briggs family was the first to permanently settle on the original townsite of Springfield. Many other settlers took donation land claims on the rich prairie land between the Willamette and McKenzie rivers in the early 1850s, creating a community with a small commercial district. The farmers raised vegetables for their families' use, and also wheat and oats, and a wide assortment of livestock.

Between 1852 and 1854, Briggs, his father Isaac, and two partners used hand tools and plows to dig a four-mile millrace and erect a gristmill and sawmill. One of the partners was Jeremiah Driggs of Linn County; the company became

Joaquin Miller, one of Lane County's most colorful characters who became world famous as the self-proclaimed "Poet of the Sierras." Courtesy of the Lane County Historical Society, GN9016.

Drawing of Elias M. Briggs, Springfield pioneer. Courtesy of the Springfield Museum.

Elijah Bristow (1788–1872)

Born in Virginia; served with distinction in War of 1812—exhibiting his excellent marksmanship

Skilled hatter, blacksmith, gunsmith, and farmer

Arrived in Lane County in 1846 by way of California, becoming one of Lane County's first settlers; joined by his family in 1848

Donated five acres for a church building, school, and cemetery in 1849

Organized Pleasant Hill Church of Christ in 1850—Lane County's first church

Built Lane County's first school in 1850, with his son and daughter-in-law serving as first teachers

Married Susanna in 1812; 15 children

The 1854 Springfield mill, constructed under the supervision of an experienced millwright. Courtesy of the Springfield Museum.

Elijah Bristow (pictured) and his wife, Susanna, were grandparents in their fifties when they settled in Pleasant Hill with their extended family. They were blessed with four more children after their arrival, bringing their total number of children to 15. Courtesy of the Lane County Historical Museum, GN4980.

known as Driggs and Briggs Company. Several years later the company sold out to B. J. Pengra and his partners, who formed the Springfield Manufacturing Company. The gristmill produced Snowball Flour, a well-known brand of flour considered the best at that time in the Willamette Valley.

The Springfield School District was established in 1854. Two schools were in operation in the adjacent Thurston area. The Baptists were the first to organize a church in the Springfield area, but not until 1865.

According to the 1860 U.S. Census, there were over 45 families settled in the area south and southeast of Springfield. Pleasant Hill had the largest concentration of people, but settlers were also located in the Fall Creek, Lost Valley, and Lowell areas. The James Parvin family arrived in Lost Valley in 1853 and was influential in the development of nearby Dexter in later years.

One of the Bristow's sons, William Wilshire Bristow, became a prominent citizen of Pleasant Hill. Among several other positions, he was a delegate to the state convention in 1858, helped draft the state constitution, served as a state senator, and was one of the founders of the University of Oregon.

John Whiteaker, Oregon's first state governor, moved his family to Pleasant Hill in 1859 from their original homestead in the Spencer Butte area. Besides his many public service activities, he was a farmer. (Whiteaker's biography appears in the Introduction.)

Junction City and Franklin

Before the disastrous flood of 1861 and the resultant changes in the course of the Willamette River, there was a river port called Woody's Landing or Woodyville. It featured a river dock, a saloon, other businesses, and a few residences. When Eugene was unreachable due to low water levels, Woody's Landing served as the head of navigation on the Willamette. In 1862, with the Willamette River then running one mile to the east, the town of Lancaster was established as an inland town, but only a small community remains in the area today.

In 1858, just to the north, the Freedom post office was established serving more than 80 families in the area, and a few more in the area of present-day Junction City. There were over 70 families settled near present-day Franklin and the adjacent Long Tom River portion of the Willamette Valley. Enos Elmaker, R. V. Howard, and Daniel Smith were among the early 1850s settlers. The Edward Adkins family settled in present-day Alvadore; they opened up their home to their neighbors for prayer and Bible study meetings. In 1855 the Grand Prairie Church was organized; the congregation began meeting in the Grand Prairie schoolhouse after it was built in 1856.

Creswell, Cottage Grove, Crow, and Lorane

There were a number of settlers located south of Spencer Butte in the early 1850s, attracted to the area by the year-round springs. Farther south, William R. Jones laid out the townsite of Cloverdale, located between Pleasant Hill and Creswell. The town had a gristmill and general store operated by Jones and John T. Gilfry. Cloverdale disappeared after Creswell developed in the 1870s. Charles G. Martin was the first to take a donation land claim in the Creswell area in 1850. Settlers from three wagon trains who joined him in the area included members of the Buoy family.

With available lands in the northern Willamette Valley becoming scarce in the late 1840s, settlers started moving into the area of Cottage Grove. John Cochran, Royal H. Hazelton, Dave Mosby, Richard Robinson, and Henry Small were among the earliest arrivals—most with families. The settlement was called Slabtown until the mid-1860s because wooden slabs were placed in the ruts of the Coast Fork Trail to keep the wagon wheels from sinking into the mud during the rainy season.

By 1859 the town had a gristmill and sawmill located on Silk Creek, and a log schoolhouse built on a donated portion of the Smalls' claim. The school-house was also used for church services and community gatherings. The post office moved as the postmasters changed, located first in the Smalls' house and later in two communities to the north, before being returned to down-town Cottage Grove in the 1860s. In 1858 gold was discovered on the Row River east of Cottage Grove, but the development of the Bohemia Min-ing District at Sharps Creek and the subsequent gold rush there did not get underway until 1863.

James Chapin settled in the area of the present-day community of Latham in the late 1840s, opening his one-room cabin to travelers on the Coast Fork Trail. A few other families, including the Henry W. Taylor family, joined him in the early 1850s. There was a log schoolhouse built in this community of set-tlers by 1853.

According to the 1860 U.S. Census, there were more than 25 families settled in the Siuslaw Valley area between present-day Crow and Lorane. The fami-lies of Daniel Lucas, John Delameter, and the many branches of the Crow family were among the earliest arrivals in the early 1850s. The valley's fertile grazing land supported a variety of livestock, and some families grew wheat. The closest gristmill was in Cottage Grove, so those who had grain traveled

The 1853 Darius B. Cartwright House, ca. 1930, was located on the Territorial Road south of Lorane. The family lived there and welcomed passing travelers. In 1866 their son-in-law renamed it the Mountain House Hotel and operated a stage stop, post office, and telegraph station. Courtesy of the Lane County Historical Museum, GN1463.

there to have it ground into flour and others took products from their farms to trade for flour. Travel was nearly impossible during the winter months, so wild game and fish were either smoked or salted in barrels and put away for the winter. Farmers with specific trade skills offered their services to their neighbors. John Crow, for example, operated a blacksmith shop; he also was a gunsmith, wagon maker, and carpenter. Timber was abundant in the area, but the first sawmill was not built until the 1880s. By 1854 Lorane's post office was located where Gillespie Corners is located today, probably in the postmaster's home.

Sampling of Lane County Family Surnames in 1859

Eugene, Coburg, Springfield, and Pleasant Hill

Alexander	Callison	Gilbert	Jennings	Morgan	Renfrew	Teal
Allen	Calloway	Goodpasture	Jones	Mulholland	Richardson	Van Duyn
Armitage	Castleman	Gray	Killingsworth	Mulkey	Rigdon	Vaughan
Bailey	Chase	Guillford	Kincaid	Mulligan	Risdon	Walker
Blair	Christian	Hadley	Latta	Noble	Ritchie	Walton
Blakely	Cogswell	Hammitt	Littrel	Parvin	Scott	Ware
Bogart	Criswell	Hardesty	Looney	Patterson	Shaw	Warner
Bond	Davis	Harlow	Luckey	Pearce	Skinner	Watson
Brattain	Day	Heatherly	Masterson	Peek	Smith	Whiteaker
Briggs	Dodson	Henderson	McClure	Pengra	Sparks	Wilkins
Bristow	Dunn	Hendricks	McDowell	Poindexter	Spores	Williams
Brumley	Eady	Hobson	McMurry	Powers	Stanton	Winter
Buoy	Ellsworth	Huddleston	Miller	Rader	Stewart	Young
Bushnell	Gay	Hulin	Mitchell	Ramsey	Storment	Zumwalt

Junction City and Franklin areas

Adkins	Elmaker	Florence	Howard	Pilney	Smith
Bushnell	Ferguson	Hinton	Hyland	Potter	

Creswell, Cottage Grove, Crow, and Lorane

Adams	Butler	Cooley	Hamilton	Lane	Morss	Robinson	Taylor
Alexander	Cartwright	Crow	Harper	Lucas	Mosby	Scott	Thompson
Allen	Chapin	Currin	Hawley	Martin	Oglesby	Sears	Turpin
Arp	Chrisman	Davidson	Hazelton	Matheny	Ozment	Shield	Veatch
Bowers	Clark	Delameter	Hughes	McFarland	Petrie	Small	White
Boxley	Cochran	Dillard	Kelly	Miller	Petty	Southwell	Whitney
Bristow	Coleman	Gilfrey	Knox	Moore	Rhinehart	Stewart	Wooten
Bryant	Colson	Gray					

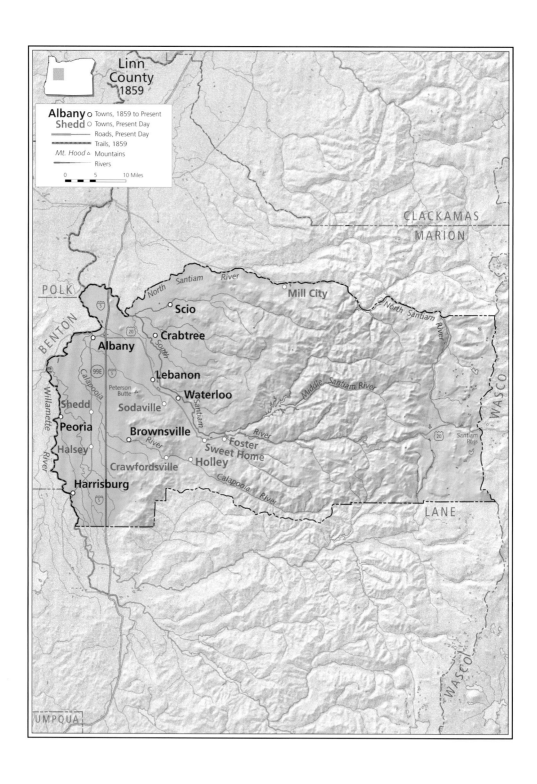

Linn
County
1859

Albany ○ Towns, 1859 to Present
Shedd ○ Towns, Present Day
——— Roads, Present Day
▤▤▤▤ Trails, 1859
Mt. Hood ▵ Mountains
——— Rivers

0   5   10 Miles

CLACKAMAS
MARION

POLK

North   Santiam   River
Mill City

Scio

North Santiam River

BENTON

Crabtree

Albany

South

Lebanon

Peterson
Butte ▵

Waterloo

Middle Santiam River

Sodaville

Santiam

Shedd

Peoria

Brownsville

River

Foster
Sweet Home

Santiam Pass

Willamette

Halsey

River

Holley

Crawfordsville

WASCO

Harrisburg

Calapooia   River

LANE

River

UMPQUA

WASCO

11 1859 LINN COUNTY

Linn County was created in 1847 from the southern portion of Champoeg (later Marion) County. Its boundaries were altered in 1851 and 1854 when Lane and Wasco counties were created. Calapooia—present-day Brownsville—served as the first county seat, but in 1851 the territorial legislature established Albany as the county seat, with approval confirmed by a special election in 1856. An octagon-shaped courthouse was built in Albany in 1853, but was destroyed by fire in 1861. According to the 1860 U.S. Census, the county population was 6772.

Since 1847 Linn County had been connected to Oregon City by the Eastside Territorial Road, which ended at Brownsville at that time. When the road was extended to Coburg in Lane County in 1851, it passed through Brownsville and Union Point, avoiding as many large streams as possible by following the east edge of the valley along Gap Road. A few county roads, like Spicer Drive between Albany and Lebanon, were constructed in the mid-1850s, and many trails and private roads ran east to west between farms. During the rainy season these roads became soggy and impassable, so travel by steamboat on the Willamette River became the chief means of transportation.

In September of 1859, John Bradenburg, John Gray, and Andrew Wiley discovered the Santiam Pass through the Cascade Range. They, along with local ranchers, formed the Willamette Valley and Cascade Mountain Wagon Road Company to build a road to connect the Willamette Valley to the pasture lands of central Oregon. The Santiam Wagon Road was completed in the mid-1860s, just in time to meet the increased demand for beef created by the gold miners in eastern Oregon and Idaho.

Early History

The lifeways of the Kalapuyans, including the Santiam, Upper Santiam, and Northern Molalla living along the Calapooia, Willamette, and Santiam rivers in Linn County, was similar to that of the other native inhabitants of the Willamette Valley. They were also peaceful, friendly, and helpful to the early pioneers.

Before settlers arrived in the 1840s and until the Indians were removed to the Grand Ronde Reservation in 1856, the survivors of the epidemics of the

Sites to Visit in Linn County

Albany Regional Museum
136 SW Lyon St, Albany
541·967·7122

Albany Visitors Association
(walking tour maps available)
250 Broadalbin SW, Albany
541·928·0911

Angell-Brewster House, ca. 1857
(private residence)
34191 Brewster Rd, Lebanon

Atavista Farm, ca. 1876, pioneer's
home (private B & B)
35580 Hwy 228, Brownsville
541·466·5566

Boston/Thompson's Mills State
Heritage Site
1½ miles east of Shedd on Boston
Mill Rd
541·491·3611

Canyon Life Museum
143 Wall St, Mill City
503·897·4088

Claypool-Elkins House, ca. 1856
(private residence)
194 Main St, Lebanon

East Linn Museum
746 Long St, Sweet Home
541·367·4580

Harrisburg Area Museum
490 Smith St, Harrisburg
541·995·4844

Humphrey House, ca. 1850s
(private residence)
265 7th St, Harrisburg

Linn County Historical Museum
(walking tour maps available)
101 Park Ave, Brownsville
541·466·3390

Monteith House, ca. 1849
518 2nd Ave SW, Albany
541·928·0911

Moyer House, ca. 1881, pioneer's
home
204 N Main St, Brownsville
541·466·3390

Scio Depot Museum
39004 NE 1st Ave, Scio
503·394·2199

Shedd Museum
29990 1st St E, Shedd

Waters House, ca. 1850s (private
residence)
205 S 4th St, Harrisburg

Indian Lize, ca. 1912, the last of the native Kalapuya Indians to live in Linn County, never moved to a reservation. Courtesy of the Linn County Historical Museum, Brownsville, Oregon.

1830s lived in the vicinity of present-day Albany, Lebanon, Brownsville, Sweet Home, and the western Cascade foothills. The Sweet Home Valley was difficult for early settlers to access, thus Indian encampments remained along the banks of the Santiam River until the mid-1860s.

Albany, Crabtree, and Scio

Between 1845 and 1846 Crill Burkhart, Abner Hackleman, and Hiram Smead were the first settlers to arrive in the area of Albany. The following year brothers Thomas and Walter Monteith arrived from Albany, New York, taking separate donation land claims. In 1848 they abandoned those claims and purchased Smead's claim, and an adjacent claim. They had their land surveyed, laid out town lots near the Willamette River, and named it New Albany. They built a cabin first and in 1849 built the first frame house in Albany. It remains today as a restored house museum, open to the public.

Abner Hackleman returned to Iowa in 1846 to accompany his family to their new home in Oregon. However, he died unexpectedly in Iowa, so it was his son Abram who settled his father's claim in 1847. In the early 1850s Hackleman laid out several additions east of the Monteith brothers' townsite. The two districts became known as the Hackleman and Monteith districts and soon developed political, business, and social demarcations that divided the town throughout the mid-1800s.

Most of the Hackleman district residents were working-class Democrats who sided with the South on the issue of slavery. Residents of the Monteith district tended to be the merchants and professionals who held Union sympathies. Most were members of the Whig Party until the Oregon Republican Party was founded in 1857 in the Monteiths' house.

The rivalry between the two districts likely had origins in 1853 over the name of the town. The Hackleman district lobbied the territorial legislature to change the name to Takenah, a Kalapuya word describing the deep pool where the Calapooia River meets the Willamette River. But two years later the Monteith brothers were able to convince the legislature to change the name to Albany, because Takenah was often incorrectly translated to mean hole in the ground, which they deemed inappropriate for a rapidly developing town.

Albany's early economy was based on its agricultural products, especially the growing and processing of wheat. In 1851 the Magnolia Flouring Mill was

The 1849 Monteith House, ca. 1905, served as the Monteith brothers' home and store in its earliest years, but later became the home of Thomas Monteith and his wife, Christine M. Dunbar. The couple hosted numerous religious, political, and social meetings in their home— many of them of historical significance. Courtesy of the Monteith Historical Society.

The Monteith's second store faced Water Avenue at the corner of Ferry Street, ca. 1858. Courtesy of the Albany Regional Museum.

built on the Calapooia River and by 1852 steamboats were stopping at Albany's landing on the Willamette to pick up the flour for delivery to Portland and beyond. The steamboats delivered goods needed by Albany residents. Development of both the Monteith and Hackleman districts soon followed with the establishment of competing stores and mills, ensuring a robust economy. Three families—the Monteiths, Hacklemans, and Burkharts (of the Hackelman District)—were generous promoters of the town through donations of land and money.

Albany's first school was a private school established in 1851; in 1855 the first public school was constructed—Central School. The Methodists built the first church building in Albany; the Presbyterians met in the courthouse and several other congregations, including the United Brethren, were meeting in homes. Albany's first newspaper appeared

The Magnolia Flouring Mill, as seen from today's Bryant Park, ca. 1851. Walter and Thomas Monteith, Samuel Althouse, Jeremiah Driggs, and Samuel Hill were the original owners. Courtesy of the Albany Regional Museum.

in 1859, when the first edition of the *Oregon Democrat* was published.

Southwest of Albany, Isaac Moore established the short-lived town of Orleans in 1851, directly across the Willamette River from Corvallis in Benton County. It had a steamboat landing, the typical pioneer-era businesses, and a ferry that connected Orleans with Corvallis. Prussian-born Gustav Hodes established the Hodes Brewery in Orleans in 1857, but during the 1861–62 winter flood the entire town was swept away.

In 1852 the Central post office was opened in Joel Ketchum's home "centrally" located between Albany and Lebanon. The Central Church was established in 1851, meeting in the homes of its congregants, including several related Powell families. The post office was in operation until 1861.

Knox Butte was another early community east of Albany. Among its early settlers were the related Chambers, Haight, and James Knox families. Methodist church services were held in the Knox cabin and later in various schoolhouses. Anderson Cox operated a sawmill near the South Santiam River.

In 1846, north of Knox Butte, at a location about one-and-one-half miles south of Jefferson in Marion County, Milton Hale established the first ferry across the Santiam River. Several years later he founded the town of Syracuse on his donation land claim. However, by 1850 the town was beset by a series of setbacks: rival ferry operators, a rival town—Santiam City—across the river in Marion County; and flooding in 1850–51 and 1860–61. Although Syracuse continued to exist throughout the 1850s, it steadily declined and soon disappeared entirely. The Hales eventually moved to Albany.

To the east of Knox Butte, the small communities of Crabtree, the Forks of the Santiam, and Scio developed from the mid-1840s on. The John J. Crabtree family arrived first and bought the squatter's rights of William Packwood, who may have been the first settler in all of Linn County in 1844. (Packwood then moved to the Washington Territory.)

Dr. Thomas Condon (pictured) and his wife, Cornelia Holt, came to Oregon in 1852 as missionaries. Condon was a pastor in Albany, Forest Grove, St. Helens, and The Dalles. The Condons lived in Albany from 1855 to 1861. While living in The Dalles, Condon made his first visit to the present-day John Day Fossil Beds, leading to a career change that secured his place in Oregon history. He became the state's first geologist and a renowned science professor and researcher at the University of Oregon. Image courtesy of Special Collections and University Archives, University of Oregon libraries.

Reverend Joab Powell
(1799–1873)

Born in Tennessee; began preaching career at age 24

Arrived in Oregon in 1852 and took donation land claim at Forks of the Santiam near Scio

Renowned Baptist circuit rider in 1850s and '60s who visited scattered settlements throughout Willamette and Umpqua valleys, reportedly converting over 3000 lost souls

Related well with fellow farmers

His wife, Ann Beeler, and oldest sons (12 children) operated farm in his absence

Poor reader so his wife read the Bible to him; he memorized scripture and hymns

The Santiam Academy, chartered as a co-educational Methodist preparatory school, never had any boarding facilities. Courtesy of the Linn County Historical Museum, Brownsville, Oregon.

The James Curl, William Cyrus, William Deakins, and Haman Shelton families arrived in 1847, followed by more members of the Crabtree family and others in the early 1850s. Another early resident, E. B. McInnish, served as the county commissioner in 1857 and as a state representative in 1858. Cyrus held several public offices after 1859.

The original town of Scio was laid out on the north side of Thomas Creek in 1856; several years later William Bilyeu and E. E. Wheeler laid out additions on the south side of Thomas Creek on portions of their property. A gristmill was built in Scio in 1856 and several other businesses were in operation by 1859, including a drugstore and a hotel owned and operated by Edward Grimes. Dr. Jacob Boice taught school and practiced medicine.

In 1853 Reverends Joab Powell, J. C. Berkley, and Richmond Cheadle organized the United Baptist Church of Providence at the Forks of the Santiam. Reverend Powell was the senior pastor, but Reverend Berkley performed most of his day-to-day duties when Powell was on the preaching circuit.

In 1852 the Powell brothers—John A. and Alfred—established the Christian Church in Scio. This Powell family was not related to Joab Powell and originally spelled their surname with only one "l"—Powel.

Mill City northeast of Scio did not have its first settlers until 1860 and soon became a logging and mining community.

Lebanon, Sodaville, Waterloo, and Sweet Home

Around 1848 the Jeremiah Ralston family settled east of Albany on the rich grassy prairies between the Willamette and South Santiam rivers. The settlement that developed was known by many different names before becoming Lebanon, including Peterson's Gap, Pinhook, Pin Head, and Santyam. Before the post office became the Lebanon post office in 1859, it was called Washington Butte, the former name of Peterson Butte.

Ralston brought a supply of staple goods and merchandise across the Oregon Trail and immediately established a trading post; Luther Elkins opened a store. Once the Ralstons and the other early settlers established their farms for growing hay and wheat and raising stock, the settlement became a regional trade center supplying the gold miners in California and later, southern Oregon. In 1852 Ralston laid out and platted the town on land that he and Morgan Kees contributed. Two 1850s houses are extant in Lebanon: the 1856 Claypool-Elkins House and the 1857 Angell-Brewster House.

Ralston and Kees also donated the land on which the Santiam Academy was built. Before its completion in 1854, Reverend Luther T. Woodward and his wife taught classes in their log church building.

Sand Ridge was a community settled four miles west of Lebanon on the west side of Peterson Butte. Reverend John A. Powell from the Central Church led church services, which were held in Ephraim and Jane Barnett's home.

Captain Henry Peterson established a nursery on Peterson Butte in 1845. He imported a plum variety that became known as the Peterson plum; the fruit was dried and shipped to the mines in southern Oregon.

In 1846 gold flakes were noted glittering in the sands of Dry Gulch about 25 miles east of Lebanon, but the first legal claim was not filed in the Quartzville area until 1863 by Jeremiah Driggs of Albany.

Reuben Coyle arrived in the vicinity of present-day Sodaville in 1847 and began farming on his donation land claim. A community developed following discovery of a spring of pungent mineral water flowing from a rocky hillside. However, the town of Sodaville was not platted until resolution of an 18-year legal dispute over the rightful ownership of the springs, with title being awarded to Thomas Summers in 1871.

Linn County's first Baptist congregation was organized at Sodaville in 1848, but a schism in 1853 led to the dismissal of some of its members who then organized the Pleasant Butte Baptist Church and began meeting at Pleasant Butte School north of Brownsville. A school was established in Sodaville in 1851.

Waterloo was first known as Kees Mills. Elmore Kees arrived in 1847, taking a donation land claim which included the falls and soda spring on both sides of the Santiam River. He and one or two other members of the Kees family built a ferry, gristmill, and sawmill.

A small group of Mormons escaping religious persecution arrived in the Sweet Home Valley in 1852, led by Lowell Ames. The families took donation land claims throughout the valley—the Ames and Moss families between present-day Holley and Sweet Home; the Andrew Wiley family at the base of Whiskey Butte on Wiley Creek; the John Gilliland family at the east end of the valley; the Pickens brothers along the Santiam River near present-day

Foster; and other families in the area of present-day Clark Mill Road. Nearby towns were scarce and farms were far apart so children were home schooled, if at all. The Ames and A. P. Morris families organized a Latter Day Saints congregation, which met at the members' homes until a church was built on the South Santiam River.

Ames built a sawmill in 1856, and in 1858 a bridge was built across the Santiam River near the site of today's Pleasant Valley Road bridge. The Pleasant Valley Baptist Church was founded in 1856, and Protestants began settling in the area.

Brownsville, Crawfordsville, and Holley

Between 1845 and 1846 settlers began taking claims in the area that later became Brownsville. Originally called Kirk's Ferry because Alexander Kirk established a ferry across the Calapooia River in 1846, the name was changed to Calapooia when a post office was opened in 1850. The ferry discontinued service when a bridge was built just upriver around 1853. Captain James Blakely laid out a town plat on his claim south of the river in 1853 and named the town after his uncle and business partner, Hugh L. Brown. The Brownsville name became official in 1859.

Blakely and Brown opened the first general store, co-founded the first flour mill in Brownsville, and promoted the Brownsville Woolen Mill. Blakely raised stock, was a captain in the Rogue River Indian War, and served one term as a state legislator. Brown held local government offices and also served in the state legislature. Brown and his wife, Clarissa Browning, parents of eight children, built the 1876 Italianate-style house known today as the Atavista Farm Bed & Breakfast.

Today a walking tour of Brownsville showcases a number of historic homes and buildings, including two houses built in the 1850s, and also the millrace dug in 1858. (A map is available at the Linn County Historical Museum.) A wooden dam was built three miles north of the Calapooia River to provide water power for the industrial development that followed in the 1860s with the establishment of a tannery and various mills.

Reverend Henry H. Spalding (variously spelled Spaulding) platted the town of Amelia, named after his youngest daughter, on the north side of the Calapooia River in 1858. (In later years another area north of the river became known as North Brownsville and the original Brownsville became South Brownsville. In 1895 all three communities were incorporated together as Brownsville.)

In 1849 Spalding established the first school in Linn County, a private school located east of Brownsville. Community meetings were held in the schoolhouse, and the Congregational Church met there on Sundays. Spalding was the pastor of the church until September of 1859, when he and his second wife, Rachel Smith, left Oregon to resume the missionary work that brought Spalding west with Dr. Marcus Whitman in 1836.

Two other churches were established in Brownsville by 1859. Reverend "Father" John McKinney established a Methodist meeting house on his claim west of Brownsville around 1847, which officially became the Methodist Episcopal Church after the Annual Methodist Conference met at Corvallis in 1857. Brownsville gained a Baptist church when the Pleasant Butte Baptist Church was formed from the Sodaville congregation; this church later became the First Baptist Church of Brownsville.

Union Point, several miles south of Brownsville on the Gap Road, became a community of 200 to 300 people in the early 1850s, featuring several businesses, a school, the Union Point Academy, and a church. At this time the Presbyterian denomination had two branches—the Associate and the Associate Reformed. In 1852 the Union Point Associate Reformed Church united with the Willamette Associate Presbyterian Church of Oakville, becoming the United

John M. Moyer (1829–1904)

Born in Ohio; arrived in Brownsville in 1852

Began as a carpenter building houses in Brownsville area; met his wife while helping her father, Hugh L. Brown, build his house on Blakely Avenue

After marrying, couple bought lots in Brownsville and a farm outside town, but soon moved into town and Moyer resumed carpentry trade

Owned or was partner in a sash and door factory, Bank of Brownsville, and Brownsville Woolen Mill

Served as town mayor

Built Italianate-style house in 1881 that is an historic house museum today

Six children with Elizabeth Brown

Mill Street, North Brownsville, ca. 1865–70.
Courtesy of the Linn County Historical Museum, Brownsville, Oregon.

Reverend Wilson L. Blain
(1813–1861)

Born in Ohio; educated at Missouri University

Arrived in Oregon City in 1848 as Presbyterian minister for Associate Reformed Church

Served as editor of *Oregon Spectator*, printer for territorial government, and territorial legislator

Organized Union Point Associate Reformed Church in 1849

Moved with family to Union Point in 1850 and built church on hillside above Gap Road

Instrumental in effecting merger of two branches of Presbyterians to form United Presbyterian Church of Oregon

Established and taught in Union Point's first school and also at Union Point Academy, which was granted charter from territorial legislature in 1854

Married Elizabeth Wilson; six children

Presbyterian Church of Oregon; in 1858 they merged into the United Presbyterian Church of North America.

Reverend Wilson L. Blain was the driving force behind the early development of Union Point. However, in the mid-1850s neighboring Brownsville was drawing business away from Union Point. The post office was closed in 1859 and, after Reverend Blain's death in 1861, Union Point rapidly declined.

Another short-lived community was developed south of Union Point in the area of Diamond Hill, with settlers arriving in the late 1840s. Most, like David Dinwiddie and Luther White, raised stock on the open lands. Diamond Hill acquired a post office in 1858, but it closed in 1869.

A number of families and individuals took donation land claims in the areas of present-day Crawfordsville and Holley by the late 1840s, including Timothy A. Riggs and Robert Glass. Richard C. Finley completed construction of the first gristmill south of Oregon City, serving customers from as far away as the Umpqua Valley. This continued until the Magnolia Flouring Mill, built in Albany in 1851, began drawing business away from Finley's mill.

In the early 1850s Finley, Philemon V. Crawford, and William T. Templeton built three sawmills in the area. The first school was built on Riggs's property in 1853. There was

The Finley Gristmill located on the falls below the present-day McKercher Park on the Calapooia River. Finley eventually sold the mill to McKercher, thus the sign on the building. Courtesy of the Linn County Historical Museum, Brownsville, Oregon.

a small settlement of farmers in the Holley Valley, including the Splawn and Rice families.

Harrisburg, Peoria, and Shedd

In 1847 William A. Forgey, Thomas Roach, Henry Schooling, and John Wilson were among the earliest settlers to arrive in the Harrisburg area. Forgey laid out town lots on his property in 1852 and eventually sold several lots. First organized as Prairie Precinct, the settlement was variously known as Crow's Nest, Mud Flats, and Thurston, but in 1855 the post office was opened under the name of Harrisburg. Its first schoolhouse was built in 1854.

In the early 1850s steamships on the Willamette River never tried to venture beyond Corvallis, for fear of offending the Corvallis merchants who wanted Corvallis to remain the head of navigation on the Willamette—keeping their businesses booming. In 1856 the *James Clinton* became the first steamer to ascend the Willamette River as far as Eugene and on its way, it stopped at Harrisburg.

Brothers David and Asa A. McCully, who had been involved in several different commercial enterprises in Harrisburg since their arrival in 1852, immediately entered the shipping business. After securing financial backing, they built the *Surprise* sternwheeler and David McCully moved to Salem in 1858 to boost the presence of their business. A narrow strip of land that extended to the river on Asa McCully's land claim served as their dock, and they were constantly in competition with the dock and warehouse amenities at Woody's Landing on the Lane County side of the river.

Most of Harrisburg's farmers raised crops and grazed stock. In 1853 Asa McCully had driven a herd of cattle from Iowa to pasture on his land. Dr. Henry A. Davis had a farm and he eventually began growing hops. He maintained a medical practice out of his home that he built in the 1850s, and frequently made house calls.

After a slow start, Harrisburg began to develop commercially when the steamboats reached the area, and greatly benefited from the destruction of Woody's Landing in the flood of 1861–62, which brought more farmers to Harrisburg with their produce for shipping down river.

Harrisburg has two extant houses that were built during the 1850s: the Alfred Humphrey House and the Abner Waters House, both private residences.

Between 1846 and 1847 settlers such as Owen Bear, J. M. Coon, and John W. Smith took donation land claims along the Willamette River in the area between present-day Halsey and Peoria. Farms were established on the open prairie land. Others soon followed and Burlington became the first named

Mr. and Mrs. Philemon V. Crawford, ca. 1880. He was a co-owner and millwright of Boston Mills. Courtesy of the Linn County Historical Museum, Brownsville, Oregon.

community in 1851. Smith established a ferry and the town had two stores, a blacksmith shop, and a schoolhouse. In 1854 Burlington was named as the terminus of a road that connected with the Territorial Road leading up the valley, but it was generally bypassed and as the river channel shifted, the town disappeared. In 1857 a post office was opened in an adjacent community and named Peoria; it had a steamboat landing on the Willamette River. (Halsey was not laid out until 1871 when the railroad came through.)

Settlers began arriving in the area of present-day Shedd as early as 1846, taking donation land claims along the Calapooia River. Several churches were organized, including the Willamette Church in the Oakville community with Dr. S. G. Irvine serving as the pastor. This church united with the Union Point Church in 1852, becoming the United Presbyterian Church of Oregon. Today the Oakville-Willamette United Presbyterian Church remains the oldest Presbyterian church congregation on the Pacific Coast.

Amanda Gardener Johnson had been a slave in Missouri belonging to the Anderson Deckard family. They freed her before they departed for Oregon in 1853, but she asked to accompany them. For five years she lived in Oakville caring for the children of her deceased mistress. After her marriage to blacksmith Ben Johnson, also a former slave, she lived in Albany until her death at the age of 93.

In 1858 Alexander Brandon, Philemon V. Crawford, and Richard C. Finley completed construction of the Boston Mills on property they purchased from Americus Savage and Robert Elder. They were hoping to attract the business that had been siphoned off from Finley's mill located east of Brownsville after a mill was built in Albany in 1851.

In 1862 a fire destroyed Boston Mills. It was believed that the blaze originated in the carding mill built in the late 1850s across from the Boston Mills millrace. The mill was rebuilt and the newly platted town of Boston Mills attracted a few other businesses. However, when a railroad station was built one-and-one-half miles to the west, giving rise to the town of Shedd in 1871, the town of Boston Mills disappeared.

Today Boston/Thompson's Mills, which includes some

more recent structures, is an agricultural and architectural landmark. The Boston Mill Society, in cooperation with the Oregon State Parks & Recreation Department, has plans to develop a heritage site at the location.

Sampling of Linn County Family Surnames in 1859

Albany, Crabtree, and Scio

Althouse	Cochran	Deakins	Grimes	Irvine	McDonald	Pollard	Simpson
Beach	Condon	Deckard	Hackleman	Jackson	McFarland	Powell	Smead
Berkley	Connor	Driggs	Haight	Kendall	McInnish	Price	Smith
Bilyeu	Cox	Earl	Hale	Knox	Miller	Propst	Thomas
Blevins	Crabtree	Fanning	Haley	Layton	Monteith	Ralston	Unphrey
Boice	Cranor	Ferry	Hamilton	Lilliard	Moore	Randall	Wakefield
Brown	Crawford	Fleischner	Hendricson	Lincoln	Mulky	Richardson	Westlake
Burkhart	Crooks	Foster	Hill	Marshall	Munkers	Sage	Wheeler
Chambers	Curl	Froman	Houston	Maxwell	Payne	Settlemire	White
Cheadle	Cyrus	Gearhart	Hughes	McConnell	Pearce	Shelton	Young
Cline	Davis	Gray	Hutchins	McCoy	Peterson	Shephard	

Lebanon, Sodaville, Waterloo, and Sweet Home

Ames	Cheadle	Elkins	Grisham	Klum	Nye	Settle	Usher
Angell	Clark	Faulkner	Hardman	Leever	Peterson	Simons	Wakefield
Backus	Claypool	Fronk	Helm	Marks	Pickens	Smith	Wasson
Ballard	Clymer	Gallagher	Hill	McDonald	Ralston	Sperry	Wheeler
Baltimore	Cochran	George	Hyde	McKinney	Ridgeway	Stringer	Whitson
Bell	Cooper	Gilliland	Irvine	Miller	Russell	Summers	Wiley
Burge	Courtney	Gore	Kees	Morris	Saltmarsh	Swank	Woodward
Burkhart	Coyle	Griggs	Ketchum	Moss			

Brownsville, Crawfordsville, and Holley

Baird	Crawford	Hawk	Malone	Montgom-	Riggs	Stannard
Blain	Deal	Henderson	McCaw	ery	Robinette	Templeton
Blakely	Dinwiddie	Isom	McCoy	Moyer	Seeley	Walters
Brown	Finley	Johnson	McHargue	Osborne	Shanks	White
Carey	Geary	Keeney	McKinney	Philpot	Smith	Wilson
Cooley	Glass	Kirk	Miller	Rice	Splawn	Woodfin

Harrisburg, Peoria, and Shedd

Alford	Busey	DuPree	Houston	Martin	Millhollen	Robbins	Sherrill
Allingham	Butler	Elder	Irvine	McCartney	Morgan	Robinett	Smith
Barr	Clark	Farwell	Junkins	McCormick	Parrish	Rodgers	Sommerville
Barrons	Cochran	Forgey	Keeney	McCoy	Porter	Roth	Sprenger
Bateman	Coon	Gray	Kendall	McCully	Pugh	Savage	Thompson
Bramwell	Davidson	Hamilton	Kesling	McCune	Purdy	Schooling	Willoughby
Brock	Davis	Harris	Lane	Mealey	Ramsey	Shearer	Wilson
Buchanan	Deckard	Hogue	Love	Miller	Roach	Shepherd	Yarbrough

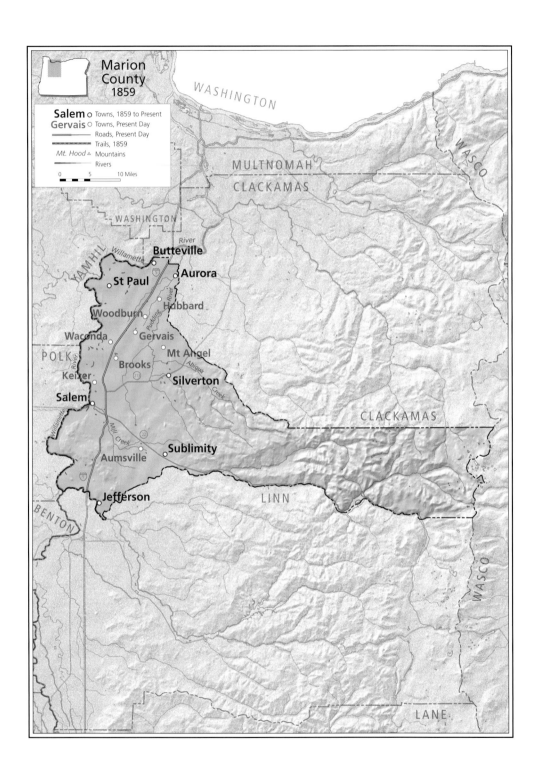

Marion
County
1859

Salem ○ Towns, 1859 to Present
Gervais ○ Towns, Present Day
——— Roads, Present Day
======= Trails, 1859
Mt. Hood △ Mountains
——— Rivers

0   5   10 Miles

WASHINGTON

MULTNOMAH

CLACKAMAS

WASCO

WASHINGTON

Willamette River

Butteville

Aurora

St Paul

Pudding River

Woodburn

Hubbard

Waconda

Gervais

Mt Angel

Brooks

Abiqua Creek

Keizer

Silverton

Willamette River

Salem

POLK

Mill Creek

CLACKAMAS

Sublimity

Aumsville

Jefferson

LINN

BENTON

WASCO

LANE

12 1859 MARION COUNTY

Marion County was created in 1843 as Champooick District and later Champoeg. In 1845 it was redesignated a county and in 1849 it was renamed Marion County. Originally much larger, Marion County's present geographical boundaries were established in 1856 following the creation of several other counties. Salem became the county seat in 1849; the first county courthouse, a wood-frame structure, was built in 1854. According to the 1860 U.S. Census, the county population was 7088.

In 1850 the territorial government authorized the building of a road from Salem to Champoeg. By 1857 three stage lines and Stuart Express Company were using this road known as the Salem–St. Paul–Champoeg stage road. Various other roads were constructed, including two into Yamhill County— one between Champoeg and present-day Newberg and another between Salem and Lafayette. In 1851 when the Eastside Territorial Road was extended to Coburg, it passed through the eastern edge of the valley. However, until the arrival of the railroad, the Willamette River steamboats were the chief mode of transportation in Marion County.

Early History

The Kalapuya—the Northern Molalla, Pudding River, and Champoeg Indians—had lived within the area of present-day Marion County for centuries before Euro-Americans arrived. They congregated near present-day Champoeg, Salem, Aumsville, and Sublimity. The region around Salem was especially favored for winter encampments.

In 1812 fur trappers were the first Euro-Americans to arrive in Marion County, building a log dwelling on some undetermined location on the Willamette River near Salem. In 1834 the Methodist Mission was established north of Salem, bringing many new Euro-Americans to the area over the next five years.

Unlike the rest of the Willamette Valley, there was at least one recorded skirmish in 1848 between the settlers and Indians. Known as the Battle of Abiqua, but hardly warranting such a characterization, it took place near Abiqua Creek in present-day Silverton between some pioneers and a group of Molalla and Klamath Indians, some of whom were killed. Disease plagued

Sites to Visit in Marion County

Antique Powerland Museum
3995 Brooklake Rd NE, Brooks
503·393·2424

Bonesteele Upland Prairie Park
Aumsville Hwy & Joseph St,
Salem/Aumsville

Brown House, ca. 1858 (private
residence)
12878 Hwy 99E, Gervais

Bush House, ca. 1878, pioneer's
home
600 Mission St SE, Salem
503·363·4714

Butteville General Store, ca. 1871
10767 Butte St NE, Butteville
503·678·1605

Champoeg State Park Visitor Cen-
ter/Museum & Bookstore
8239 Champoeg Rd, NE, St Paul
503·678·1251 or 503·678·1649

Conser House, ca. 1854 (public
library)
128 N Main St, Jefferson

Geer Farmhouse, ca. 1854 (Geer-
Crest Farm-private residence)
12390 Sunnyview Rd NE, Salem

Keizer Heritage Museum
980 Chemawa Rd NE, Keizer
503·393·9660

Marion County Historical Society
Museum
1313 Mill St SE, Salem
503·364·2128

McMenamins Boon's Treasury, ca.
1860 (restaurant)
888 Liberty St. NE, Salem
503·399·9062

Mission Mill Museum & Village
(four ca. 1840 and '50s structures)
1313 Mill St SE, Salem
503·585·7012

Newell House Museum Complex,
ca. 1852
8089 Champoeg Rd NE, St. Paul
503·678·5537

Old Aurora Colony Museum
15008 2nd St, Aurora
503·678·5754

Oregon State Capitol
900 Court St NE, Salem
503·986·1388

Pioneer Mother's Memorial Cabin
8035 Champoeg Rd NE, St Paul
503·633·2237

St. Paul Catholic Church, ca. 1846
20217 Christie St NE, St Paul
503·633·4611

Santiam Historical Society
Museum
260 N 2nd Ave, Stayton

Silverton Country Historical
Museum
428 S Water St, Silverton
503·873·7070

Smith-Fry House, ca. 1859/1947
(private residence)
606 High St, Salem

Willamette Mission State Park
10991 Wheatland Rd NE, Gervais
503·393·1172

The Willamette Queen
Sternwheeler
City Dock Riverfront Park, Salem
503·371·1103

Willamette University
900 State St, Salem
503·370·6340

the Indians in this region and they eventually were required to remove to the Grand Ronde Reservation.

Salem and Keizer

In 1841 the Methodist missionaries became the first permanent American set-tlers of Salem, relocating their mission from its original site on Mission Bot-tom after heavy flooding. They built a combination gristmill and sawmill on Mill Creek, and also a house and parsonage for the missionaries. Until the Indian Manual Training School was completed, classes were held in the parsonage.

Failing again in their efforts to convert the Kalapuya Indians to Christianity at their new location, the missionaries decided instead to lay out a town and sell lots to finance a school for the education of the settlers' children. In 1842 Reverend Jason Lee founded the Oregon Institute, the first school for non-Indians west of Missouri and later the first institution of higher education in the West. In 1853 the name was changed to Wallamet University, which continued in use until 1870 when the current spelling of Willamette was adopted. In 1859 Reverend Francis S. Hoyt was the president of the university and Emily J. York became its first graduate.

The Methodist mission was disbanded in 1844 and the parsonage was given to the Methodist Church. Today Lee's house, the parsonage, and two other pre-1860 restored buildings—all moved from their original locations—are located on the grounds of the Mission Mill Museum in Salem.

One of the other restored buildings is the 1847 John D. Boon House. Boon, a Methodist minister, was one of the few missionaries who remained in Salem after the mission closed. He served as Oregon's first treasurer, serving from 1851 to 1855, and again from 1856 to 1862. Sometime around 1860, Boon built a two-story brick building on his property for his dry goods store. A small sign at the rear of the extant building reads "Est. 1853," but most believe that it was built in 1860 or shortly thereafter. It is known that after Boon opened his store he conducted his state treasury duties there, being careful to separate the public's money from his own. Boon's property was completely surrounded by Mill Creek and the millrace at the time and was called Island Salem or Boon's Island. Boon was involved in bringing the telegraph and railroad to Salem.

The town of Salem, originally called Chemeketa, developed slowly until successful gold miners returning from California infused the economy with their newly found wealth. With the arrival of steamboats moving up and down the Willamette River by 1851, river commerce spurred

Chief Quinaby of the Chemeketa Indians, whose village was located in Salem. He refused to live on the Grand Ronde Reservation, choosing instead to live on hand-outs from Salem residents until his death in the 1870s or '80s. Courtesy of the Oregon Historical Society, OrHi 76207.

The Reverend Jason Lee House, the first house in Salem. Courtesy of the Oregon Historical Society, OrHi 39916.

John D. Boon's general store, ca. 1860. Today the restored building is known as Boon's Treasury and houses McMenamins Boon's Treasury Restaurant. The residence at the left belonged to Harry Kelly. Courtesy of the Marion County Historical Society, #2004.10.490.

Salem in 1858, showing the first Commercial Street bridge spanning North Mill Creek. By Kuchel & Dresel Lithographers, San Francisco. Courtesy of the Marion County Historical Society, #2007.2.1.

Benjamin F. Bonham (1828–1906)

Born in Tennessee; educated in Indiana

Arrived in Oregon in 1853; taught school on French Prairie and in Salem for two years

Studied law and in 1856 was admitted to the bar

Held territorial offices of auditor, librarian, and legislator

State legislator and superintendent of schools for Marion County

Partner in two law firms

Elected to state supreme court, serving as chief justice from 1874 to 1876

Appointed by President Grover Cleveland to consul-generalship to British India, representing the United States at Calcutta for four years

Served as postmaster of Salem from 1894 to 1898

Married Mildred A. Baker; seven children

further growth and prosperity. Salem was also connected to other parts of the state by stage line and the telegraph.

In 1852 the territorial capital was moved from Oregon City to Salem. Controversy and political maneuvering continued for another dozen years; the new location was not officially affirmed by voters until 1864. When Oregon became a state in 1859, the state government offices were located in several downtown Salem locations, as the first territorial capitol had been destroyed by fire in 1855, shortly after it was built. Construction on the second capitol did not even start until 1872.

The Willamette Woolen Manufacturing Company Mill was built in 1857, becoming the Pacific Coast's first woolen mill. The founders of the mill included E. M. Barnum, W. H. Rector, Daniel Waldo, Ahio S. Watt, and Joseph Watt.

Lafayette F. Grover was one of the directors of the mill from 1856 to 1871. Grover served as the first U.S. representative to Congress, governor from 1870 to 1877, and U.S. senator from 1877 to 1883. At one time he lived in the house known today as the Smith-Fry House, which was built in 1859 and extensively remodeled in 1947.

Salem had at least one public school for its children by 1857. The Methodist Church had the largest congregation in 1859, but several other Protestant denominations were also organized.

Willamette Woolen Manufacturing Company Mill, the leading industry in Salem until an 1876 fire closed it permanently. Courtesy of the Salem Public Library, Ben Maxwell Collection, #873.

Methodist Mission House, established in 1834 by Reverend Jason Lee at Mission Bottom. Today the former mission house, which was severely damaged in the flood of 1861, has been rebuilt as a ghost structure—an open-sided metal structure which depicts the mission building—on the original site located on the grounds of the Willamette Mission State Park. Sketch by Lieutenant Henry Eld Jr. Image courtesy of Special Collections and University Archives, University of Oregon libraries.

Like all other towns located along the Willamette River, Salem experienced seasonal flooding. The 1861 flood destroyed nearby farms and parts of the business district, but most of Salem's other structures survived.

The community of Keizer, located directly north of Salem, began with the arrival of the Thomas D. Kaizur and J. B. Kaizur families in 1843. (Fifteen different versions of spelling the family surname existed, with Keizer being

Asahel Bush (1824–1913)

Born in Massachusetts; apprenticed as printer in New York at 17; studied law and passed the bar in Massachusetts in 1850

Arrived in Portland in 1850 by ship, sponsored by Democratic Party; moved to Oregon City and became editor of *Oregon Statesman* in 1851; moved newspaper to Salem when it became territorial capital

Served as territorial printer, regent of University of Oregon, and trustee of Willamette University

Co-founded Ladd and Bush Bank with William S. Ladd in 1867; became sole owner in 1877

Involved in other financial and civic activities, especially Democratic politics

Married Eugenia Zieber; four children before she died of tuberculosis in 1863

Built mansion in 1878, which today is a house museum, open to the public

Asahel Bush, a leading Oregon journalist, politician, and banker. His 1878 mansion was not completed until after his wife's death. As he never remarried, his second daughter, Sally Bush, was the mistress of the house. Courtesy of the Oregon Historical Society, OrHi 70286.

"Doc" Robert Newell (1807–1869)

Born in Ohio; one of the Mountain Men as young adult

With Joseph L. Meek, brought first wagon across plains to Willamette Valley by way of Columbia River in 1841

Friend to Indians and fluent in their dialects, which led to appointment as peace commissioner after Whitman Massacre in 1847; as special interpreter and commissioner at U.S. Army post in Lapwai, Idaho in 1862; and as Indian agent in Lewiston, Idaho in 1868

Director of first literary society in Oregon, the Lyceum, in 1842; and director of first newspaper publishing organization on Pacific Coast, Oregon Printing Association, that published *Spectator* in 1845

Served on legislative committee that framed first laws of Oregon territorial government; elected to state legislature in 1860

Prospected for gold in California; returned to Champoeg by 1850 with funds to invest in business enterprises, including store, flour mill, and real estate investment

Prominent civic leader who often entertained in his home

Impoverished by property losses following 1861 flood and from generous assistance he gave to flood victims

Sold his land holdings and moved to Lapwai, Idaho

Married three times, first to Nez Perce woman and later to women both of French descent; 16 children

adopted in a later generation.) Many other pioneer families arrived throughout the 1840s and early 1850s. The Alanson Beers family settled on a claim purchased after the Methodist Mission disbanded in 1844, including the former mission hospital and granary. Several families built landings where steamboats stopped with passengers and freight.

Growth in the Keizer area was slowed because of the frequent flooding from the Willamette River. Keizer, which remained a suburb of Salem until it incorporated in 1982, included parts of other present-day communities, including Hayesville where Adam Stephens bought property in 1849. He built the future town's first school in 1858.

French Prairie, including Butteville, Champoeg, and St. Paul

The area between the east bank of the Willamette River and present-day Highway 99E in northern Marion County came to be known as French Prairie. (The settlements west of present-day Interstate 5 are discussed under this heading; those established east of the freeway and to the county line are discussed in the heading "Silverton, Mount Angel, Gervais, and Aurora.")

Between 1828 and 1832 retired French-Canadian Hudson's Bay Company (HBC) employees Joseph Gervais, Louis La Bonte, Etienne Lucier, and J. B. McKay settled as farmers in the area with their Indian wives; they were followed by many more of their former co-workers. Their former boss, Dr. John McLoughlin, had encouraged them to settle there, even though it was against company policy. At first their wheat and produce were exported to the Sandwich Islands, Peru, and other faraway locations, but when gold was discovered in California, it became the primary market.

By 1859 Marion County had over 30 landings on the Willamette River. Well-established landings had warehouses, but most were primitive platform docks with no storage facilities.

In the 1840s George Abernethy of Oregon City and Alanson Beers of Keizer established Butteville, first called La Butte by its early French-speaking Canadian residents. It soon had a river landing, a warehouse to store the grain products of the French Prairie farmers, a store operated by Francois X. Matthieu, and several homes.

The Episcopalians met in homes until a church was built in 1860. The state legislature chartered the Butteville Academy in 1859; it likely was only a small schoolhouse which was later relocated to the grounds of the Newell House Museum in Champoeg. (The 1849-era jail built in Butteville was also moved to this site.)

After steamboats began operating on the Willamette River in 1851, Butteville and the neighboring town to the west, Champoeg, became arch-rivals in competition for the shipping services needed by the French Prairie farmers. When the 1861 flood struck, Butteville suffered damage, but was not washed away like Champoeg. It developed into a thriving river port until the railroad arrived, bypassing Butteville and supplanting river commerce.

In 1852 Robert Newell and Andre Longtain platted the townsite of Champoeg, but Champoeg had earlier been the name of a larger area that included St. Paul, Fairfield Landing, and Wheatland across the river in Yamhill County. In 1843 Champoeg was the site of the historic meetings that led to the establishment of the provisional government.

Champoeg's residents represented a wide variety of nationalities and trades. Figures cited for the number of buildings standing in Champoeg by 1859 vary, but there were more than a hundred, including a Masonic Hall, a schoolhouse, an Episcopal church, and a bowling alley owned and operated by the Zorn family, immigrants from Germany. The Allan, McKinlay and Company of Oregon City, owned by George T. Allan, Archibald McKinlay, and Thomas Lowe, had recently acquired the Champoeg Flour Mill built by Newell in 1855. The mill continued to grind flour for shipment by the steamboats that stopped at Champoeg daily.

In the early 1830s French-Canadian trappers and their Indian wives settled the St. Paul community. When Americans began arriving in the 1840s, they either took claims on unclaimed land or purchased land from the French-Canadians.

Robert Newell had no medical training, but he was so skilled at simple surgical procedures and curing illnesses that he was called "Doc" Newell. Courtesy of the Salem Public Library, Ben Maxwell Collection, #3903.

Robert Newell's 1852 house, ca. 1956. It was the only building in Champoeg to survive the 1861 flood. Built on a bluff above the town, it served as a refuge for several families during and after the flood. The Oregon State Society Daughters of the American Revolution operate the restored residence as a house museum today. Courtesy of the Salem Public Library, Ben Maxwell Collection, #3652.

Hugh Cosgrove was among the early settlers; he opened a general store in St. Paul. Charles F. Ray farmed and operated a ferry from a landing on his property. Steamboats docked at two different landings at St. Paul on a regular schedule and in 1859 the steamboat *Saint Clair* was built at Davidson's Landing. Several Catholic institutions were established in St. Paul in the early days, but by 1859 only the St. Paul Catholic Church remained, with Father Fabian Malo serving as the priest. (A school founded in 1844 was reopened in 1860.)

In 1851 Fairfield Landing was established on the J. C. Peebles land claim south of St. Paul. It soon developed into a major grain-shipping port with two warehouses, several stores, a post office, and a school. Small farms with orchards and livestock dotted the landscape. Fairfield Landing survived the 1861 flood, but later declined after improved roads and the railroad supplanted river commerce.

French Prairie, including Silverton, Gervais, and Aurora

During the 1840s numerous communities developed east of Salem. In 1843 the Daniel Waldo family founded the Waldo Settlement—the area now known as the Waldo Hills. Arriving from Virginia, his family group included his slaves, one of whom was the mother of his child, America Waldo. Waldo grazed cattle on his land and planted the first wheat in the area. He held several public offices, and served as a director of the Salem woolen mill and a trustee of Willamette University.

Daniel Delaney, a slaveholder from Tennessee, settled near the Waldos with his family and at least one slave, Rachel Beldon. Rachel continued to live with and work for the Delaneys until the end of the Civil War.

Dr. Benjamin Davenport took a donation land claim in the Waldo Hills and offered his medical services to his neighbors in eastern Marion County. His son, Timothy, farmed and held several public offices, including county surveyor in the 1860s.

Timothy's first father-in-law was Ralph C. Geer who, in 1854, completed his farmhouse which remains as a private residence today southwest of Silverton. Geer was a successful nurseryman in Marion County. (The same house was the 1867 birthplace and boyhood home of Homer Davenport, the famous cartoonist, author, and "favorite son" of Silverton.)

A few families were settled between the branches of the Pudding River in the area known today as Howell Prairie. The John Howell family was the first to settle there in 1843.

John Barger and James Smith established a sawmill at a settlement called

Main Street, Silverton, ca. 1863, showcasing the treasured oak tree that disappeared in the 1870s. Courtesy of the Marion County Historical Society, #1996.5.1.2.56.

Rose Jackson, at her own request, was smuggled across the Oregon Trail by her slave owner, Dr. Allen, in 1849. After Dr. Allen's death in 1850, Rose saved the surviving family from poverty by working as a laundress in Oregon City for up to $12 a day. Later she married John Jackson, a groom for stagecoach horses in Canemah. The couple moved to Waldo Hills, where they raised two children. Courtesy of the Oregon Historical Society, OrHi 105967.

Milford about two miles upstream from where Silverton developed in 1852 after the arrival of more than 30 families. The Silver Creek post office was established in 1854, but Polly Crandall Coon Price changed the name to Silverton when she began selling town lots from her late husband's donation land claim. Silverton became an important trading center with several general stores, a gristmill, and a sawmill.

A small community located just west of Silverton was known as Bethany. In 1851 the Bethany Church organized and met in the home of Elias Cox until a church building was constructed on his property in 1858. A few families settled in the area of today's Mount Angel, including the Benjamin Cleaver and Samuel Allen families. The Abiqua Baptist Church organized in 1850.

Two small communities—Parkersville and Belle Passi—developed in the vicinity of present-day Gervais, but both towns disappeared once the railroad came to the valley in 1870. William Parker settled on the Pudding River southeast of Gervais in 1846; the Parkersville post office was established in 1852. Parker operated a general store, gristmill, saloon, and sawmill. Belle Passi, with a post office, school, store, and the Cumberland Presbyterian Church, was located northeast of Gervais.

Joseph Gervais, a former HBC trapper who arrived in Oregon in 1811 with the Wilson Price Hunt Expedition, was among the first to settle on the portion of French Prairie where the town of Gervais later developed. He and his Indian wife grew wheat and raised horses and hogs.

The Samuel Brown family arrived in 1846 and built a log cabin and sawmill. Lured to California by the discovery of gold in 1848, the whole family departed, but returned the following year with a large sum of cash. They purchased more land to add to their original donation land claim, amassing over a thousand acres in the Gervais area. (Brown founded Gervais in the 1870s.)

St. Louis, located about three miles northwest of Gervais, began in the early 1840s when a Jesuit parish was organized there. Waconda and Brooks, both located south of St. Louis, were established in the early 1850s, with Linus Brooks among the first to arrive.

As early as 1845 settlement of the northeastern portion of Marion County occurred with the arrival of French-Canadian Jean B. Ducharm, who claimed land east of present-day Woodburn. Bradford Bonney, Eli Cooley, and George Leisure soon joined him.

In 1848 Charles Hubbard Jr. and his family settled in the area where the town of Hubbard was later platted after the railroad arrived. His son, William, and his wife developed the family's property while Charles operated

The 1858 Samuel Brown House still stands on the Pacific Highway near Gervais. After the California-Oregon Stage began in 1860, it served as a stagecoach station. Courtesy of the Oregon State Library.

a gristmill in Oregon City. He returned in 1868 when he heard about the impending railroad, offering land to the railroad for a station site and right-of-way and platting the town of Hubbard.

In 1856 Dr. William Keil established a German Christian colony along Mill Creek above its confluence with the Pudding River. Known as Aurora Mills until the name was changed to Aurora in 1894, the self-sustaining communal settlement grew rapidly and prospered economically. It continued operating the gristmills and sawmills purchased from the previous landowners; manufactured finely crafted furniture, clothing, and household items; and tended productive gardens and orchards. Once the needs of the colony were met, members were allowed to offer their surplus for sale to the public. Travelers passing through the area looked forward to stopping at the colony store. The colony was famous for its hospitality, delicious German cooking, and entertaining brass bands.

Aumsville, Sublimity, and Jefferson

By 1859 several communities were established southeast of Salem. In the early 1840s a number of families settled in the area that later became Aumsville in 1868, including the Allen J. Davie, Reuben Lewis, John McHaley, William Porter, Henry Smith, and Henry L. Turner families. Davie built a sawmill and all of the families engaged in farming and grazing stock on the fields, which earlier occupants of the area—the Kalapuya Indians—had carefully prepared by annual burning.

Lewis, Porter, and Smith built the first schools in the area in the mid-1850s. The Mill Creek Church of Christ met in the schoolhouse that Porter built until a larger building was constructed in 1858. In the same year Reverend Philip Condit founded the Pleasant Grove Presbyterian Church. Today the restored building is located on the grounds of the Mission Mill Museum in Salem; it is the oldest extant Presbyterian Church building in the Pacific Northwest.

Sublimity started out as a trading post called Hobson Corner when Hadley Hobson arrived in 1848 and settled on Mill Creek. In 1850 James M. Denny took a donation land claim nearby and named the town Sublimity in 1852 after opening a post office. In the mid-1850s a school was built and by 1859 Sublimity had enough settlers to support a variety of stores and businesses, and also two churches—the Methodists and the United Brethren in Christ, a branch of the Mennonite Church.

The United Brethren contributed to the early growth of Sublimity in 1858 when they received a charter from the legislature for Sublimity College—a

1854 Jacob Conser House, ca. 1955. Later it became the Jefferson Hotel and for a number of years during the 20th century it served as the City Hall. Today it houses the town's public library. Courtesy of the Salem Public Library, Ben Maxwell Collection, #6369.

semi-public school built on land donated by Denny for the primary grades through high school. Milton Wright, who later fathered pioneer aviators Wilbur and Orville Wright after returning to Indiana, served for two years as the first teacher and president of the college.

Jefferson was first known as Conser's Ferry after Jacob Conser built a ferry across the Santiam River there in 1851. In 1858 the Jefferson Institute, a primary and secondary private school, opened on land donated by Conser and J. M. Bates; by 1861 the town's name changed to Jefferson.

Conser first arrived in Oregon in 1848 and built a sawmill and ferry at the future site of Santiam City—the town Samuel S. Miller founded. In 1850 the Miller family acquired a license to operate a ferry in competition with Milton Hale's ferry in Syracuse across the river in Linn County. The county commissioners allowed the Millers to offer lower fares. When the winter flood of 1850–51 struck, Santiam City suffered less damage than Syracuse because it was on higher ground. It continued to prosper in other ways—all at the expense of Syracuse. However, by the late 1850s, Santiam City began facing stiff competition from the developing town of Jefferson; Santiam City's demise was completed when it was swept away by the flood of 1861. Today the former sites of both Santiam City and Syracuse lie under the gravel bed of the Santiam River.

Sampling of Marion County Family Surnames in 1859

Salem and Keizer

Baker	Brown	Ford	Kaizur	Pugh	Roberts	Waite
Beers	Bush	Grover	Lesley	Purdy	Simpson	Walker
Belt	Claggett	Hirsch	Morris	Reed	Smart	Waller
Boise	Cox	Holman	Penter	Rickey	Smith	Willson
Bonham	Fisher	Hoyt	Pickard	Robb	Stevenson	Zieber
Boon	Force					

French Prairie, including Butteville, Champoeg, and St. Paul

Ady	Cone	Fackler	Hauxhurst	Lawrence	Newell	Scheil
Bernier	Cook	Ferris	Hibler	Lebrun	Petitt	Servant
Bisconett	Cooley	Flannery	Hickey	Longtain	Pichet	Shiel
Butler	Cosgrove	Gauthier	Heifer	Manson	Ray	Smith
Case	Costello	Gearin	Jette	McKay	Raymond	Waggoner
Chamberlain	Coyle	Geer	Lacourse	McPherson	Rees	Weston
Childers	Crawford	Goodell	Laferte	Mongrain	Rhoades	Whitney
Clery	Davidson	Grimm	Lambert	Murphy	Ryan	Zorn

French Prairie, including Silverton, Gervais, and Aurora

Allen	Crandall	Harpole	Lewis	Parker	Simmons
Barger	Cranston	Hartman	Lipscomb	Pittman	Simpson
Beardsley	Darst	Heater	Mascher	Plummer	Smith
Bell	Davenport	Hedrick	McAlpin	Pooler	Stipp
Black	Delaney	Hendrick	Miller	Powell	Symons
Bonney	Dinsmore	Hicks	Milster	Price	Tucker
Brooks	Dudley	Hirsch	Moore	Putnam	Veazey
Brown	Dunbar	Hobart	Morrison	Sappingfield	Waldo
Bullin	Eldriedge	Howell	Moser	Sconce	Walker
Burnett	Elliott	Hubbard	Murray	Scott	White
Chapman	Fuller	Hutton	Newsom	Settlemier	Wilcox
Churchill	Geer	Keil	Norton	Shannon	Wolfard
Cleaver	Gervais	King	Osborne	Shaw	Wood
Cline	Guerin	Leonard	Palmer	Shepard	Woolen
Coolidge	Hamilton				

Aumsville, Sublimity, and Jefferson

Alberson	Conner	Harding	Looney	Porter	Taylor
Bates	Darby	Hobson	McHaley	Reed	Tucker
Coffey	Davis	Hunt	Miller	Rudolph	Wright
Condit	Denny	Kenoyer	Neal	Stayton	

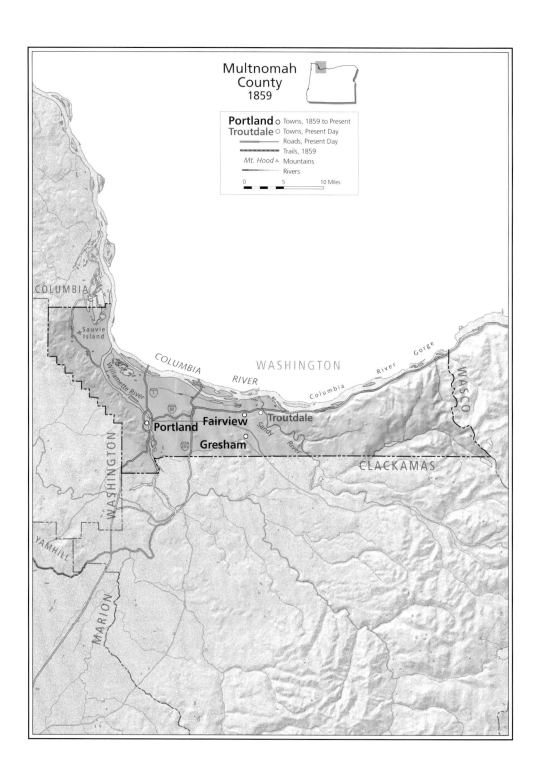

Multnomah
County
1859

Portland ○ Towns, 1859 to Present
Troutdale ○ Towns, Present Day
Roads, Present Day
Trails, 1859
Mt. Hood △ Mountains
Rivers

0   5   10 Miles

COLUMBIA

Sauvie
Island

COLUMBIA

WASHINGTON

River   Gorge

Willamette River

RIVER

Columbia

WASCO

WASHINGTON

Portland

Fairview

Troutdale

Sandy

Gresham

River

CLACKAMAS

YAMHILL

MARION

13 1859 MULTNOMAH COUNTY

Multnomah County was created in 1854 from the eastern portion of Washington County and the northern part of Clackamas County. The borders have remained relatively unchanged since then. Portland was incorporated in 1851 and became the county seat in 1854. The first courthouse was built in 1866. According to the 1860 U.S. Census, the county population was 4150.

In the 1850s, Portland had wooden sidewalks and tamped dirt streets. Paving of selected streets did not begin until 1865. Washington Street was one of the first named streets. In 1846 Francis Pettygrove extended it west toward Tualatin Plains. The bumpy road known as Tuality Road paralleled today's West Burnside Street.

In 1849 Daniel Lownsdale selected a shorter route with an easier grade that passed directly in front of his tannery and approximated today's Canyon Road to Beaverton. In 1850 the territorial legislature chartered the Portland–Tualatin Valley Plank Road Company to add planks to the road. Bankruptcy brought construction to a halt, but in 1855 subscriptions were sold to raise money and a toll was charged. Upon completion in 1860, it became known as the Great Plank Road.

Another wagon road was built in 1852 on the west bank of the Willamette, passing Baker's Landing. The Sauvie Island-Tualatin Plains Trail was the former Indian trail leading from the mouth of the Willamette to the Tualatin Plains. Hudson's Bay Company (HBC) trappers had used it and Reverend Jason Lee traveled the trail on the way to his mission in present-day Marion County.

There are several accounts regarding the ferry that connected East Portland to Portland and later became known as the Stark Street Ferry. James B. Stephens was the first operator in either 1853 or 1855, but may have been ferrying emigrants across the Willamette River on either a barge or in a canoe as early as the mid-1840s. The ferry departed and arrived at the foot of Stark Street.

In 1849 paddle-wheel riverboat traffic began around Portland, and in 1850 the first steamer, the *Columbia*, linked Portland with Astoria. Portland prevailed in the townsite competition to become the chief shipping center or the head of navigation, primarily because it was the farthest point inland on the Columbia/Willamette river system that was accessible year round. In addi-

Sites to Visit in Multnomah County

Gresham History Museum
410 N Main St, Gresham
503·661·0347

Howell Territorial Park & Bybee
   House, ca. 1858
13901 NW Howell Park Rd, Sauvie
   Island
503·797·1850

Multnomah Falls & Visitor Center
I-84 Exit 31, Historic Columbia
   River, Bridal Veil
503·695·2372

Oaks Pioneer Church, ca. 1851
455 SE Spokane St, Portland
503·234·3570

Oregon Historical Society Museum
1200 SW Park Ave, Portland
503·222·1741

Oregon Jewish Museum
310 NW Davis St, Portland
503·226·3600

Oregon Maritime Museum
Foot of SW Pine St, Portland, on
   sternwheeler *Portland*
503·224·7724

Pittock Mansion, ca. 1919, pioneer's home
3229 NW Pittock Dr, Portland
503·823·3624

Portland Oregon Information
   Center
Pioneer Courthouse Square
701 SW 6th Ave, Portland
503·275·8355

Troutdale Historical Society
   Museums
726 E Historic Columbia River Hwy,
   Troutdale
503·661·2164

Tryon Creek State Park Nature
   Center
11321 SW Terwilliger Blvd, Portland
503·378·6305

Vista House at Crown Point State
   Park
40700 E Historic Columbia River
   Hwy, near Troutdale
503·695·2230

Wells Fargo History Exhibit, Lobby
1300 SW 5th Ave, Portland
503·886·1102

Front Avenue looking south from Oak, ca. 1852.
Courtesy of the Oregon Historical Society, OrHi 946.

Portland's Stark Street Ferry operated for over 30 years—
until shortly after the first Morrison Bridge was built in 1887.
Courtesy of the Oregon Historical Society, OrHi 104766.

tion, it was directly connected to the Tualatin Valley by Canyon Road and the Willamette Valley by the Willamette River and the Territorial Road. Possibly the first steamer to be entirely constructed at Portland was the *Eliza Anderson*, launched in 1858.

Early History

For centuries, two bands of Upper Chinook Indians had inhabited present-day Multnomah County. The Multnomah lived on Sauvie Island and in the area where Portland developed; the Cascades settled along the Columbia Gorge. The Upper Chinookans fished and traded along the river and gathered berries and root plants, especially wapato, on Sauvie Island. A trail led from Sauvie Island at the mouth of the Willamette into prime hunting grounds on the Tualatin Plains.

Historians disagree about how a one-acre piece of land located in the vicinity of present-day Portland was cleared. It became known as "the clearing" and some believe that Indians and trappers cleared it over the years as they gathered wood for their campfires while on trading journeys between the Columbia and Willamette rivers.

The earliest Europeans to discover the area within Multnomah County were members of British Captain George Vancouver's mapping expedition in 1792. Lieutenant William Robert Broughton is credited with being the first to see Sauvie Island and the confluence of the Sandy and Columbia rivers. (He also saw Mount Hood in the distance, located in present-day Hood River County.)

The Lewis and Clark Corps of Discovery passed through Multnomah County along the Columbia River in 1805 and 1806, followed by the Astor party, the Northwest Company, and the HBC. In 1841 the HBC established farming operations on the island that Captain William Clark named Wappato Island, now Sauvie Island, because of the abundance of wapato.

Less than a hundred Indians remained in the region by the 1850s. They never recovered from the various epidemics they were exposed to during the years of exploration and early settlement. The few who did remain were a party to the Kalapuya and Confederated Bands of the Willamette Valley Treaty of 1855, ceding their lands to the U.S. government. In 1856 they were removed to the Grand Ronde Reservation.

Portland, Sauvie Island, and East Portland

Before becoming Oregon's chief shipping center in the 1850s, Portland developed slowly with land claims changing hands several times. Although people

Captain John and Caroline Couch. He was a mariner, merchant, and involved in numerous business ventures in Portland. He also served in several public offices, including provisional treasurer and county commissioner. Courtesy of the Oregon Historical Society, OrHi 4301.

Benjamin Stark, first a territorial legislator, later was appointed by Governor Whiteaker to serve the unexpired U.S. senatorial term of E. D. Baker (1861–62). Courtesy of the Oregon Historical Society, OrHi 48436.

Panorama of Portland, 1858. By Kuchel & Dresel Lithographers, San Francisco. Courtesy of the Oregon Historical Society, OrHi 24308.

had been stopping at the place called the clearing for years when traveling between Oregon City and Fort Vancouver, no one took a claim here until 1843. Captain John H. Couch recognized the suitability of the location as a port as early as 1840, but it was Asa L. Lovejoy and William Overton who filed the first land claim on the clearing. Originally, Lovejoy had no serious interest in the property, except that he advanced the 25-cent filing fee and had the legal acumen that Overton lacked. Lovejoy returned to his business interests in Oregon City while Overton built a shack near the river and began manufacturing shingles. In 1844 Overton sold his half of the claim to Francis W. Pettygrove, a merchant in Oregon City, and moved to the Southwest. Pettygrove immediately began development of a new city, deciding the name by a coin toss with Lovejoy. (Lovejoy was from Massachusetts and wanted it named Boston, but Pettygrove, from Maine, won the toss, so the city was named after the original capital of his state—Portland.)

Soon Pettygrove had the land surveyed, a road constructed to the Willamette Valley, a wharf and warehouse established at the foot of Washington Street and Front Avenue, and a house built for his family by John L. Morrison. Two more ownership changes occurred: In 1846, Lovejoy sold his interest in the townsite to Benjamin Stark, and when gold was discovered in California in 1848, Pettygrove sold his portion of the claim to Daniel Lownsdale, and then left to seek his fortune.

Some of Portland's early buildings were prefabricated structures shipped around Cape Horn, but most were built from lumber milled in Oregon—in Portland after 1850 when a steam sawmill was built. In addition to individual homes, other structures included churches, hotels, professional offices, rooming houses, schools, stores, tradesmen's shops, warehouses, and wharves. In addition to the sawmill, Portland had a flour mill, a planing mill, a tannery, and two breweries operated by German immigrants.

Numerous merchants from New England arrived during the 1850s, establishing stores stocked with goods from the supply houses of their former employers. Young Jewish merchants from Germany also opened shops. They had supply agents in San Francisco and New York.

By 1859 key components of urbanization were developing in Portland, such as a volunteer fire department and water works. In 1859 Henry Green and Washington Irving Leonard founded the Portland Gas Light Company. When the equipment arrived by ship from New York the following year, gaslights illuminated Portland's streets for the first time.

Judge Matthew Paul Deady, political leader, writer, and founder of Multnomah County Library. Courtesy of the Oregon Historical Society, OrHi 81679.

Judge Matthew Paul Deady (1824–1893)

Born in Maryland; studied law in Ohio, passing the bar in 1847

Arrived in Lafayette in 1849 where he taught and practiced law

Presided over state constitutional convention in 1857

Elected and appointed to numerous public offices, including territorial legislature, territorial supreme court, and U.S. district court

Moved to Portland in 1859; became one of the founders of Multnomah County Library

Popular public speaker and prolific writer, including *General Laws of Oregon 1843–1872*

University of Oregon Regent for 20 years—Deady Hall on university campus named in his honor

Married Lucy A. Henderson; three children

1858 T. J. Holmes House. Holmes served as the mayor of Portland in 1866 and 1867. By Kuchel & Dresel Lithographers, San Francisco. Courtesy of the Oregon Historical Society, OrHi 44360.

Wells Fargo opened an express office in Portland in 1857. Wells Fargo's valuables were transported by steamships on the Columbia River and by the Oregon stage line between Portland and Salem. Courtesy of the Oregon Historical Society, OrHi 50934.

Henry Lewis Pittock (1836–1919)

Born in England; educated in Pennsylvania schools and learned printing trade from his father

Arrived in Oregon in 1853 and became typesetter for *Weekly Oregonian* newspaper

Acquired ownership of paper in lieu of back wages in 1860; changed it to a daily paper, and later changed name to *The Oregonian*, its name today

Became wealthy through involvement in variety of business ventures, including real estate, banking, railroads, steamboats, sheep ranching, silver mining, and the pulp and paper industry

Married Georgiana Martin Burton, who was highly regarded for her dedication to improving lives of women and children through volunteer work with Ladies Relief Society, Women's Union, and Martha Washington Home for single, working women

Couple's 1919 mansion built on a hill overlooking Portland remains as a house museum today

Jewish immigrant Aaron Meier opened his first store on Front Avenue in 1857. Meier began his career in America as a peddler in the gold mining towns of California and Oregon. In later years, with partners, he established the Meier & Frank Co. department store chain, which retained family ownership among the two German families until it became a subsidiary of the May Department Stores Company in 1966. (In 2005, all May & Company stores, including Meier & Frank, were purchased by Federated Department Stores and were absorbed into the Macy name.) Courtesy of the Oregon Historical Society, OrHi 51815.

The several Multnomah volunteer fire companies established in 1859 functioned as exclusive social clubs, with vacancies filled only upon acceptance by the entire membership. The city provided the firehouse and equipment for each company, ca. 1865. Courtesy of the Oregon Historical Society, OrHi 3631.

Portland's first school was a private school opened in 1847, but it was short-lived, as were several other schools opened in subsequent years. Because so many of Portland's residents were young business entrepreneurs without families, it was difficult to generate the public support necessary to fund public school construction. Finally, through the efforts of Josiah Failing and Reverend Horace Lyman, public moneys and private subscriptions were raised to build Central School, which opened in 1858.

In 1851 Methodist minister Reverend James H. Wilbur, formerly with the Oregon Institute in Salem, founded the Portland Academy & Female Seminary. By 1859 its emphasis was on preparing high school students for college at the Willamette or Pacific universities.

In 1859 the Sisters of the Holy Names of Jesus and Mary arrived in Portland. They founded St. Mary's Academy, Oregon's oldest continuously operating secondary school. (In the early 1900s, St. Mary's also served as the foundation of today's Marylhurst University in Lake Oswego.)

By the late 1850s a number of churches were built along Third, Fourth, and Fifth avenues. The major Protestant denominations were represented, and congregations of Catholics and German Jews also were organized. In 1861 the Portland Jewish congregation built the first synagogue in Oregon at Fifth Avenue and Oak Street.

As early as 1852, the residents of Portland recognized the need for a city park. They planted trees and grass for 25 blocks between Park and Ninth avenues—where the South Park Blocks are located today.

By 1859 Portland had two newspapers, the *Weekly Oregonian*, owned and edited by Thomas J. Dryer, and the *Oregon Weekly Times*, owned by John O. Waterman and William D. Carter. The *Times* had recently moved from Milwaukie, where it had been called the *Western Star*.

In 1845 Daniel Lownsdale settled in the King's Hill area northwest of the early business district. He built a tannery in 1846, utilizing the area's plentiful hemlock trees that are integral to the hide tanning process. In 1848 Lownsdale sold the rights to his tannery to two men, but when they were

Henry and Georgiana Pittock 1860 wedding, beginning a 58-year life together of raising their family and serving the community. The couple had a great love for the outdoors; Georgiana was one of the founders of Portland's annual Rose Festival and Henry was a member of the first party to climb Mount Hood. Courtesy of the Pittock Mansion.

Daniel H. Lownsdale, an early tanner in Oregon, bought Pettygrove's Portland claim in 1848 for $5000 worth of leather. Courtesy of the Oregon Historical Society, OrHi 13420.

James Francis Bybee built the Bybee-Howell House on Sauvie Island, maintained by Regional Metro Parks & Greenspaces, but currently closed to the public. Courtesy of the Oregon Historical Society, OrHi 75580.

James Francis Bybee (1818–1901)

Born in Kentucky; arrived in Oregon in 1845 with Stephen H. L. Meek wagon train

Made profitable trip to California gold fields around 1848

Served as Multnomah County Commissioner in 1854 and unsuccessfully ran for governor

Built extant Bybee-Howell House in 1858, which he later sold to Dr. Benjamin Howell

Horse racing enthusiast, credited with introducing the sport to Portland

Depleted his wealth with his gambling, land prospecting, and race horse ownerships

Married Julia, from whom he was later estranged; 18 children, six of whom died as children

lured to California by the gold rush, Amos Nahum King and his wife, Melinda, purchased the tannery and a portion of Lownsdale's property. In later years the Kings developed the elite King's Heights district in today's West Hills.

According to Howard McKinley Corning in his *Willamette Landings: Ghost Towns of the River*, Baker's Landing was a wharf built by W. H. Baker in the early 1850s on the west side of the Willamette River, northwest of Portland. It was an ideal location to load wheat onto steamships, and it expanded when Baker sold it in 1859 to Comstock and Company owned by Creesus B. Comstock and La Fayette Scoggins. A warehouse for wheat, a general store, and a few houses were built and the name was changed to the Port of Springville. It rapidly declined after a fire destroyed the warehouse in 1872.

Two other towns were established northwest of Portland along the Columbia. In 1843 Linnton was founded by General Morton M. McCarver and Peter H. Burnett, the first American governor of California. In 1850 James Johns established St. Johns. Both towns were hailed as future centers for the shipping trade on the Columbia River, but soon were absorbed as neighborhoods of Portland as it expanded.

Farther to the northwest, the upstream portion of Sauvie Island lies within Multnomah County. Several former HBC employees remained on the island after the company withdrew its interests in 1848 under the terms of the 1846 boundary treaty.

By 1856 American settlers had staked out most of Sauvie Island, including the Charlton, Howell, Jewett, and Reeder families. The settlers engaged in agricultural pursuits, especially dairy farming that had been so successful for the HBC. They also raised stock and partook of the abundance of wild game and fish. In a canoe built by the Cathlamet Indians, Simon M. Reeder regularly paddled four miles to Vancouver, Washington, for supplies. The canoe is on display at the Alsea Bay Bridge Interpretive Center in Waldport in Lincoln County.

The Mouth of Willamette post office was established in 1851; the name was changed to Souvies Island in 1852.

This post office was discontinued in 1860, and when a new post office was established in 1866, it was renamed Sauvie Island.

By 1859 development of the eastern outskirts of Portland directly across the Willamette River had begun. In 1851 James B. Stephens laid out East Portland along the bank of the Willamette River. He operated a ferry across the river, was one of the organizers of the Pacific Telegraph Company in 1855, and made many other contributions to East Portland's growth.

Gilmer Kelly was another early settler in East Portland. A furniture and cabinet maker, he marketed his home-grown apples, packed in boxes he crafted, in Portland.

By 1855 all of the land surrounding Mount Tabor was claimed. Early arrivals included Elijah B. Davidson, Newton D. Gilham, Dr. Samuel Nelson, and Benjamin F. Starr. Dr. Perry Prettyman, a Methodist naturopath, is said to have introduced the dandelion to the Northwest, bringing it to Oregon for medicinal purposes. Most of the Mount Tabor settlers were farmers with fruit orchards. They profited handsomely during the California gold rush.

Gresham, Fairview, and Troutdale

Although early pioneers had regularly passed through the east end of Multnomah County on their way to the Willamette Valley, the first settlers did not cut a trail through the virgin, fir-covered wilderness where Fairview, Gresham, and Troutdale are located today until 1851. In 1852 the Powell brothers, Jackson and James, and their families were the first to begin settling the community that was originally known as Powell's Valley before the Camp Ground post office was established in 1871. In 1884 the name was changed to Gresham. (Today's Powell Valley is located southeast of Gresham and is not to be confused with the former Powell's Valley.)

More families soon arrived—the Catheys, Metzgers, Stanleys, and Wilkes. A number of businesses opened, including a blacksmith shop, gristmill, and a small store. Each family cleared enough timber off their property to cultivate

Jackson Powell, regarded by historians as the founder of Gresham. Courtesy of the Gresham Historical Society.

Dr. John Parker Powell
(1822–1909)

Born in North Carolina; became physician in 1844, married, and moved to Missouri

Treated sick along Oregon Trail, advocating digging fresh wells to avoid contracting cholera

Took donation land claim in Powell's Valley, which probably was named after unrelated Powell brothers

Practiced medicine and pharmacy in area for rest of century, often compensated by food or labor around his property

Donated engineering services for construction of Main Street in Gresham and served as county coroner

One of founders of Gresham public school and Methodist Church and taught in both

Married Adaline Duvall; three children

Chief John, known as Indian John, lived peacefully with the settlers. Courtesy of the Gresham Historical Society.

Beacon Rock, located across the river from the present-day community of Dodson, marked the last leg of the Oregon Trail for emigrants. They placed their wagons on log rafts at The Dalles for the dangerous route down the Columbia. By A. Burr. Courtesy of the Oregon Historical Society, OrHi 5229.

areas for growing berries, fruit trees, vegetables, and wheat. Any excess crops were sent by wagon to Portland to trade for needed household items. At least one family, the Harry Stanleys, raised sheep, spinning their wool into yarn for socks and shirts. Although there was plenty of timber to be harvested, sawmills were not built on any of the available streams until later in the 1800s.

Several early families helped organize the first school district in Gresham, and the first schoolhouse was built in 1854. The most popular denomination appears to have been Methodist; services were held at the schoolhouse or in different homes with sermons delivered by circuit riders or locals well-versed in the scriptures. The First Methodist Church was chartered in 1853, but a permanent church was not built until 1876.

Chief John lived along the Sandy River and was one of the few Multnomah Indians remaining in the area, reportedly living beyond his 100th birthday, although his date of death varies among historical accounts. He tanned hides and worked odd jobs for the farmers in the area.

By the late 1840s, some of the settlers continuing along the Columbia River route rather than the Barlow Road departed from the Columbia at the mouth of the Sandy River and continued overland to Oregon City. By 1850, a few families decided to settle in the area of present-day Troutdale and Fairview. One of these—David F. Buxton— filed a donation land claim in 1853 in the center of today's Troutdale.

Addison C. Dunbar and his extended family settled on the future site of Fairview. The Dunbar family was community-minded, offering help to new arrivals and starting a school and church. Dr. John Crosby, a Methodist minister, often hosted the church services in his home. When Emsley R. Scott became the first postmaster around 1858, the post office was called Sandy, but had no connection to present-day Sandy in Clackamas County. Later the name changed to Cleone, and finally, Fairview.

Sampling of Multnomah County Family Surnames in 1859

Portland, Sauvie Island, and East Portland

Abraham	Caruthers	Foster	Humphrey	Meier	Reed	Strowbridge
Abrams	Cason	Frank	Jewett	Menzies	Reeder	Stump
Ainsworth	Caywood	Frush	Johns	Millard	Rennison	Taylor
Allard	Clary	Gates	Johnson	Miller	Reynolds	Terwilliger
Ankeny	Cline	Gatton	Kelly	Moar	Richards	Thomas
Backenstos	Coffin	Gibbs	Kern	Morgan	Robinson	Thompson
Baker	Collins	Gillihan	King	Murray	Royal	Thornton
Balch	Corbett	Goddard	Kittredge	Myers	Saxer	Tibbetts
Barnhart	Cornell	Goodwin	Knapp	Nelson	Schramm	Tice
Barr	Couch	Gradon	Ladd	Northrup	Scott	Tigard
Barrell	Cully	Gray	Lawrence	Page	Shattuck	Tomlinson
Blackiston	Deady	Green	Lewis	Parrish	Shaw	Wakefield
Blaumauer	Dennison	Guild	Loomis	Pearcy	Simon	Walker
Bloch	Doane	Haas	Lownsdale	Pennoyer	Skidmore	Warren
Bottler	Donner	Hall	Luther	Perkins	Slavin	Wasserman
Buchtel	Dryer	Hamilton	Marquam	Pittock	Smith	Waterman
Burton	East	Hawthorne	Maxey	Pointer	Stark	Weinshank
Buxton	Failing	Hay	May	Potter	Stephens	White
Bybee	Farrar	Hicks	McCarver	Powell	Stephenson	Williams
Campbell	Field	Hill	McIntire	Powers	Stevens	Wilmott
Caples	Fitch	Holmes	McKeown	Prettyman	Stevenson	Wilson
Cardwell	Flanders	Holtgrieve	McQuinn	Ramsey	Stewart	Yates
Carter	Force	Howell	Meeker	Rankin	Streibig	

Gresham, Fairview, and Troutdale

Albright	Dickenson	Hall	Lewellyn	Powell	Sullivan	Whitaker
Allyn	Douglas	Hamlin	Linnemann	Pullen	Sunderlan	Wilkes
Billups	Dufur	Harlow	Long	Quimby	Swift	Williams
Brigman	Dunbar	Hartley	Mitchell	Richey	Talbot	Wilmot
Cathey	Duvall	Heslin	Moore	Roberts	Taylor	Wilson
Cook	Frazer	Hicklin	Morgan	Royal	Thomas	Windle
Cornutt	Gates	Johnson	Nelson	Smith	Toohill	Wing
Corwin	Giese	Jones	Page	Stanley	Webber	Witten
Crosby	Gilham	Kelly	Payne	Stott	Welch	Zimmerman
Culbertson	Hale	Lent				

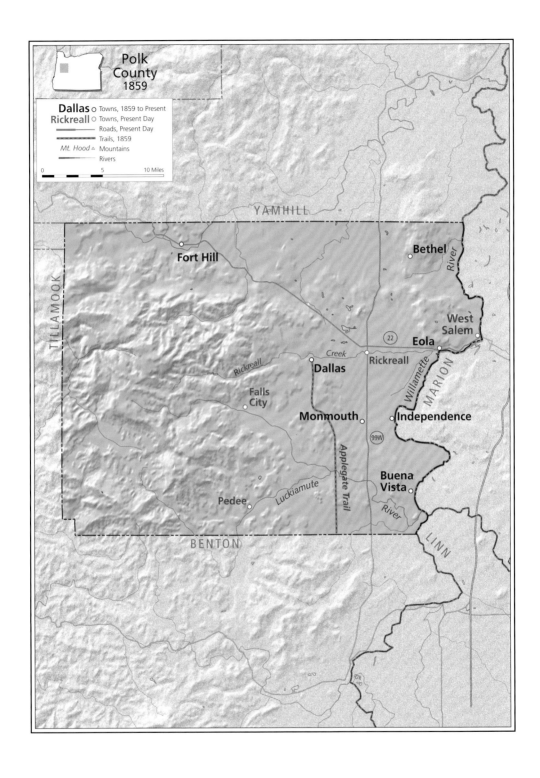

Polk
County
1859

Dallas ○ Towns, 1859 to Present
Rickreall ○ Towns, Present Day
——— Roads, Present Day
▬▬▬ Trails, 1859
Mt. Hood △ Mountains
——— Rivers

0   5   10 Miles

YAMHILL

Fort Hill

Bethel

TILLAMOOK

West
Salem

22   Eola

Creek   Rickreall

Rickreall   Dallas

MARION

Falls
City

Monmouth   Independence

99W

Buena
Vista

Pedee   *Luckiamute*

Applegate Trail

River

BENTON

LINN

Willamette

14 1859 POLK COUNTY

Polk County was created from all but a small northern portion of Yamhill District in 1845. Boundary changes in 1847 and 1853 reduced the county to its current size. The first county seat was a settlement on the north side of La Creole Creek—today's Rickreall Creek—named Cynthian (also known as Cynthia Ann). In 1852, when the growth of Dallas on the south side of the creek began to outpace Cynthian's, the county seat was moved to Dallas. According to the 1860 U.S. Census, the county population was 3625.

River navigation was Polk County's chief form of transportation in 1859. A portion of the Territorial Road connected Dallas with Salem, and primitive wagon roads connected some of the other communities. The Applegate Trail unofficially terminated in Dallas.

Early History

The Dallas area and the eastern portion of present-day Polk County along the Willamette River, especially in the areas of Independence and West Salem, had been home to various bands of the Kalapuya. They frequented the present-day Falls City area to hunt, fish, and dig and process camas bulbs.

Hudson's Bay Company (HBC) trappers and traders ventured into the area of Polk County in the 1820s, accompanied by botanist David Douglas in 1826. Settlers began arriving in 1841. After the Grand Ronde Reservation was established in 1856, trade between the Indians from the reservation and the settlers in Falls City was common, as it was only a day's travel between the two locations.

Dallas, Rickreall, and West Salem

The first settlers began arriving in present-day Dallas in 1845. The establishment of La Creole Academy in 1855–56 spurred the early development of the town. The founders and first trustees of the school, which offered classes for all ages, included James Frederick, Nicholas Lee, Isaac Levens, William Lewis, John Lyle, Solomon Shelton, and Frederick Waymire. Town lots were sold to raise construction funds.

Three Christian denominations organized churches in Dallas in the 1850s.

1859 Polk County Courthouse in Dallas, said to have been modeled after the state capitol in Richmond, Virginia. Courtesy of the Salem Public Library, Ben Maxwell Collection, #3452.

Nathaniel and Lucinda Ford, ca. 1844. Mr. Ford served as a territorial legislator and surveyed the line between Oregon and California. Courtesy of the Polk County Historical Society.

Nicholas Lee was the preacher of the Methodist Episcopal Church, and other early pioneers organized a Baptist and Christian Church.

Some settlement occurred just northwest of Dallas in an area later known as Ellendale. The community developed around the gristmill built by James A. O'Neal in 1844. The mill's ownership had changed hands several times by 1859. In 1854 Ezra Halleck and Luther Tutthill built a dam and sawmill above the gristmill.

A few families settled in the area of present-day Rickreall in 1844, including James W. Nesmith and Nathaniel Ford. Ford brought his slaves with him from Missouri. Robin and Polly Holmes were the parents of Mary Jane Holmes Shipley. (She was living in Philomath by 1859; her biography appears in the Benton County chapter.) When the parents gained their freedom from Ford in 1849, they established their own residence and a nursery business in Salem. Their children were finally freed in 1853, after Mr. and Mrs. Holmes won a court action against Ford, prompted by the death of one of their children in his custody. The 1853 decision handed down by Oregon Supreme Court Justice George H. Williams was the first Oregon court decision against slavery.

One church was organized in Rickreall by 1859—the Cumberland Presbyterian Church. Reverend J. A. Cornwall organized it, although he was not a local resident.

The once prosperous community of Eola was located in the vicinity of present-day West Salem. (Although West Salem is located in Polk County, since 1950 it has been part of the city of Salem located across the Willamette River in Marion County—the two towns merging at that time.) When the community was first settled in 1848 on the donation land claim of William Duran, it was called Cincinnati, but when the territorial legislature incorporated it in 1856, it already had taken the name of Eola. Joseph B. V. Butler, William Hayden, Alva C. R. Shaw, and Joshua "Sheep" Shaw are considered to be the town fathers. Butler opened one of the first two stores in Eola and still owned it in 1859, but he resided in Monmouth and operated another store in Portland. The Shaws—father and son—were the first to herd sheep over the Oregon Trail in 1844, an important addition to the culture because until then animal hides were the only other local material available for clothing, although dry goods such as cotton and linen could be purchased from the HBC.

Eola had the usual businesses of a rising community, including a gristmill, sawmill, and tanyard. It became a busy shipping port, with riverboats arriving at Rickreall Creek.

In 1859 Hugh McNary Waller was the pastor of the Disciples of Christ Church organized in 1856. Eola School was built in 1853 and was replaced in 1858 after fire destroyed the first one. The school's first teacher was Abigail Scott, who later became Abigail Scott Duniway and an advocate of women's suffrage. (Duniway's biography appears in the Yamhill County chapter.)

When Harrison and Emily Brunk arrived in Oregon in 1845, they took a donation land claim northwest of Rickreall, but in 1856 they bought Waller's claim in Eola, later known as Brunk's Corner. In 1861 they completed their new home, which today is the Brunk House museum, open to the public.

James W. Nesmith (1820–1885)

Born in New Brunswick, Canada; educated in New England, Ohio, and Oregon

Arrived in Oregon in 1843 with Dr. Marcus Whitman

Forced ashore during severe windstorm on Columbia River below cascades at what now is known as Nesmith Point

Took donation land claim in Polk County in 1844

Served as captain in Cayuse and Rogue River Indian wars, and colonel in Yakima Indian War

Mined for gold in California in 1848, and upon returning bought flour mill on Rickreall Creek

Partner in first law firm in Polk County

Participant in formation of provisional government and Polk County

Served as provisional government judge, territorial legislator, U.S. marshal for Oregon Territory, Superintendent of Indian Affairs for combined agencies of Oregon and Washington (1857–1859), U.S. senator, and U.S. congressman

Married Pauline Goff; seven children

James W. Nesmith, when he was not serving as a public official for Polk County or the state of Oregon, farmed just south of Rickreall. Courtesy of the Salem Public Library, Ben Maxwell Collection, #3899.

Jessie and Julia Harritt settled into a log cabin at the north end of West Salem in 1845. Jessie was among the many settlers in Polk County who ventured to California after the discovery of gold in 1848. When he returned home he could afford to build a plantation-style house for Julia; they were from Kentucky and this was the style of house she dreamed of. The 1858 Harritt House remains today, extensively remodeled, as a private business.

Falls City, Monmouth, Independence, and Buena Vista

In 1844 Major John Thorpe (or Thorp) and his extended family and friends from Missouri settled southwest of Dallas where Falls City is located today. In the early 1850s he and his son Theodore built a gristmill at the falls on the Luckiamute River with money they acquired in the California gold fields. The community had several names before becoming Falls City in later years.

Monmouth was settled in 1852 by members of the Disciples of Christ from Monmouth, Illinois, who moved to Oregon specifically to establish a Christian college. Some of them donated land for a townsite and lots were sold to raise construction funds. Elijah Davidson and John E. Murphy were among the founders of the First Christian Church of Monmouth in 1856, and when Monmouth University was established, its first classes were held in the small church building. In 1858 the university's first building was constructed on property donated by Thomas H. Lucas, John B. Smith, and Squire S. Whitman.

Joseph B. V. Butler became one of the financial supporters of Monmouth University, but he arrived in Oregon earlier than the group from Illinois. Before moving to Monmouth in 1857 and opening a store, he and his wife lived in Portland in the early 1850s and in Eola in the mid-1850s. Butler retained ownership of the two stores he had opened in those locales. A post office was established in Monmouth in 1859 and several other stores were in operation, including a harness shop and a sash and door shop.

In the early 1850s, Elvin A. Thorp (or Thorpe) platted the town of Independence east of Monmouth. It soon featured many businesses, including a sawmill and a brick factory. Located on the Willamette River, boat docks and several warehouses were built to store the grain products delivered by local farmers for shipment by steamship or barge. In 1853 Independence also acquired its first licensed ferry service.

Independence had its own resident physician, Dr. James W. Boyle. He also provided his services to adjacent communities until his death in 1864 at age 49 after a fall from his carriage.

In the 1850s a city government was established in Independence. One of the services it provided was oversight of a circulating library operated out of various private homes. Independence did not escape the 1861 flood unscathed; a new town was platted south of the original townsite.

To the southeast of Independence, Reason B. Hall settled along the Willamette River and in 1850 founded the town of Buena Vista. The town had a warehouse, a gristmill, and two general stores, one owned by James O'Neal, formerly of Ellendale. In 1852 Hall began operating Hall's Ferry. Buena Vista became an important shipping point on the river. By 1859, a one-room log house served as a school during the week and as a church on Sundays.

Settlement was occurring to the west of Buena Vista— enough for the Luckiamute and Bloomington post offices to be established in the early 1850s. Harrison Linville was one of the first settlers in 1847. His property was surrounded by the Luckiamute River on three sides. Deciding not to establish a town, he farmed, raised cattle, and operated a store and ferry across the river. He also served as an elder when the Luckiamute Church was established and hosted the church services in his home. Farther west near present-day Pedee, M. D. S. Gilliam, John Johnson, and Charles Moore established homesteads.

First building of Monmouth University, known today as Western Oregon University after six name changes between 1865 and 1997. Courtesy of Western Oregon University Archives. All rights reserved.

Lincoln and Bethel

North of West Salem, there was settlement along the Willamette River where the community of Lincoln is located today. Andrew Jackson Doak operated a ferry so the settlement was known as Doak's Ferry until he sold his land claim and ferry to Jesse Walling in 1860. Walling laid out the town of Lincoln, which developed into a major wheat shipping center during the steamboat era.

Numerous families settled between the Spring and Plum valleys in the 1840s and '50s, including Reverend Glen O. Burnett, Amos Harvey, Dr. Nathaniel Hudson, Ira S. Townsend, and Sanford Watson. Each valley had its own post office by 1854, but only one town developed— Bethel, situated between the two valleys.

Reverend Burnett organized the Bethel Church where, in

Bethel Institute, later Bethel College, was built in 1855 and chartered in 1856. By 1859 college courses were being offered. Two dormitories were built near this two-story building. Courtesy of the Oregon Historical Society, OrHi 4125.

1859, Reverend George W. Richardson was the minister, as Burnett had moved to Yamhill County. In 1852 Dr. Hudson established Bethel Academy in a log schoolhouse built on his donation land claim. When he sold his squatter's rights in 1854 and moved to another claim west of Dallas, the community immediately began planning for a replacement facility.

Burnett and Amos Harvey both donated portions of their land claims for a townsite and college. The sale of the town lots financed the construction of Bethel Institute in 1855. The institute later joined with Monmouth University in 1865. (When the railroad bypassed Bethel in the 1870s, the town declined.)

Fort Hill and Fort Yamhill

The settlers in the community that came to be known as Fort Hill built a blockhouse in 1855 to protect themselves from the Indians. U.S. Army troops built Fort Yamhill adjacent to the blockhouse the following year; it became a fully staffed military post for keeping the Indians recently removed to the nearby Grand Ronde Reservation on the reservation and the settlers out.

The 4th Infantry officers stationed at Fort Yamhill included Captain D. A. Russell and Lieutenant Philip H.

Fort Yamhill blockhouse, at one time located at the Grand Ronde Agency. Today it is located in Dayton in Yamhill County. Courtesy of the Oregon Historical Society, OrHi 62683.

Sheridan. Benjamin Simpson operated a store and sawmill on the fort grounds before becoming an Indian agent at the Siletz Agency in 1863. (When Fort Yamhill was abandoned as a military post in the 1860s, the blockhouse built by the Fort Hill settlers was moved to the Grand Ronde Agency just north of the Polk and Yamhill county lines for use as a jail.)

Sampling of Polk County Family Surnames in 1859

Allen	Downer	Harvey	Levens	O'Neal	Tetherow
Ball	Faulconer	Hayden	Lewis	Pigg	Thompson
Brunk	Ford	Hedges	Linville	Richardson	Thorp (Thorpe)
Burbank	Frazer	Hill	Lovelady	Ritner	Townsend
Burch	Frederick	Hirsch	Lyle	Robb	Tutthill
Burford	Frizzell	Holmes	Mason	Rowland	Waller
Butler	Galloway	Hudson	McCarty	Russell	Warriner
Clark	Gilliam	Jeffries	McKinley	Scott	Watson
Cluff	Ground	Johnson	McNary	Shelton	Waymire
Cook	Hall	Jones	Moore	Shreve	Wells
Cooper	Halleck	Kennedy	Murphy	Simpson	Whitman
Davidson	Harris	Ladd	Nesmith	Smith	Williams
Denny	Harritt	Lee	Nicholas	Stump	Wolverton
Doak					

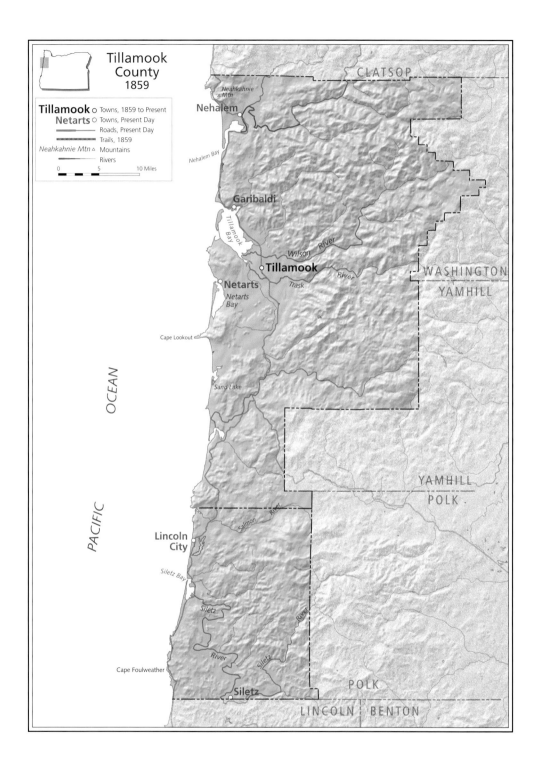

Tillamook County 1859

Tillamook ○ Towns, 1859 to Present
Netarts ○ Towns, Present Day
── Roads, Present Day
═══ Trails, 1859
Neahkahnie Mtn △ Mountains
── Rivers

0   5   10 Miles

CLATSOP

Neahkahnie Mtn △

Nehalem

Nehalem Bay

Garibaldi

Tillamook Bay

Wilson River

Tillamook

Trask

River

WASHINGTON

YAMHILL

Netarts

Netarts Bay

Cape Lookout

Sand Lake

OCEAN

YAMHILL

POLK

PACIFIC

Salmon River

Lincoln City

Siletz Bay

Siletz

River

Siletz

Cape Foulweather

POLK

Siletz

LINCOLN | BENTON

15 1859 TILLAMOOK COUNTY

Tillamook County was created in 1853 out of southern Clatsop County and the western portions of Yamhill and Polk counties; it included the northern portion of present-day Lincoln County. There were several minor boundary changes with neighboring counties between 1855 and 1898, and in 1893, Lincoln County was created out of the southern portion of Tillamook County and the western portion of Benton County. In 1859 the county court was still meeting in private homes in the town of Lincoln, which later was renamed Tillamook, but Tillamook was not officially made the county seat until 1873. There was very little development in Tillamook County until the 1860s and '70s. According to the 1860 U.S. Census, the county population was a mere 95 persons, with most living around Tillamook Bay and along the rivers.

In Present-Day Tillamook County

Early settlers in Tillamook County arrived by Indian trails along the coast or paths that crossed the Coast Range from the Willamette Valley. A few arrived on small sailing vessels after cajoling a ship's captain to make the risky trip by sea into Tillamook Bay.

Early History

The Nehalem, Tillamook, and Nestucca Indians had occupied the areas along the coast of present-day Tillamook County for at least 3000 years. In her *At the Foot of the Mountain*, Jane Comerford writes that from spring to late fall they lived in small temporary villages near Neahkahnie Mountain where they fished and hunted to stockpile food for the winter. Every few years they burned the slopes of the mountain to encourage new growth of grasslands where the deer and herds of elk grazed. During the winter months the Tillamook returned to their permanent villages near Tillamook Bay. They traded with other tribes up and down the coast, traveling along a network of trails.

American Captain Robert Gray was the first explorer to enter Tillamook Bay in 1788, nearly four years before he discovered the Columbia River. On their way to the Willamette Valley in 1841 Reverend John H. Frost, from

Sites to Visit in Tillamook County

Garibaldi Museum
112 Garibaldi Ave, Garibaldi
503·322·8411

Morning Star Replica at Tillamook
  Cheese Visitor Center
4175 Hwy 101 N, Tillamook
503·815·1300

Tillamook County Pioneer Museum
2106 2nd St, Tillamook
503·842·4553

the mission at Clatsop Plains, and Solomon H. Smith traveled along Netarts Bay, over Cape Lookout, and around Sandlake.

Exposure to diseases brought by sailors, explorers, and fur traders decimated the Tillamook Indian population. It is estimated that the population declined from 2200 in 1806, when the Lewis and Clark expedition departed, to 200 by the time settlers began arriving in the early 1850s. Yet the Tillamook were generally peaceful, friendly, and helpful to the settlers, including aiding the ship builders of *The Morning Star* in Tillamook in 1855. From a wrecked ship near Netarts Bay, the Indians salvaged ship components, including canvas for sails, and sold them to the ship builders.

The Tillamook lost all of their lands when they signed the Coast Treaty of 1855—a treaty that was never ratified. However their lands south of Cape Lookout were included in the 1855 executive order creating the Coast Reservation. The area north of the cape was opened to settlement.

Rosa Kilchis and her husband. She was the daughter of Chief Kilchis, chief of the Tillamook Indians. Courtesy of the Tillamook County Pioneer Museum.

Tillamook, Netarts, and Garibaldi

The town of present-day Tillamook was not laid out until 1861, but the slowly developing community was known successively as Lincoln and Hoquarton before later taking the name of the local Indians in 1891.

Joseph C. Champion was the first settler in the county in 1851, arriving by boat from Astoria. Within a few years he was joined by several other bachelors and two families, the Nathan Dougherty and Elbridge Trask families.

Extremely isolated geographically, the settlers in the Tillamook and Nehalem valleys were hardy pioneers. All of their supplies had to be packed in over the steep and rugged Neahkahnie Mountain. Numerous shipwrecks along the coast deterred the inexperienced from wanting to travel by ship and most captains refused to sail into Tillamook Bay because of the risks involved.

The region, with an abundance of lush grass year round, was immediately identified as ideal land for dairy farming. Growing crops was difficult because of the laborious land clearing required; the wet, cool climate; and the short growing season. Depending on the weather in a given year, the farmers had modest success with potatoes and grain.

Joseph C. Champion, Tillamook County's first county clerk. Local lore depicts him as the man who lived in the hollowed-out tree stump among the Indians. Courtesy of the Tillamook County Pioneer Museum.

With at least one cow per farm, there soon was a surplus of milk, so the settlers began butter production and, by the mid-1850s, cheese processing. William W. Raymond, who settled in the vicinity of present-day Netarts, is believed to have produced the first vat of cheese around 1856.

The marketing of dairy products and salted salmon was the settlers' only source of income, but they were limited by the lack of transportation. In 1853 a group of farmers and fishermen made the first of several attempts to acquire a reliable ship for transporting their products to Portland. In his *The Tillamook Way: A History of the Tillamook County Creamery Association*, Archie Satterfield gives a detailed account of the two ships they purchased and *The Morning Star* that they built and launched in the Kilchis River in 1855. Financial circumstances forced the sale of *The Morning Star*, but its short-lived service sustained the settlers for a few years and contributed to the development of the county.

Elbridge Trask (1815–1863)

Born in Massachusetts; fur trapper and one of the Mountain Men

Arrived in Oregon by ship in 1834 with Nathaniel J. Wyeth; worked at Wyeth's fur trading post on Sauvie Island through following year

Resumed fur trapping in Rockies until meeting Dr. Elijah White's wagon train in Snake River Valley; served as guide and met his future wife and her infant

Settled on Clatsop Plains in 1843, working at Hunt's Mill until 1852 when family moved to Tillamook County and settled along Trask River

Farmed and worked as blacksmith and teacher

Developed trust among Indians, who allowed him to mediate disputes

Established one of first three dairies in Tillamook County by 1859

Served as justice of the peace and county commissioner

Married widow Hanna Able in Oregon City in 1842; ten children

Popularized in 1960 historical novel *Trask* and two sequels by Don Berry

Henry W. Wilson (1800s)

Born in England

Settled along Wilson River in 1851 as bachelor

Brought first cattle into area in 1852, driving them from Clatsop County

Trained as a printer; worked on *Statesman* newspaper in Salem in late 1850s

Believed to have presented bill to territorial legislature for creation of Tillamook County

Advocated for county in territorial legislature

Married Veronica Manning in 1854

The Morning Star II, built in 1959 to commemorate Oregon's centennial. This ship sailed to Portland to participate in centennial festivities, but it later fell into disrepair, so a second replica of *The Morning Star* was built and dedicated in 1992. It stands on the grounds of the Tillamook Cheese Visitor Center and its likeness serves as the company's logo. Courtesy of the Tillamook County Creamery Association.

Three of the men who built the two-masted schooner were still living in the area in 1859—O. S. Thomas, Warren N. Vaughn, and Peter Morgan, the latter a Danish shipbuilder who was persuaded to move to Tillamook and lend his skills to the project.

The first permanent settler in Garibaldi arrived by accident in 1856. Charley Farwell was the cook on a ship that ran aground in Tillamook Bay because of Farwell's erroneous directions. The captain threatened to kill him, but Farwell agreed to be put ashore before the captain located his pistol.

Because the portion of Tillamook County south of Cape Lookout was reservation land, there was no Euro-American settlement there until an 1875 Congressional act took the land north of Cascade Head.

Sampling of Tillamook County Family Surnames in 1859

Allen	Dougherty	Morgan	Trask	Wilson
Champion	Farwell	Thomas	Vaughn	

In Northern Portion of Present-Day Lincoln County

Early History

For thousands of years before their homeland became part of the Coast Reservation in 1855, the Siletz Indians had lived along the Siletz River and the Siletz Bay. The Salmon River Indians lived along the Salmon River. Both tribes lived off of the land and sea, partaking of the abundance of salmon, shellfish, sea mammals, venison, wild berries, and roots. By the 1840s their numbers were greatly reduced from foreign diseases.

English navigator Captain James Cook sighted and named Cape Foulweather in 1778, but the land area of this part of today's Lincoln County had no known Euro-American visitors until the 1820s. Fur traders explored the area, trading with the Indians along the way. In 1837 recently married missionaries Jason Lee and Cyrus Shepard, along with their brides and guide Joseph Gervais, camped where present-day Lincoln City is located. The U.S. Army expedition led by Lieutenant Theodore Talbot passed along the coast in 1849.

Because the Coast (Siletz) Reservation encompassed all but the eastern-most portion of present-day Lincoln County, settlement of the area did not occur until after enactment of the Dawes Act of 1887, which caused lands not allotted to the Indians to become available for purchase and settlement.

Siletz Reservation

In 1855 an executive order signed by U.S. President Franklin Pierce created the Coast Reservation. The reservation orig-

Sites to Visit in North Lincoln County

Siletz Tribal Cultural Center
Government Hill off Logsden Rd, Siletz
541·444·2532

North Lincoln County Historical Museum
4907 SW Hwy 101, Lincoln City
541·996·6698

inally stretched from Cape Lookout in Tillamook County to the south side of the Siltcoos River in southern Lane County, but since the Congressional act of 1875, it has been located on different and significantly reduced acreage and called the Siletz Reservation. By 1859 nearly all of the coastal Indians and some of the Indians from the Willamette, Umpqua, and Rogue valleys were resettled to the Coast Reservation. Additional bands and tribes from northern California and the southern portion of the Washington Territory eventually arrived, some by treaty and others by forced removal. This commingling of people with many language and cultural differences created chaotic conditions, leading to outbreaks of violence on the reservation. Within two years, the reported death rate among the Indians was in the hundreds from hunger, disease, exposure to the cold and wet climate, physical abuse, violence, or depression of spirits.

Until the late 1850s, the reservation comprised crude shelters and the U.S. Army blockhouse. Eventually, an office, warehouse, drug store, blacksmith shop, schoolhouse, storehouses, log cabins, and a hospital were built.

In 1859 the Coast Reservation was under the control of Indian sub-Agent Robert Metcalfe. His staff included a farmer, doctor, miller, and teachers. The teachers and Methodist and Catholic missionaries attempted to "civilize and Christianize" the Indians.

The isolated location of the Siletz Agency created many cost overruns. Transportation costs were high and room and board for the employees had to be furnished because there were no nearby communities where they could establish homes of their own. The U.S. Army was in charge of maintaining order at the reservation, which was plagued by thefts and excessive alcohol consumption.

The dire conditions under which the Indians on the Coast Reservation lived are verified in various documents held by the U.S. National Archives and Records Administration and are viewable on the Native American Document Project Web site. For example, the "Report of the speeches made by the Chiefs, 24–26 May 1862" details the chiefs' complaints about hunger, the lack of clothing, blankets, and compensation for their hard labor; the confiscation of personal property and supplies intended for delivery to them; unfair restrictions; and the general disregard for the terms of the treaty. At least one Indian expressed his people's interest in remaining on the reservation if they could be provided with the means to live decently and earn an income—provision of utensils to cook with, a wagon and two yoke of cattle, carts so the women would not have to pack supplies on their backs (Indian women were forced to travel the long, rugged mountain trail to Fort Hoskins to pick up

100-pound sacks of flour to carry back to the reservation), and guns to hunt with—just to name a few.

Siletz agents' letters written to the Office of Indian Affairs in Washington, D.C. during the early 1860s further document the lack of food, clothing, and supplies available to the Indians. Also noted were the failure of the farms to produce adequate crops and the lack of grazing lands for livestock.

The Web site of the Confederated Tribes of Siletz and the publication "A Travel Guide to Indian Country" available at most visitor centers in Oregon provide details about the later history of the reservation. Today the Siletz Reservation consists of close to 4000 acres of scattered parcels within Lincoln County.

Charley and Mary Bradford, Rogue Indians on the Coast (Siletz) Reservation. Courtesy of the Josephine County Historical Society.

Emmeline John, a Takelma Indian of the Rogue Valley, was married to Klamath John, a Shasta leader in several Indian wars. She lived on the Coast (Siletz) Reservation. Photo provided by the Lincoln County Historical Society.

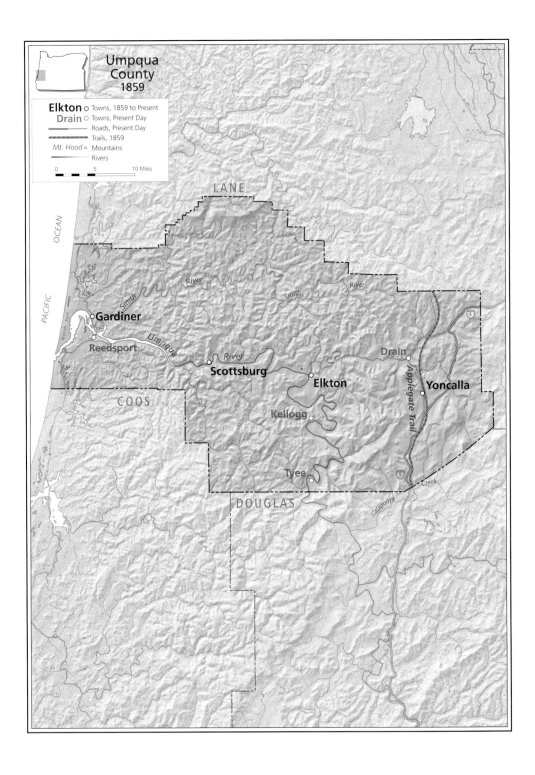

LANE

OCEAN

PACIFIC

River

Smith

River

Smith

○ Gardiner

Umpqua

Reedsport

River

Scottsburg

Drain

Elkton

Applegate Trail

Yoncalla

COOS

Kellogg

Tyee

DOUGLAS

Creek

Calapooya

16 1859 UMPQUA COUNTY

The short-lived Umpqua County was formed in 1851 from the southern portion of Benton County and the western portion of Lane County. Portions of Umpqua County were annexed to other counties—Douglas County in 1852 and Coos and Lane counties in 1853.

The county seat alternated between Elkton and Scottsburg until 1855 when Elkton became the seat. Umpqua County never had a courthouse; proceedings were held in a dwelling on Judge Underwood's property. According to the 1860 U.S. Census, the county population was 1250.

When the southern Oregon gold rush waned, the commercial trade that had helped the economy to prosper in the early 1850s was lost and the county struggled. Maintenance of a county government became increasingly difficult. In 1862 Umpqua County was incorporated into Douglas County and ceased to exist.

With the gold rush fueling Oregon's economy in the early 1850s, the U.S. Congress was convinced that federal appropriations would be well spent on navigational improvements at the mouth of the Umpqua River. A number of ships had been wrecked there. Three appropriations totaling $35,000 were made for various harbor projects, including the 1857 lighthouse.

In 1854 Colonel Joe Hooker supervised the construction of the Scottsburg–Myrtle Creek Military Wagon Road—a portion of the Southern Oregon Military Road. In 1855 the county improved the Scottsburg to Winchester portion of the road, used by pack trains, with funds derived from a property tax and free labor provided by property owners in lieu of taxes.

South of Elkton where the Umpqua River winds back and forth and numerous creeks fan out across the valley, bridges and ferries were needed. John Ambrose Fryer Sr. built a bridge across Elk Creek at Elkton and several other bridges throughout the county. The bridge across Elk Creek displaced a ferry, but three to five other ferries were always operating. One of the county commissioners' most time-consuming jobs was to review applications for ferry licenses. There was fierce competition between several operators, including Ziba Dimmick and his son-in-law James T. Cooper; Edward P. Drew, James Laughlin, and William Robertson.

Yoncalla Chief Halo and the Applegate family members had a mutual respect and admiration for one another. Courtesy of the Oregon Historical Society, CN 022580.

Early History

The area within the former Umpqua County had long been the home of the Lower Umpqua and the Yoncalla band of the Kalapuya. A few Klickitats also lived in the Yoncalla area and hunted in the Umpqua Valley.

The Lower Umpqua lived off the abundance of the Umpqua River estuary and its shoreline near present-day Reedsport. The river provided clams, crabs, seals, and fish. Another important fishing site was at the waterfalls on the Smith River.

The Yoncalla lived along the Calapooya Creek in the Coles Valley, in Yoncalla and its surrounding valleys, and in the Kellogg and Elkton areas, especially along Elk Creek. The writings of several Applegate family members, including Anne Applegate Kruse's book, *The Halo Trail, Yoncalla, Oregon*, provide first-hand accounts of the Indians who lived in the Yoncalla and Scott valleys.

A number of European explorers entered the mouth of the Umpqua River. In 1828 trappers arriving from Fort Vancouver explored the area and the Jedediah Smith expedition had its fatal encounter with Indians at the confluence of the Smith and Umpqua rivers. Smith and three of his men were the only survivors.

Missionaries Jason Lee and Gustavus Hines traveled to the mouth of the Umpqua River in 1840 to hold services for the local tribes. The following year, a patrol of the U.S. Exploring Expedition ventured into the area.

By the 1840s the Indian population in this region dwindled from exposure to disease brought by Euro-American travelers and settlers. Nonetheless, relationships between the surviving Indians and the settlers were amicable, with only a few exceptions. The Indians were often helpful to the settlers, transporting them across rivers and creeks and providing them with freshly caught fish.

When the Kalapuya Indians were sent to the Grand Ronde Reservation in 1856, Yoncalla Chief Halo refused to leave his home in Yoncalla. Members of his family were allowed to return shortly thereafter. The Applegate family sponsored Chief Halo's family through the U.S. citizenship process, which permitted them to be allotted tracts of land. They chose the surname of Fearn to qualify for land ownership.

Elkton, Scottsburg, Reedsport, Gardiner, and Winchester Bay

In 1850 the Umpqua Exploring Expedition from the San Francisco trading company of Winchester, Payne & Co. laid out Elkton on land donated by James F. Levins. Although it was the designated county seat and had a post office, it remained essentially a rural community throughout the 1850s. Many of the early settlers were Europeans who arrived by ship from San Francisco. Farms were established on the river bottom land near the Indian trail to the coast. Fields of wheat were planted, the orchard formerly belonging to the Hudson's Bay Company (HBC) was tended, and the livestock trade started by the HBC was continued.

There was some logging and lumbering to supply local residents, but inadequate transportation limited these operations. A log schoolhouse was located on Ira Wells's property, and the Methodist Church held services in the home of his father, Aseph Wells.

Across the river from Elkton near the confluence of Elk Creek and the Umpqua River stood the Fort Umpqua that the HBC built in the early 1830s until it burned in 1852. Several places have been known as Fort Umpqua; this one was a fur trading post where HBC employees lived, farmed, and raised livestock.

In 1850, to the west of Elkton, the Umpqua Exploring Expedition, along with Captain Levi Scott, established the town of Scottsburg. Only 26 miles from the coast, Scottsburg soon became the major point of delivery for supplies and equipment bound for the gold mines of southern Oregon and northern California. Ocean-going schooners docked and unloaded their freight for the pack trains and freight wagons that would then haul the goods over trails to the mining districts.

Scottsburg also was an arrival and departure point for passengers arriving from San Francisco or Coos Bay or

Captain Levi Scott (1797–1890)

Arrived from Iowa in 1844 with son John; first settled in Dallas in Polk County

With Jesse and Lindsay Applegate in 1846, blazed Applegate Trail, an alternative to Columbia River route and Barlow Road; led first wagon train to Willamette Valley in 1847

Commissioned as captain in 1848 during Cayuse War, carrying dispatches to California

Settled on Elk Creek in Scotts Valley east of Yoncalla in 1848

With Umpqua Exploring Expedition, founded Scottsburg on Umpqua River in 1850 and established several of his own businesses

Member of territorial legislature and state constitutional convention

Wrote his memoirs at age 92

Widowed before arriving in Oregon; two children

Captain Levi Scott, road builder and town founder. Courtesy of the Oregon Historical Society, OrHi 5437.

headed out from the interior valleys or gold fields. With all of this dock activity, Scottsburg quickly developed into a prosperous community, with wharves, numerous mercantile businesses, saloons and gambling houses, and several hotels operating out of private residences. A Lower and Upper Scottsburg eventually developed, with the two frequently engaging in fierce competition. (According to one author, Harold A. Minter, there also was a Middle Scottsburg.) An extant building in Upper Scottsburg served as the school building between 1859 and 1943 and today houses the Scottsburg Historical Center, marked by an interpretive sign.

A few ships were built in Scottsburg. Resident William E. Rackleff and his father, Captain William R. Rackleff, built the schooner *Twin Sisters* in 1858. The father sailed this ship into the mouth of the Coquille River the following year, reaching Myrtle Point where settlers, desperately in need

Cyrus Hedden and the original Hedden Store in Scottsburg.
Courtesy of the Douglas County Museum, N726.

of supplies, hailed the schooner's arrival. William E. Rackleff made many additional trips from the Lower Umpqua to Myrtle Point and San Francisco loaded with cargo.

The decline of Scottsburg began when shipping points developed closer to the mines, especially after Crescent City in northern California was established in 1854. Many of the mercantile businesses closed and residents left the area. However, in his *Umpqua: The Lost County of Oregon*, Jerry Winterbotham writes that in 1858 new settlers still were arriving and that trade to San Francisco took an upswing in 1859 when Scottsburg merchants started shipping potatoes and pork. But any dreams for a full recovery were swept away by the winter flood of 1860–61.

Several families were settled just east of Scottsburg in an area known as Long Prairie. The Ephraim H. Burchard family moved there in 1854. He served as justice of the peace for the Scottsburg precinct and as the county assessor of Umpqua County in 1859 and 1860. One other settlement located above the mouth of the Umpqua was Middleton, occupied by a few families.

An unfortunate shipwreck on the Umpqua Bar at the mouth of the Umpqua River in 1850 led to the founding of Gardiner City, known today as Gardiner. Starting out as a center of trade and industry supported by the gold rush of the 1850s, it later developed into a lumbering and fishing community.

When the Umpqua U.S. Customs District was established, Gardiner became the port of entry. Barclay J. Burns was serving as the collector of customs in 1859.

In 1850 the Umpqua Exploring Expedition established Umpqua City on the spit just north of the mouth of the Umpqua River. Another town, West Umpqua, was planned for the other side of the river. There was some development at both sites, but with intense competition upriver from Scottsburg and Gardiner, neither ever became successful commercially and both disappeared during the 1860s.

In July of 1856, just north of Umpqua City, the 3rd U.S. Artillery built Fort Umpqua on the east side of the North Spit. The fort was built as a southern boundary outpost for the Coast Reservation and was under the command of Major John B. Scott. The fort included a blockhouse, quarters for the officers and enlistees, a hospital, and a variety of miscellaneous buildings.

The military soon removed hundreds of Coos and Lower Umpqua Indians to a reserve near Fort Umpqua under the jurisdiction of a new sub-agency— the Umpqua Sub-Agency. Food shortages, alcohol abuse, and exposure to new diseases, including sexually transmitted ones, impacted the Indian population over the ensuing years. Four hundred sixty surviving Indians were

Fort Umpqua blockhouse located on the north spit of the Umpqua River.
Courtesy of the Oregon Historical Society, OrHi 1658-A.

forced to march up the coast in 1859 to a new sub-agency site—the Alsea Sub-Agency at Yachats in present-day southern Lincoln County. Several years later, Fort Umpqua was abandoned.

The first lighthouse to be built on the Oregon coast was built in 1857 on the sand at the mouth of the Umpqua River on the south side. It replaced the beacon that had been in use. However, in 1864 it toppled into the river during a storm. The present Umpqua River Lighthouse did not replace it until 1894.

Drain and Yoncalla

A few settlers took land claims east of Elkton in the Putnam Valley where the communities were called Tin Pot or Sunnydale, and in the area where Drain was established in the 1870s when the railroad came through. Warren Goodell was one of the first to arrive in 1847; he and most of the other settlers raised sheep. Charles C. Drain Sr. purchased Goodell's land in 1861 and it later became the Drain townsite.

The Robert Cowan family may have been the first to settle in the Yoncalla Valley in 1848. Different members of the Applegate family arrived soon after, and George A. Burt's donation land claim of 1850 became the site of the Yoncalla townsite. A school and courthouse were built in the late 1850s, funded by subscriptions from Yoncalla's residents, but when Elkton was chosen as the county seat, the courthouse also became a school.

In 1859 Lindsay Applegate, his son E. Lindsay Applegate, John Long, James Miller, and W. H. Wilson were trustees of the newly established Yoncalla Institute, a private school.

Donation land claims were taken and settled in the numerous adjacent valleys, including Pleasant, Scotts, and Rice valleys. These settlers were ranchers and farmers.

Lindsay Applegate (1808–1892)

Born in Kentucky; arrived in Oregon in 1843 from Missouri

Built first ferry in Polk County in 1844

Inspired by tragic loss of one of his sons on Columbia River, he helped open up alternate southern route to Willamette Valley—Applegate Trail—in 1846

Settled in Yoncalla and established gristmill on Halo Creek

Prospected on Applegate Creek in Rogue Valley on way to California mines in 1848

Special Indian agent for Superintendent Joel Palmer in 1855

Founded Yoncalla Institute with his wife, Elizabeth Miller, in 1859

Built toll road over Siskiyous with several partners; sold his Yoncalla property to his brothers, Charles and Jesse, and moved his family southeast of Ashland to begin operating toll road in 1860

Member of state legislature in 1862

Sold toll road and moved to Klamath Falls in 1862, serving as

Indian agent at Fort Klamath from 1865–1869

Acquired large piece of property in Ashland; later sold to Southern Pacific and moved back to Klamath Falls

Several of his sons contributed significantly to early development of Oregon

Lindsay Applegate, trail blazer and Indian agent. Courtesy of the Oregon Historical Society, OrHi 46.

Jesse Applegate (1811–1888)

Born in Kentucky; developed teaching and surveying skills in Missouri, before leaving for Oregon with his wife, children, and brothers' families in 1843

Initially settled in Polk County, farming, operating mill, and working as surveyor

Participated in organization of provisional and territorial governments, and served as member of state constitutional convention

Like his brother, Lindsay, also lost a son on the Columbia River; the loss inspired him to help open an alternate southern route to Willamette Valley—Applegate Trail—in 1846

Settled in Yoncalla in 1849 to farm and raise cattle; first teacher in Yoncalla

Surveyed road over Siskiyous in late 1850s for his brother and other investors

Suffered financial losses in 1866; moved to California in 1872

Returned to Yoncalla after recouping his losses; established first vineyard in area

Married to Cynthia Parker; twelve children

Jesse Applegate, trail blazer, surveyor, and Yoncalla pioneer. (This sketch of his likeness was made from memory by his nephew, George, in 1908.) Courtesy of the Oregon Historical Society, OrHi 45.

The Applegate House built by Charles Applegate between 1852 and 1857 still stands today in Yoncalla. It was the gathering place for several generations of the Applegate family. Courtesy of the Douglas County Museum, Peret Collection, N12798.

Coles Valley and Kellogg

The Coles Valley straddled the Umpqua/Douglas County line before Umpqua County was absorbed into Douglas County in 1862, with Calapooya Creek serving generally as the boundary line between the two counties. French-Canadians, presumably former HBC employees, were settled on the west side of the valley, but do not appear in the 1860 census.

A number of American settlers were in the valley, including Dr. James Cole, who arrived in 1851. He raised cattle and also practiced medicine. He was the only physician and surgeon in the area and made frequent house calls throughout Coles and adjacent valleys. Benjamin J. Grubbe helped organize the first school. In 1852 the Ebenezer Stephens family took a donation land claim on the Calapooya Creek. Stephens served as assessor of Umpqua County and after the county became part of Douglas County, he served as county clerk and deputy sheriff.

To the north in Green Valley, Joseph Gilbert started a school in his log cabin in 1852. The early pioneers in all of these remote valleys hunted and harvested the abundant natural resources to feed their families.

South of Elkton, John J. Kellogg and his two eldest sons, Adna and Lyman, each took donation land claims along the Umpqua River in the area of the present-day hamlet of Kellogg. They built the first gristmill and sawmill in the area. A number of other families settled nearby, farming and raising sheep. A few of the settlers provided lodging and feed for the many pack trains stopping on their way to the southern Oregon gold mines.

Gottlieb Mehl established his homestead along Mehl Creek and built a gristmill and saw and furniture factory. John Ambrose Fryer Sr. owned the first threshing machine in the lower Umpqua Valley. Cyrus Hedden of Scottsburg arranged for it to be delivered around Cape Horn in the mid-1850s.

Sampling of Former Umpqua County Family Surnames in 1859

Allen	Butler	Drew	Hart	Langdon	Ogle	Sloan
Allensworth	Chism	Driver	Hatfield	Laughlin	Paine	Smith
Ambrose	Churchill	Ensley	Hathaway	Learn	Parker	Snyder
Andrew	Clark	Estes	Hayhurst	Letsom	Patterson	Stephens
Applegate	Clayton	Farmer	Hedden	Levins	Price	Swearingen
Baker	Cole	Fearn	Hedrick	Long	Putnam	Test
Barnard	Colvin	Forrest	Helbert	Lyons	Rackleff	Thiele
Bavington	Cooper	Frary	Henderer	Marshall	Rice	Turner
Bay	Cowan	Fryer	Howard	Maxey	Rich	Underwood
Beckley	Cozad	Gagnier	Hudson	McDonald	Ritchey	Van Riper
Brackett	Dagan	Gardiner	Huntington	Medley	Savery	Weaver
Breen	Daley	Goff	Jeffrey	Mehl	Sawyers	Wells
Brown	Dean	Haines	Jones	Merrick	Scott	West
Burchard	Dimmick	Hall	Kellogg	Miller	Sherrit	Williams
Burns	Dodge	Hancock	Kelly	Mills	Shupe	Wilson
Burt	Drain	Hanna	Kent	Moore		

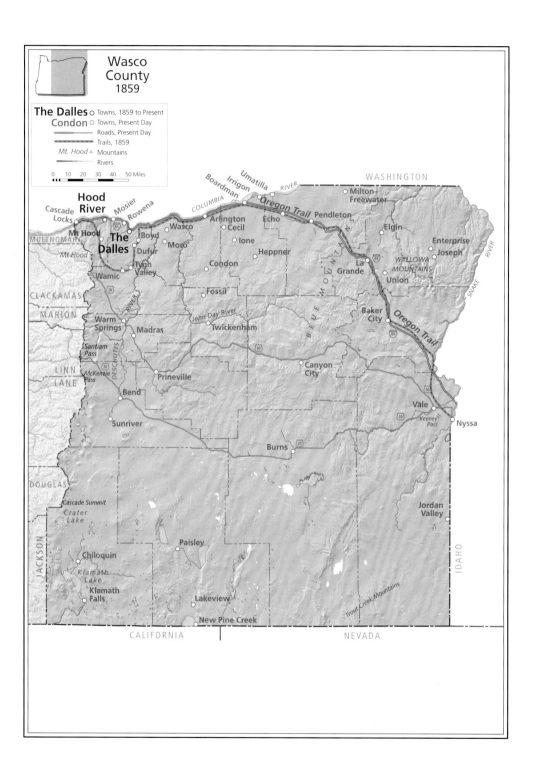

Wasco County 1859

The Dalles ○ Towns, 1859 to Present
Condon ○ Towns, Present Day
　　　　　━━━ Roads, Present Day
　　　　　━━━ Trails, 1859
Mt. Hood △ Mountains
　　　　　━━━ Rivers

0　10　20　30　40　50 Miles

WASHINGTON

Hood River

Cascade Locks　Mosier　Rowena

COLUMBIA　RIVER

Umatilla
Boardman　Irrigon
Milton-Freewater

Oregon Trail

Pendleton

MULTNOMAH

Mt Hood
Mt Hood
The Dalles
Boyd
Wasco
Arlington
Cecil
Echo

Elgin

Enterprise
Joseph

Dufur　Moro　Ione
Heppner

WALLOWA MOUNTAINS

Tygh Valley
Condon
La Grande
Union

SNAKE RIVER

CLACKAMAS
Wamic
Fossil

MARION
John Day River

Warm Springs
Madras
Twickenham

Baker City

Oregon Trail

DESCHUTES RIVER

Santiam Pass

Canyon City

LINN
McKenzie Pass

LANE
Prineville

Bend

Vale
Keeney Pass
Nyssa

Sunriver

Burns

DOUGLAS

Cascade Summit
Crater Lake

Jordan Valley

JACKSON
Paisley

Chiloquin
Klamath Lake

IDAHO

Klamath Falls
Lakeview
Trout Creek Mountains

New Pine Creek

CALIFORNIA　　　　　NEVADA

17 1859 WASCO COUNTY

The emigrants who arrived in Oregon on the Oregon Trail were bound for the Willamette Valley and paid little attention to the rolling hills covered with bunchgrass in eastern Oregon. The Whitman Massacre in 1847 near present-day Walla Walla, Washington, and the lack of adequate military protection until the mid-1850s had chilled any interest in settling the area.

In 1856 U.S. Army General John E. Wool issued an order forbidding settlement east of the Cascade Range to keep the settlers separate from the Indians. However, settlers already in the areas of present-day Wasco and Hood River counties were permitted to stay. By the late 1850s, Willamette Valley cattle ranchers were looking for new grazing land for their livestock. In 1858 General William S. Harney responded by revoking the 1856 order.

Shortly after statehood, a few stockmen started the reverse migration of settlers from the Willamette Valley eastward, and soon newly arriving Oregon Trail emigrants began choosing to settle east of the Cascade Range instead of continuing on to the Willamette Valley. Some of the Indians in central and eastern Oregon were placed on reservations created in 1855, but many remained in their homelands until the 1860s when the deluge of gold miners and settlers taking advantage of the 1862 Homestead Act enacted by the U.S. Congress changed the landscape forever.

Wasco County was created from portions of Clackamas, Marion, Linn, and Lane counties in 1854 and comprised all of the Oregon Territory east of the Cascade Range between the California border on the south and the Washington Territory on the north. At the time it was the largest county ever formed in the United States. Over the years, seventeen new counties were created from this county. The Dalles was designated the county seat in 1857. According to the 1860 U.S. Census, the county population was 1689, with almost all of it concentrated within present-day Wasco and Hood River counties.

In Present-Day Wasco County

When the post-1846 Oregon Trail emigrants arrived in present-day Wasco County, they could choose their route to the Willamette Valley: either proceed down the treacherous waters of the Columbia on a raft or take the Bar-

The 1859 Wasco County courthouse in The Dalles remains today as an historical landmark open to the public at its fifth location. Courtesy of the Oregon State Archives.

low Road. If they elected the latter, they would continue south through present-day Dufur, Tygh Valley, and Wamic to reach the tollgate and begin the arduous trek across the south slope of Mount Hood. The Barlow Road continued in operation until 1918.

By 1856 the partnership of Orlando Humason, John Simms, and Indian Agent Robert R. Thompson had improved a primitive portage road around Celilo Falls and controlled the freight and passenger traffic along this part of the Columbia. Called The Dalles Portage Road, it terminated at Deschutes Landing where a store, cafe, warehouse, and several other buildings were located.

By 1855 steamboats began running on a regular schedule between Portland and The Dalles, and in 1858 the *Colonel Wright* made the first trip upstream. Thompson and Lawrence W. Coe built the sternwheeler to haul freight; Captain Leonard White operated it from Celilo Landing to Wallula above the mouth of the Walla Walla River in the Washington Territory.

Early History

For more than 10,000 years, the Wasco (or Wascopam) Indians lived in villages in the vicinity of The Dalles, sustaining themselves on the abundance of salmon, roots, and berries. The Tenino and Tygh Indians lived south of the Wascos.

Celilo Falls, located on the Columbia River about twelve miles above The Dalles, served as a fishing, trading, and gathering center for tribes from all over the Northwest. In 1957 it was inundated by the rising waters of The Dalles Dam built by the U.S. Corps of Engineers. Indians have retained the right to dip-net for salmon near the dam and the nearby bridge, but the cultural loss of Celilo Falls continues to be mourned. Memaloose Island, located below The Dalles and substantially reduced in size following construction of the Bonneville Dam in 1938, was once a burial ground for the Chinooks of the Columbia Gorge.

The Lewis and Clark Corps of Discovery camped along the Columbia River on their way to and from the Pacific

The Dalles, also called the Grand Dalles, the Great Falls, and Celilo Falls by the Indians, referred to the rapids east of the town. Painting by John Mix Stanley, Courtesy of the Oregon Historical Society, OrHi 87276.

Ocean in 1805 and 1806. Several landmarks detailing their encampments and activities are situated along today's Interstate 84. Fur traders employed by Astor's Pacific Fur Company and the Hudson's Bay Company (HBC) followed Lewis and Clark during the next two decades. According to the book published by *The Dalles Chronicle* and edited by Dan Spartz entitled *Wasco County*, in 1829 the HBC established Fort The Dalles (not to be confused with the U.S. Army's later Fort Dalles) as a means of claiming the region's fur trade.

The many explorers and fur traders passing through the area along the Columbia River exposed the Indians to disease that decimated their population. By the early 19th century, entire villages had been wiped out.

The Cayuse War fought in the region triggered sporadic localized Indian attacks, but otherwise the Indians in the region were peaceable and friendly. With the signing of the Treaty of the Tribes of Middle Oregon in 1855, the Indians were relocated to the Warm Springs Indian Reservation.

The pioneers who chose to take the Barlow Road around Mount Hood camped in the Tygh Valley and traded with the local Tygh Indians. In 1855 Lieutenants Robert S. Williamson and Henry L. Abbot of the U.S. Army Corps of Topographical Engineers led the Pacific Railroad Survey expedition through this valley that Abbot referred to as Tysch Prairie.

Mount Hood from Tysch Prairie, a lithograph based on a watercolor by Robert S. Young, the artist accompanying the 1855 Pacific Railroad Survey expedition. Courtesy of the Oregon Historical Society, OrHi 104903.

The Dalles

In 1838, Reverend Jason Lee's nephew, Reverend Daniel Lee, along with Reverend H. K. W. Perkins, established the Methodist Wascopam Mission at the future site of The Dalles. Intended as a branch of the Salem mission for ministering to the Indians, it became a rescue facility for the thousands of sick and starving Oregon Trail emigrants. There are several conflicting accounts about the mission's status in 1847, but it appears that it was sold to the Presbyterian Church and that Dr. Marcus Whitman planned to move there from the Waiilatpu Mission in the Washington Territory. However, after the infamous massacre later that year that killed Whitman, his wife, and 12 others, the American Board of Commissioners for Foreign Missions closed all of their missions in the Oregon Country.

In 1848 a volunteer militia occupied the abandoned mission, calling it Fort Wascopam or Fort Lee. In 1850 the U.S. Army established Camp Drum on the same site to protect the incoming wagon trains preparing to board rafts for passage down the Columbia River. In 1853 it became known as Fort Drum and later Fort Dalles. It was only a primitive post until Indian unrest increased following the signing of the 1855 treaties affecting this region. The fort soon developed into a central military headquarters and depot for supplies. To accommodate its new stature, Fort Dalles was rebuilt between 1856 and 1857. Under the direction of Assistant Quartermaster Captain Thomas

Jordan, German civil engineer Louis Scholl Sr. drew up the plans for the construction of a number of elaborate buildings in the Gothic Revival style of architect Andrew Jackson Downing.

By the late 1850s Fort Dalles gradually declined in importance. With most of the Indians in the region removed to the Warm Springs Indian Reservation and the Yakima Indian War of 1855–58 in the Washington Territory over, the fort was no longer needed. The fort closed in 1868, after most of the U.S. Army troops had been sent to fight in the Civil War. However, the federal funds that were infused into the economy during its decade of operation spurred the growth of the local community.

Nathan Olney was the first permanent Euro-American settler in The Dalles in 1847. Living in a small cabin along Chenoweth Creek with his Indian wife, Annette, he operated a trading post and ferry service. Former HBC employee Edward Crate arrived in 1851 with his Indian wife, Sophia. In addition to raising cattle, he also offered transport services along the Columbia River to emigrants and The Dalles merchants. Charles Denton arrived in 1854 and planted the first orchard in the area.

The Rorick House, named for its later era owners, is extant in The Dalles and includes a two-room portion built around 1850 by a non-commissioned officer from Fort Dalles. The

The 1857 Fort Dalles Surgeon's House, one of the buildings constructed during the fort's transformation, was the only significant building to survive destruction by fire. Today it houses a museum open to the public. Courtesy of the Oregon Historical Society, OrHi 5352.

Methodist Wascopam Mission established in 1838, ca. 1849.
Courtesy of the Oregon Historical Society, OrHi 58874.

Victor Trevitt (1827–1883)

Born in New Hampshire; attended school in Ohio, learning printer's trade

Served in Mexican War in 1847 and with U.S. Mounted Rifles in Oregon

Worked for newspaper publisher Asahel Bush in Oregon City

Moved to The Dalles in 1854; laid out portion of town, sold lots, and operated tavern

Served as state representative and state senator

Married twice, first to Indian/Spanish woman and then to widow Mary W. H. Miller

Trusted Indians more than his own peers; buried in Indian burial site on Memaloose Island in accordance with his wishes

(The Euro-American style of his gravesite prompted the Indians to abandon the burial grounds.)

Justin Chenoweth (1825–1898)

Born in Illinois; educated as surgeon

Arrived in Oregon as civilian with First U.S. Mounted Rifles in 1849

Taught school in Willamette Valley, clerked for territorial legislature, and worked in territorial library

Settled on land claim west of The Dalles along Chenoweth Creek in 1852

Carried mail by boat between The Dalles and the Cascades downriver

Surveyed public land for settlers and townsites

Married Mary H. Vickers; four children

house is owned by the Wasco County Historical Society and is open to the public on specific days during the year.

The town of Fort Dalles was laid out in 1854, and lots were sold. When the city was incorporated in 1857, it became Dalles City, but by 1860 The Dalles became the name most commonly used.

In 1859 The Dalles was still in the midst of the boom that started the year before with the beginning of reverse migration from the Willamette Valley. James Fulton and his family likely were the first to arrive from the Willamette Valley in 1857, taking land on Tenmile Creek close to The Dalles. Fulton was one of the first farmers to raise wheat in Wasco County.

Commercial enterprises in The Dalles included gambling saloons, three sawmills, and the Umatilla House—considered by many the best hotel north of San Francisco with its extravagant décor and hospitality. Henry Isaacs built the hotel on the Columbia riverfront in 1857; it was destroyed by fire and rebuilt twice before it was demolished in 1929. The fire department and school district for The Dalles were both established in 1859.

That same year Captain Jordan, quartermaster at the fort, published *The Dalles Journal*, the first Oregon newspaper east of the Cascade Range. The following year he sold it to W. H. Newell, who changed the name to *The Dalles Weekly* and later the *Mountaineer*.

Several religious denominations were active in The Dalles by 1859. The Catholic Church had established a mission in 1848 and the Episcopalians began holding services in 1855. A Methodist Church was established in 1856, and the Congregational Church organized in 1859.

Before the Wascopam Mission was closed, Methodist missionaries used a 20-foot high stone pillar as an elevated platform. Pulpit Rock remains standing today on 12th Street, surrounded by pavement.

In 1854 the Josiah Marsh family took a donation land claim west of The Dalles near the current location of Rowena. In the same year Jonah H. Mosier and his family settled on Mosier Creek where present-day Mosier is located. Between 1854 and 1858 Mosier built three different sawmills near the falls on the creek, each one being washed away by floods. He later became a cattle rancher and in 1878 was elected to the state legislature.

There were scattered settlements south of The Dalles. In 1854 the Daniel Bolton family took a donation land claim in the area of the former town of Boyd. In 1852 L. P. Henderson settled where the town of Dufur later developed, and the William R. Menefee family arrived in 1855, joining other settlers at that location. Menefee farmed and served as a justice of the peace.

Farther south in the Tygh Valley, the George Hayes family was among the earliest to settle in 1853. John Y. Todd arrived in 1857 with the cattle he drove over the Barlow Road from the Willamette Valley.

In Present-Day Baker County

Baker County was created from part of Wasco County in 1862. Baker City is the county seat.

For nearly 10,000 years the Cayuse, Umatilla, and Nez Perce Indians occupied the area within present-day Baker County. They lived in small villages in the river valleys during the winter, moved to the upland prairies and streams during the spring and summer, and hunted and gathered in the mountain foothills in the fall.

In 1811 members of the Astor party led by Wilson Price Hunt were the first group of Euro-Americans to enter the area of Baker County in search of a shortcut to the Columbia River. They stopped near present-day Huntington, as did later explorers Captain B. L. E. Bonneville, Captain John C. Frémont, and Nathaniel J. Wyeth. Burnt River was noted in 1825 by the explorer and fur trader Peter Skene Ogden.

Most of the Oregon Trail pioneers stopped for rest near Huntington and then continued northwest through the treacherous Burnt River Valley. The Baker Valley, with its abundant bunchgrass, wood, and water, served as a respite prior to the Blue Mountain crossing which loomed in the distance.

Sites to Visit in Baker County

Eastern Oregon Museum
610 3rd St, Haines
541·856·3233

National Historic Oregon Trail Interpretive Center
22267 Hwy 86, I-84 Exit 302, Baker City
541·523·1843

Oregon Trail Regional Museum
2480 Grove St, Baker City
541·523·9308

Sumpter Municipal Museum
245 S Mill, Sumpter
541·894·2314

Grave Beside the Trail, evidence of the nearly one in ten who did not survive the rigors of the Oregon Trail. Courtesy of the Oregon Historical Society, OrHi 26389.

As in other areas, the Indian population began declining after exposure to new diseases from the Euro-Americans passing through the region. With the signing of the Treaty of the Cayuse, Umatilla, and Walla Walla Indians in 1855, the Indians within Baker County ceded a large portion of their land to the United States and by 1861 were removed to the Umatilla Indian Reservation. Under the treaty, they retained rights to hunt, fish, gather plants, and graze stock in parts of Baker County.

In 1861 gold was discovered in Griffin Gulch south of present-day Baker City by four men searching for the legendary Blue Bucket Mine, supposedly found in 1845 by settlers in a Lost Wagon Train led by Stephen H. L. Meek. This discovery and the subsequent one at Canyon City in present-day Grant County in 1862 led to the gold rush that spurred settlement east of the Cascade Range.

In Present-Day Crook County

Sites to Visit in Crook County

A. R. Bowman Memorial Museum
246 N Main St, Prineville
541·447·3715

Peter Skene Ogden, a Scottish explorer and fur trapper working for the Hudson's Bay Company. Courtesy of the Oregon Historical Society, OrHi 707.

Crook County was created in 1882 from the southern part of then Wasco County. Prineville is the county seat.

For centuries the Northern Paiute migrated seasonally to survive the hot, dry summers and harsh winters of this region. They fished along the Columbia and Snake rivers, gathered roots and berries in the foothills, and hunted in the Columbia-Snake River drainage. They rarely established permanent villages.

In 1825 the HBC trappers led by Peter Skene Ogden were the first Euro-Americans to enter the area within present-day Crook County. Ogden made subsequent expeditions through the Crooked River Valley. Other visitors included John C. Frémont and Kit Carson in 1843, and Stephen H. L. Meek in 1845, seeking a shorter route to the central and southern parts of the Willamette Valley for his Lost Wagon Train. Several military expeditions in the 1850s scouted the area for railroad routes and wagon roads—the Pacific Railroad Survey party led by Lieutenants Williamson and Abbot in 1855, and Captain H. D. Wallen's wagon road expedition in 1859. Settlement of Crook County did not begin until after completion of the wagon road over the Santiam Pass in Linn County in the 1860s.

The Northern Paiute escaped confinement to a reservation in 1856 and in 1859 they still held vast stretches of central and southeastern Oregon. They had been largely unaffected by the arrival of the Euro-Americans in Oregon, although foreign diseases had reduced their population. However, beginning in the 1860s, they endured an equally grim history that continued into the 20th century.

In Present-Day Deschutes County

Deschutes County was created from the western portion of Crook County in 1916. Bend is the county seat.

The Northern Paiute and Molalla Indians either had temporary villages within present-day Deschutes County or traveled through the area with the changing of the seasons. Indian trails led north toward the Warm Springs Indian Reservation and others crossed the McKenzie and Santiam passes of the Cascade Range to the Willamette Valley.

A fur trading party from the American Fur Trading Company began exploring Deschutes County as early as 1813, searching for beaver. Other early explorers and fur traders between the 1820s and 1840s included Kit Carson, Thomas "Broken Hand" Fitzpatrick, John C. Frémont, Finan McDonald, Thomas McKay, Peter Skene Ogden, and Nathaniel J. Wyeth.

Several pioneer wagon trains seeking a shortcut to the Willamette Valley passed through Deschutes County, including Stephen Meek's in 1845, Elijah Elliott's in 1853, and William Macy's in 1854. Pioneers referred to the location along the Deschutes River where Bend is located today as Farewell Bend because it was one of the few fordable points along the river.

The Indians in the area were removed to the Warm Springs Indian Reservation under the 1855 Treaty of the Tribes of Middle Oregon. Settlement did not begin in Deschutes County until the 1860s with the reverse migration of people seeking to escape the crowding of settlers in the Willamette Valley.

Sites to Visit in Deschutes County

Des Chutes Historical Center
129 NW Idaho Ave, Bend
541·389·1813

The High Desert Museum
59800 S Hwy 97, Bend
541·382·4754

Stephen H. L. Meek, mountain guide, fur trapper, and brother of Joseph L. Meek.
Courtesy of the Oregon Historical Society, OrHi 19905.

In Present-Day Gilliam County

Sites to Visit in Gilliam County

Gilliam County Historical Society
 Museum Complex
Hwy 19 at Burns Park, Condon
541·384·4233

Gilliam County was created in 1885 from the eastern half of then Wasco County. Condon is the county seat.

For thousands of years, the Umatilla had followed Indian trails leading to fishing, hunting, gathering, and trading spots within present-day Gilliam County. They were a party to the 1855 agreements of the Cayuse, Umatilla, and Walla Walla Indians creating the Umatilla Indian Reservation as their new place of residence. Indians remained along the John Day River until the reservation became operational in 1861.

The inaccessibility of the area within Gilliam County deterred the early explorers, although Lewis and Clark passed through along the Columbia River. The Oregon Trail crossed the northern part of the county through bunchgrass and sagebrush. Fourmile Canyon was a difficult portion of the trail, but fresh water awaited the pioneers at Cedar Springs and a well-traveled ford allowed them to safely cross the John Day River. Today wagon wheel ruts are still visible in the canyons between Cecil and Arlington.

In 1858 Tom Scott established a ferry service across the John Day River. Settlers began arriving by 1859—many from the Willamette Valley.

In Present-Day Grant County

Sites to Visit in Grant County

Dewitt Museum & Prairie City
 Depot
Main & Bridge streets, Prairie City

Grant County Historical Museum
101 S Canyon City Blvd (Hwy 395),
 Canyon City

Kam Wah Chung & Co. Museum
Hwy 395 & Hwy 26, John Day
541·575·2800

Grant County was created in 1864 from portions of Wasco and Umatilla counties. Canyon City is the county seat.

The northern portion of present-day Grant County had been home to the Umatilla Indians. The Northern Paiute lived along the John Day River in the southern part of the county.

Fur trappers and traders, including Peter Skene Ogden, frequented the Grant County area in the early 1800s.

The Umatilla were included in the Cayuse, Umatilla, and Walla Walla Treaty negotiations of 1855. The Northern Paiute in the region were not affected by the arrival of Euro-Americans until after the discovery of gold.

Gold was discovered in Canyon Creek in 1862, bringing the first permanent settlers to the region. It may never be known if the legendary Blue Bucket Mine ever existed, but it was the legend that led to the discovery at the future Canyon City.

In Present-Day Harney County

Harney County was created from the southern two-thirds of Grant County in 1889. Burns is the county seat.

Archaeological studies place Indians in the Trout Creek Mountains in the southeast portion of present-day Harney County over 9000 years ago. It also is known that Native American Indians from as far east as Ohio traded for obsidian originating from the Glass Buttes located west of present-day Burns. The Northern Paiute frequented the area near present-day Drewsey for fishing, hunting, and foraging for various natural roots.

Fur trappers explored the area within Harney County in the early 1800s. The three wagon trains seeking a shorter route to the Willamette Valley also passed through the county—the Meek, Elliott, and Macy trains. Settlers began arriving in the early 1860s to establish cattle ranches.

In Present-Day Hood River County

Hood River County was established in 1908 from the northwestern portion of Wasco County. Hood River, platted in 1881, is the county seat.

Early History

Some Northern Molalla Indians roamed the southern portion of present-day Hood River County. The Wasco and Cascade Indians had lived along the Columbia River for at least 9000 years before Euro-Americans began arriving. They nourished themselves with the abundant natural resources available and traveled along the river in their dugout canoes to trade with neighboring tribes.

In 1805 the Lewis and Clark Corps of Discovery traveled

Sites to Visit in Harney County

Harney County Historical Museum
18 W D St, Burns
541·573·5618

Oard's Museum & Gift Shop
42456 Hwy 20E, near Burns
541·493·2535

through Hood River County, followed by fur traders. The mission established at The Dalles in Wasco County in 1838 used the Indian trails across the upper Hood River Valley to transport cattle and supplies from the home mission near Salem. The emigrants traveling the Oregon Trail were journeying by raft or in canoes on the Columbia River at this point, but teamsters herded the settlers' cattle single file along the shore.

By 1861 most of the Indian survivors of the epidemics that occurred during the years of exploration were removed to the Warm Springs Indian Reservation under the terms of the 1855 treaty, but a few like Indian George managed to remain and become a part of the newly developing community of settlers.

Hood River and Cascade Locks

Hood River (both the river and the future city) was called Dog River until 1858. The families of Nathan and James Benson, Nathaniel Coe, and William Jenkins became the first permanent settlers in 1854, all having been acquaintances in New York. The Benson brothers and Jenkins had enjoyed good fortune in the California gold fields.

In 1852 Dr. Freeman Farnsworth and M. C. Laughlin unsuccessfully attempted to fatten up a herd of oxen and cattle purchased from Oregon Trail emigrants. They both built

George Tomileck Chinidere, known as Indian George, was nearly 100 years old when he died in 1917. *Courtesy of the Hood River County Historical Museum, 54.016.*

The 1854 Nathaniel and Mary Coe home served as the community center, courthouse, precinct, church, and funeral parlor. *Courtesy of the Hood River County Historical Museum, 95.002.*

cabins for their families to live in, but when most of the herd died, they vacated the area. The Coes initially resided in the Laughlin's cabin and Jenkins moved his family into the Farnsworth cabin. After the Coes built a larger house in 1854, the Laughlin cabin was used as a storehouse on their farm. The Coes farmed, and the Jenkins and Bensons raised cattle and oxen.

The settlers befriended the Indians in the area, trading goods for deer and wild fowl and hiring them to work on their farms. In 1856 when several bands of Indians from the Washington Territory across the river attacked the emigrants at the portage around the Cascades west of Hood River, the local Indians prevented the hostile Indians from landing at the settlement. They also transported the Hood River families by canoe to The Dalles for safety. Once the Indian troubles subsided, the families were able to return to their homes. By the late 1850s, there had been peace in the area for several years and other families arrived, but substantive development of the city did not take place until after the railroad was completed through the Columbia Gorge in 1882.

A few families settled at the site of present-day Cascade Locks in 1853. They always were willing to assist the pioneers

Captain Nathaniel Coe
(1788–1868)

Born in New Jersey; served as captain in War of 1812 and in New York legislature

Arrived in Oregon in 1851; served as postal agent responsible for letting contracts for mail routes and establishing post offices throughout entire Oregon Territory; used steamer *Canemah* as his postal headquarters on Columbia and Willamette rivers; traveled on horseback when river travel unavailable

Postal agent appointment ended in 1853

Wife and children arrived by ship from New York to establish home in Hood River in 1854

First to plant fruit trees in Hood River Valley in 1855 obtained from Luelling brothers' stock in Milwaukie; also grew grain, hay, and vegetables

Married Mary T. White; six children, including Captain Lawrence W. Coe who was prominent in steamer industry—co-founder of Oregon Steam Navigation Company and builder of four ships

The Cascades of Columbia were the white-water rapids located on a section of the Columbia River opposite today's town of Cascade Locks. Until the locks were built in 1896, travelers had to disembark from their boats and make a rocky portage around the Cascades. (The Bonneville Lock and Dam, built in 1938, submerged all but the upper portion of the locks.) Courtesy of the Hood River County Historical Museum, 87.052.

traveling on the river make the portage around the cascades, first on foot, and from 1856 to 1862 assisted by mule-drawn rail cars that carried the freight. The first passenger car was added in 1859.

The Roger G. Attwell (or Atwill) family was one of the early families to settle in Cascade Locks. In 1852 Dr. Hiram A. Leavens began a medical practice with his wife, Pluma, as his office nurse, but they may have left by 1859.

In Present-Day Jefferson County

Sites to Visit in Jefferson County

Jefferson County Historical Society
& Museum
34 SE D St, Madras
541·475·3808

The Museum at Warm Springs
2186 Hwy 26, Warm Springs
541·553·3331

Jefferson County was created in 1914 from the northern portion of Crook County. Madras serves as the county seat.

With its remote location, fur trappers and explorers did not visit the area within present-day Jefferson County, nor did the Oregon Trail pass through there. Jefferson County was one of the last homesteading regions in the United States.

Warm Springs Indian Reservation
The Tygh and Tenino Indians residing within Jefferson County signed the 1855 Treaty of the Tribes of Middle Oregon and became part of the confederated bands of Indians

This view of Mount Hood, ca. 1875, is from the Columbia River in Hood River County, where the mountain is located. It could be viewed from many far away places, including the Warm Springs Indian Reservation. Courtesy of the Hood River County Historical Museum, 81.083.001.

removed to the Warm Springs Indian Reservation. The reservation was located in the southwestern portion of present-day Wasco County and the northwestern part of Jefferson County. The confederated bands included the Wascoes on the Columbia River and, after 1879, the Paiute living in the southern part of the county.

The Treaty of the Tribes of Middle Oregon ceded ten million acres of land south of the Columbia River lying between the Cascade and Blue Mountain ranges to the U.S. government. In exchange, the Warm Springs Indians received $150,000 to be paid over 20 years, and a pledge for the provision of facilities and services to help them adjust to reservation life. The treaty also reserved the right to hunt, fish, and gather food on traditional lands outside the reservation boundaries.

Colonel A. P. Dennison arrived in 1857 to assume his duties as the first Indian agent for the reservation. He chose to live in The Dalles in Wasco County, so Dr. Thomas Fitch, the physician assigned to the reservation, supervised the administrative personnel. The U.S. Senate did not ratify the Treaty of the Tribes of Middle Oregon until 1859, so the U.S. government did not immediately fulfill many of the terms of the treaty.

In the early years on the reservation, the Indians lived in traditional dwellings they built themselves. The government provided clothing, tools, livestock, and instruction on how to grow crops and raise the livestock. Information about their standard of living is limited, but during the spring of 1859 roaming Northern Paiute became envious enough of the resources available on the reservation that they repeatedly raided it, stealing horses and cattle. A small military force was dispatched and the raids soon ceased.

In 1862 then Indian Agent William Logan reported on the status of the buildings that the U.S. government was required to build under the terms of the treaty. A saw and flour mill, one wagon and plough maker's shop, one blacksmith shop, one unfinished schoolhouse, and one unfinished hospital were noted.

Warm Springs Indian woman and traditional lodge of vertical poles. Courtesy of the Oregon Historical Society, Lot 467-29.

In Present-Day Klamath County

Klamath County was created in 1882 from the western part of Lake County. Klamath Falls is the county seat.

Early History

The Klamath, Modoc, and eastern Shasta Indians had lived within the area of present-day Klamath County for centuries prior to the arrival of Euro-Americans. Klamath congregated at the north end of Upper Klamath Lake and traveled the Klamath Trail along the Cascade Range to trade with the Molalla and Kalapuya Indians in the Willamette Valley.

An array of HBC trappers visited Klamath County, with Finan McDonald, Thomas McKay, and Peter Skene Ogden being the first in 1825. John C. Frémont and the other members of his mapping expeditions passed through the county in 1843 and 1846. In 1846 the Applegate Trail was blazed through the lower portion of the county, bringing many settlers through on their way to the Willamette Valley.

Most historians credit gold prospector John W. Hillman with the discovery of Crater Lake when he happened on it in 1853. No other Euro-Americans visited the lake until 1862.

The Indians of this region did not sign a treaty, cede property, or move onto a reservation until 1864. Their subsequent history includes a war in the 1870s, the termination of the tribe and closure of their reservation by the U.S. Congress in 1961, and, finally in 1986, the resumption of federal recognition of the Klamath Tribes.

Present-day Klamath Falls had at least one known settler before 1860; Wendolen Nus reportedly built a cabin on the west shore of Klamath Lake in 1858. Others did not arrive for another several years.

In Present-Day Lake County

In 1874 Lake County was established from the southern part of Wasco County and the eastern part of Jackson County.

Its boundary lines changed in 1882 and 1885. Lakeview is the county seat.

Early History

The Northern Paiute and some Modoc Indians lived in the area of present-day Lake County for centuries. Ancient Indian sandals over 10,000 years old were discovered in a cave near Fort Rock in the northern part of the county, and evidence of prehistoric life in caves and ancient petroglyphs exist near present-day Paisley. Later generations of Indians camped near Paisley when hunting and foraging. Near the town of present-day New Pine Creek, the Indians gathered and dried the rare native wild plum.

HBC trappers traveled through Lake County in 1832, as did the John C. Frémont party in 1843. The earliest settlement was in Lakeview in 1873.

In Present-Day Malheur County

Malheur County was created in 1887 from the southern portion of Baker County. The county seat is Vale.

Northern Paiute Indians lived within Malheur County for centuries. They migrated between the low lands and the mountains with the seasonal changes.

In 1811 the passage of the Wilson Price Hunt Expedition through Malheur County near present-day Vale marked the first time Euro-Americans set foot in the area. A few of the group returned several years later to trap beaver, and other trappers combed the areas of both Vale and Nyssa. Peter Skene Ogden of the HBC passed through in 1825 and 1826 while exploring the Snake River country.

The Oregon Trail entered Oregon at the Snake River Crossing near Nyssa—a risky undertaking—or forded the river at Fort Boise south of Nyssa. Several different paths fanned out across the valley in a northwesterly direction, heading over the steep Keeney Pass and crossing the Malheur River near Vale. The lack of safe drinking water for long stretches made this part of the Oregon Trail challenging. The hot springs located along the Malheur River at

Sites to Visit in Lake County

Lake County Museum
118 S E St, Lakeview
541·947·2220

Schminck Memorial Museum
128 S E St, Lakeview
541·947·3134

Sites to Visit in Malheur County

Four Rivers Cultural Center
676 SW 5th Ave, Ontario
541·889·8191

Oregon State Visitor Center
Off I-84 south of Exit 376, Ontario

Rhinehart Stone House Museum
255 Main St S, Vale
541·473·2070

Oregon Trail Agricultural Museum
117 Good Ave, Nyssa

An emigrant camp on the Oregon Trail. Lithograph by H. Wilcox and S. Sartain. Courtesy of the Oregon Historical Society, OrHi 5231.

Vale were popular for bathing, washing clothes, and steam-cooking fresh salmon caught from the river.

Ranchers and stockmen crowded out of the Willamette Valley were the first to settle in the county in the early 1860s. Miners soon followed after Michael M. Jordan discovered gold on creek banks in the Jordan Valley in 1863.

In Present-Day Morrow County

Sites to Visit in Morrow County

Agricultural Equipment Museum
Hwy 207 & Riverside, Heppner
541·676·5524

Columbia River Heritage Trail
Boardman Marina Park
Exit 164 off I-84, north on Main St,
   left on Marine Dr

Morrow County Museum
444 N Main St, Heppner
541·676·5524

Morrow County was created in 1885 from the western portion of Umatilla County. Heppner is the county seat.

The Umatilla and Cayuse Indians had lived within present-day Morrow County for thousands of years. The Umatilla lived in villages near the Columbia River and the Cayuse lived along the many creeks in the eastern portion of the county. Both groups partook of the abundance of fish, game, and berries available. The Cayuse were especially skilled horsemen, having acquired horses in the early 1730s.

Lewis and Clark were the first Euro-Americans to set foot in Morrow County when they camped between today's Irrigon and Boardman. The Oregon Trail passed through the northern edge of the county, with a camping stop at Wells Springs.

Stockmen were the first to begin settling in the county. George Vinson possibly was the first in 1852, filing a claim on Little Butter Creek. A number of families settled along Willow Creek near its junction with Rhea Creek, and in 1859 John Jordan built a log cabin near present-day Ione.

The Indians in this region signed the Cayuse, Umatilla, and Walla Walla Treaty in 1855 creating the Umatilla Indian Reservation and were removed there in 1861.

In Present-Day Sherman County

Sherman County was created in 1889 out of what was, by then, the northeast corner of the pared-down Wasco County. Although Wasco was originally designated the county seat, Moro is the county seat today.

For centuries, the Tenino Indians had lived and traded along the three rivers that border present-day Sherman County—the Columbia, John Day, and Deschutes rivers. They were ultimately relocated to the Warm Springs Indian Reservation.

With its northern border running along the Columbia River, Sherman County had explorers, trappers, and missionaries passing through—Lewis and Clark, the Wilson Price Hunt Expedition, including John Day; Nathanial J. Wyeth, John C. Frémont, and Methodist missionaries Jason and Daniel Lee. The Oregon Trail crossed the region from the John Day River crossing to the crossing at the mouth of the Deschutes River. Some settlers planning to travel the Barlow Road took a cut-off west of the John Day River heading southwesterly along Grass Valley Canyon to a dangerous crossing of the Deschutes River. In 1853 a ferry crossing at the mouth of the Deschutes was established.

A few stockmen began grazing their herds on the bunch-grass hills of Sherman County in 1858. That same year, William Graham, his wife, and seven children opened a hotel, likely in their home, at the Deschutes River crossing.

Sites to Visit in Sherman County

Sherman County Historical
  Museum
200 Dewey St, Moro
541·565·3232

In Present-Day Umatilla County

Umatilla County was created in 1862 from a portion of Wasco County. Although Umatilla City originally served as the county seat, an election in 1868 moved it to Pendleton.

Early History

For thousands of years, the Cayuse and Umatilla Indians had fished and traded along the Columbia and Umatilla rivers in present-day Umatilla County. The Walla Walla Indians fished and traded along the Walla Walla River. All three tribes hunted in the Blue Mountains. Some had permanent villages on the Columbia River, but others moved seasonally. The vicinity of Echo was the site of a seasonal camp and was criss-crossed by trails. The Walla Walla Valley also was a popular gathering place. The acquisition of horses in the 1730s and guns in the early 1800s added new dimensions to the culture of the Indians in the region and allowed them a new means of security.

Lewis and Clark visited the future site of Umatilla County in 1805; and explorer and fur trader Wilson Price Hunt followed in 1811. The HBC trapped and traded in the northern region of Umatilla County west of Milton Freewater from 1821 to 1846, and operated a farm there. A Roman Catholic mission was established in 1847 near present-day Pendleton, but it was abandoned soon thereafter. The Indians' numbers were greatly reduced by the Cayuse War and from exposure to Euro-American diseases.

Two favored stops along the Oregon Trail were located in Umatilla County. Near the summit of the Blue Mountains, wagon trains camped for several days and replenished their water barrels from a spring located in the vicinity of today's Emigrant Springs State Heritage Area. The pioneers crossed the Umatilla River at present-day Echo and camped at a site known as the Lower Crossing. They were able to graze and water their animals and do their laundry there before heading due west toward Wells Springs in present-day Morrow County. (Pendleton was the site of the Upper Crossing.)

In 1851 the Utilla Indian Agency and Trading Post was

Descent of the western side of the Blue Mountains along the Oregon Trail, ca. 1849.
Courtesy of the Oregon Historical Society, OrHi 35575.

Traditional Indian family dwelling.
Courtesy of the Oregon Historical
Society, OrHi 4466.

constructed on the Umatilla River across from Echo and included eastern Oregon's first post office. The structure burned during the 1855 Yakima Indian War and was replaced by Fort Henrietta, a temporary military stockade. A battle was never fought at the fort, but it served as a major supply and relay point between Fort Dalles and military camps in the field. Today a replica of the blockhouse and interpretive panels are located in Fort Henrietta Park in Echo.

In 1855 the Cayuse, Umatilla, and Walla Walla Indians ceded to the United States more than 6.4 million acres in what is now northeastern Oregon and southeastern Washington. They reserved rights for fishing, hunting, and gathering foods and retained acreage for establishment of the Umatilla Indian Reservation. Conflict—primarily in the Washington Territory with the outbreak of the Yakima Indian War in 1855—continued until 1858 and the U.S. Senate did not ratify the treaty until 1859. Consequently, it was 1861 before the reservation was occupied. Located east of Pendleton, the reservation today has gradually been reduced from the original 510,000 acres to approximately 172,000 acres because settlers during the 19th century continued to desire the prime wheat-producing lands and access to the mountains ideal for grazing livestock. Legislation enacted in the late 1800s by the U.S. Congress sanctioned the reduction.

Beginning about 1860 Echo was one of the first areas to be settled by emigrants deciding to cut short their westward journey. Even though settlement was not allowed east of the Cascade Range until 1860, a few families nevertheless settled in the Walla Walla Valley near present-day Milton Freewater in the 1850s.

In Present-Day Union County

Union County was created from Baker County in 1864. The county seat moved between Union and La Grande until it became permanently located at La Grande in 1905.

For over 7000 years, the Nez Perce, Cayuse, and Umatilla Indians had lived within present-day Union County. In the Grande Ronde Valley they gathered camas roots and berries, grazed their horses and cattle, and fished the streams. Herds of elk, deer, antelope, and bighorn sheep were hunted in the meadows and mountains. They smoked and dried the surplus of their harvest for winter use. Every fall, before leaving to winter along the Columbia plateau, the Indians set fires in the valleys to encourage new growth in the spring.

The Grande Ronde Valley served as a trading center for local tribes and for tribes from the West Coast to the Great Plains. When wagon trains began crossing through the val-

Grande Ronde Valley sketch of wagon trains coming down a hill.
Courtesy of the Oregon Historical Society, OrHi 35853.

ley, the Indians traded their food for the pioneers' manufactured goods.

In the winter of 1811–12, the Wilson Price Hunt Expedition rested at the hot springs now known as Hot Lake Springs near present-day La Grande. Other explorers, trappers, and missionaries soon followed. The Oregon Trail pioneers passed through the Powder River and Grande Ronde valleys. The lush surroundings were a welcome relief after several months of hot, dusty travel. The steep slopes of the Blue Mountains lay ahead, however—often called the most difficult part of the two thousand-mile journey west to the Willamette Valley.

Farmers, many from the Willamette Valley, began settling in the Grande Ronde Valley in the early 1860s.

In Present-Day Wallowa County

Wallowa County was established in 1887 from the eastern portion of Union County. The county seat is Enterprise.

Early History

For thousands of years the Wallowa band of the Nez Perce lived in today's Wallowa County, moving seasonally between the Snake River canyons and tributaries in the winter months, to the mountains and headwaters in the summer seeking fish, game, and wild plants. The Hells Canyon area was especially popular for its milder winters and abundant natural resources. The Nez Perce of this region traveled on the Snake and Columbia rivers to trade with other tribes, and after acquiring horses they traveled throughout a larger area considered Nez Perce territory in the present-day states of Idaho and Washington, and also hunted bison in the Great Plains.

Captain B. L. E. Bonneville may have passed through the Wallowa Valley in the early 1800s; fur trappers followed him. However, the first permanent settlers did not arrive in the valley until the 1870s.

In 1855 Old Chief Joseph of the Wallowa Valley was one of the signers of the Nez Perce Treaty of 1855 at Walla Walla.

Sites to Visit in Wallowa County

Nez Perce Historic Site-Old Chief
  Joseph Monument
North end of Wallowa Lake near
  Joseph

Wallowa Band Nez Perce Trail
  Interpretive Center
209 East 2nd St, Wallowa
541·886·3101

Wallowa County Museum
110 S Main St, Joseph
541·432·6095

Wallowa History Center
204 E 1st St, Wallowa
541·886·9695

Young Chief Joseph, nationally recognized for leading the heroic retreat of the Nez Perce in 1877. Courtesy of the Oregon Historical Society, OrHi 5172.

Young Chief Joseph (ca. 1840–1904)

Born in Wallowa Valley as Hin-mah-too-yah-lat-kekt (Thunder Rolling down the Mountain)

Son of Wallowa Nez Perce chief named Tu-eka-kas, who converted to Christianity in 1839 and received name of Joseph at his baptism—commonly known as Old Chief Joseph

Became chief of Wallowa band upon his father's death in 1871; continued policy of peacefully defying 1863 treaty requiring Wallowa Valley Nez Perce to remove to reservation in Idaho

Finally agreed to move to Idaho in 1877, recognizing his warriors were outnumbered by the U.S. military

Fled with his band to Montana, though he may have opposed the decision, following insurgency and killing of settlers by members of his band

Surrendered in October 1877 at what came to be known as the Bear Paw Battlefield of the Nez Perce War, 40 miles from Canadian border

Forced to move with the few other survivors of his band to reservation in present-day Oklahoma, where many died of disease

Removed to Colville Reservation in Washington in 1885 where he spent rest of his life trying to regain beloved Wallowa homeland for his people

Arrival of the Nez Perce at the 1855 Walla Walla Treaty Council, by Gustavus Sohon.
Courtesy of Special Collections, Washington State Historical Society, 1918.114.9.36.

The treaty ceded lands in the Oregon and Washington territories in exchange for a $200,000 payment over 20 years and the standard pledge of facilities and services for a Nez Perce reservation that was to be established on land extending from the Wallowa Valley into Washington and Idaho. The treaty was not ratified until 1859 and the first annuity payment was not made until 1861. The discovery of gold on a portion of the Nez Perce reservation in southern Idaho in

1860 prompted the U.S. government to negotiate new treaties. Although the Wallowa band never signed the new documents, the Wallowa Valley was taken from them.

The Wallowa Valley remains a significant cultural center for the Nez Perce, Umatilla, and Cayuse Indians. The Nez Perce National Historical Park has visitor centers in Idaho and Montana. A map retracing the 1170-mile Nez Perce Trail, which begins near Wallowa Lake, is available at the Wallowa Band Nez Perce Trail Interpretive Center in Wallowa. A monument to Old Chief Joseph rests at the north end of the lake at a site that is part of the Nez Perce National Historical Park. A movie—*I Will Fight No More Forever*—and several books also recount the Nez Perce story.

In Present-Day Wheeler County

Wheeler County was established in 1899 from parts of Grant, Gilliam, and Crook counties. The county seat is located in Fossil. The Northern Paiute Indians frequented this region. In 1862 a Mr. Biffel became the first Euro-American to settle in the county near the present-day hamlet of Twickenham.

Sites to Visit in Wheeler County

Fossil Museum
IOOF Building on First St, Fossil

Spray Pioneer Museum
402 Willow St, Spray
541·468·2069

Sampling of Wasco County Family Surnames in 1859

Wasco County

Bolton	Denton	Henderson	Laughlin	Menefee	Snipes
Coe	Fulton	Humason	Marsh	Mosier	Todd
Crate	Gates	Jordan	McCormick	Scholl	Trevitt

Gilliam County

Scott

Hood River County

Attwell	Ayres	Benson	Coe	Jenkins

Sherman County

Graham

Umatilla County

Arnold	Bradburn	McCoy

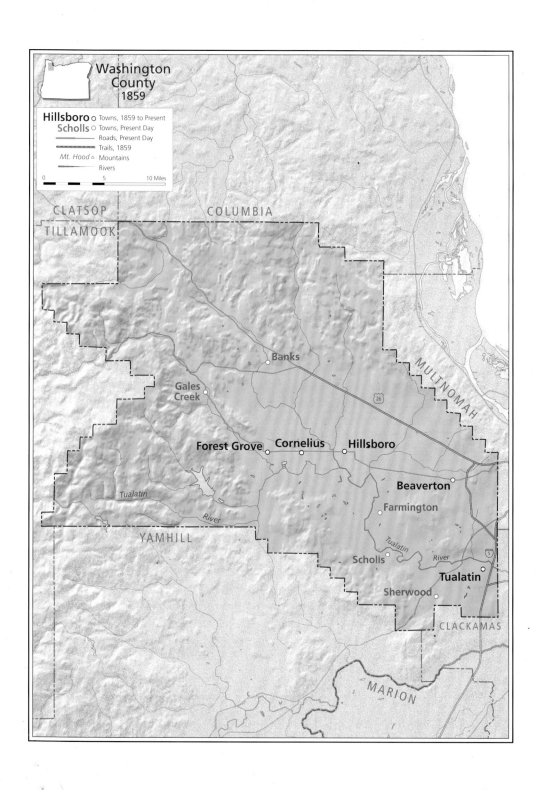

CLATSOP

COLUMBIA

TILLAMOOK

MULTNOMAH

Banks

Gales
Creek

26

Forest Grove   Cornelius   Hillsboro

Beaverton

Tualatin

Farmington

River

Tualatin

Scholls

River

5

YAMHILL

Tualatin

Sherwood

CLACKAMAS

MARION

18 1859 WASHINGTON COUNTY

In 1843 Tuality District was created as one of the four original counties. Its boundaries were changed in 1844 and 1854, "district" was changed to "county" in 1845, and in 1849 Tuality was changed to Washington. Columbia, later known as Hillsborough and Hillsboro today, became the county seat in 1850. A permanent county headquarters building was constructed in 1852, but a courthouse was not built until 1873. According to the 1860 U.S. Census, the county population was 2801.

In the early days, Washington County farmers had to travel primitive wagon roads to transport their wheat and other farm and wood products to the ports along the Willamette and Columbia rivers. In 1849 Canyon Road was constructed between Beaverton and Portland, and in 1855 the territorial legislature appropriated funds to improve another road that passed by way of the Tualatin Plains later known as the Astoria-Salem Military Road.

At different times, there were a number of ferries that crossed the Tualatin River, including those operated by Philip Harris and Peter B. Scholl in the present-day Farmington area and Samuel Galbreath's in present-day Tualatin. In 1850 Zenas J. Brown located his ferry just upriver from where today's Brown's Ferry Park is located in Tualatin. A financial setback and a false accusation led Brown and his wife to leave Oregon in 1856. In 1854 John A. Taylor built a ferry upriver from Tualatin, which his wife, Sarah, and her brother Isaac McKenzie operated while Taylor constructed Taylors Ferry Road to Portland. The road eventually connected Portland to Dayton in Yamhill County.

During the rainy season, the farmers transported their products to Oregon City and Portland by boat—actually mere rafts which they guided down the Tualatin River using long poles. Numerous bends, debris, and shallow portions of the river made this an arduous trip requiring several portages. In 1858 the territorial legislature chartered the Tualatin River Transportation and Navigation Company to dredge and straighten the river downstream from Tualatin. A small steamer, the *Hoosier*, was enlisted to transport goods to a portage point farther down the river for delivery to Linn City. However, the following year the service was terminated for lack of federal funding to maintain clearance on the river. Steam navigation did not resume on the Tualatin until 1865.

Sites to Visit in Washington County

Fanno Farmhouse, ca. 1857
8405 SW Creekside Pl, Beaverton
503·629·6355

Luster House, ca. 1857 (private
  residence)
9030 SW Sagert St, Tualatin

The New Tualatin Heritage Center
8700 SW Sweek Dr, Tualatin
503·885·1926

Pacific University Museum
Old College Hall, ca. 1851
2043 College Way, Forest Grove
503·352·6151

Sherwood Heritage Center &
  Museum
90 NW Park St, Sherwood
503·625·1236

Sweek House, ca. 1858 (private
  residence)
18815 SW Boones Ferry Rd,
  Tualatin

Washington County Historical
  Museum
Rock Creek Campus of Portland
  Community College
17677 NW Springville Rd, Portland
503·645·5353

West Union Baptist Church, ca.
  1850s (private church)
NW West Union Rd & NW Dick Rd,
  West Union (Hillsboro)

Canyon Road, also known as the Great Plank Road, was improved several times
between 1849 and 1860. Courtesy of the Oregon Historical Society, CN 018904.

Early History

For centuries the Tualatin band of the Kalapuya had lived within present-day Washington County. They lived much like the Kalapuya of the Willamette Valley, except they lacked immediate access to salmon and tended only to hunt game when their plant harvests ran low. They established permanent winter villages around Wappato Lake (a lake located in present-day Gaston until it was drained in 1880) and in the vicinity of the present-day communities of Forest Grove, Banks, Hillsboro, Cedar Mill, Beaverton, and Sherwood. The remainder of the year the Tualatin roamed from the Willamette River to the foothills of the Coast Range and from Sherwood to the Columbia River to harvest food for the following winter.

The Tualatin population declined significantly from exposure to disease from fur traders and explorers in the late 18th and early 19th centuries. By the time the first settlers arrived in the late 1830s, the survivors were concentrated around Wappato Lake, where the wapato was readily available.

In the 1820s the Hudson's Bay Company (HBC) fur traders trapped beaver in the Tualatin Valley. Washington County's earliest settlers were American fur trappers from the Rocky Mountains who arrived with their Indian wives and children after the fur trade dwindled. A few missionaries arrived in the late 1840s. The Tualatin Indians were removed to the Grand Ronde Reservation in 1856.

Hillsboro, Cornelius, Forest Grove, Gales Creek, and Banks

During the 1840s families began arriving in Hillsboro—the entire area originally called East Tualatin Plains. By 1850 there were enough residents to warrant the establishment of a post office on David Hill's land claim, which he named Columbia. Most of the early settlers established farms or were working in the developing lumber industry.

In the early 1850s the West Union Baptist Church was built on property donated by David T. Lenox. It is the oldest Baptist church building west of the Rocky Mountains

Joseph Lafayette Meek
(1810–1875)

Born in Virginia; fur trader and one of the Mountain Men during 1830s

Brought Indian wife and his children to Oregon in 1840; took land claim in Hillsboro

Elected first sheriff of Oregon Territory at Champoeg meeting in 1843

Helped form Tuality District government and served as U.S. marshal and provisional legislator

As U.S. marshal, in 1850 at Oregon City, hanged the five Indians accused of Whitman Massacre

Built first frame house in Tuality District in 1845 and became prosperous farmer

Married three times, each time to Indian women; six children

Subject of several biographies, including *River of the West* by F. F. Victor

Joseph L. Meek—trapper, one of the Mountain Men, and first elected sheriff of the Oregon Territory. Courtesy of the Washington County Historical Society, Portland, OR.

Colonel Thomas R. Cornelius (1827–1899)

Born in Missouri; arrived in Oregon in 1845 with his parents Benjamin and Elizabeth; established farm on his own donation land claim

Successfully mined for gold in California in 1848

Served in Cayuse War in 1848 and Yakima Indian War in 1855

Served in state legislature for 20 years and unsuccessfully ran for governor in 1886

Moved into town named for him in early 1870s in anticipation of arrival of railroad; owned general store, sawmill, and warehouse, while continuing his farming operations

Married Florentine Wilkes; six children; second marriage to Missouri Smith in 1866

Tabitha Moffatt Brown was honored by the 1987 Oregon State Legislature as the "Mother of Oregon" for the way in which she "represents the distinctive pioneer heritage and the charitable and compassionate nature of Oregon's people." She died in 1858. Courtesy of Pacific University.

and one of the oldest Protestant churches still standing in Oregon.

The area of present-day Cornelius west of Hillsboro was known as Free Orchards in 1859, likely inspired by the fruit orchards spread across most of Benjamin Q. Tucker's donation land claim. Tucker arrived in Oregon in 1844, and a small community of farmers soon developed, including Solomon Emerick and the extended Cornelius family.

Settlement in the Forest Grove area began in the 1840s. Originally known as West Tualatin Plains, the community developed around the Tualatin Academy, founded in 1848 by Reverend Harvey Clark, Reverend George H. Atkinson, and Tabitha Brown. The academy began as a school for Indian children established in 1842 by Reverend Clark and his wife. In 1848 the Clarks and Tabitha Brown, out of concern for the many children orphaned while traveling the Oregon Trail, opened an orphanage in the Congregational Church's log cabin. Later that year, Clark and Atkinson, who had been commissioned by the Home Missionary Society of the Congregational Church Association to found an academy, made the necessary arrangements to have the school chartered. In 1854 a new college charter was granted and the name changed to Tualatin Academy and Pacific University, making it Oregon's second oldest college.

Reverend John S. Griffin started the First Congregational Church of Oregon in 1842 in Hillsboro, but in 1845 Reverend Clark replaced him and the church was moved to Forest Grove.

A few pioneers settled in the Gales Creek and Banks area in the 1830s and '40s, including Joseph Gale and Emanuel Horner near Gales Creek, and William Mills and Peyton Wilkes where Banks later grew. Gale and others had driven hundreds of horses and mules into the Willamette Valley from California in 1843. Gale established the first gristmill and sawmill in the county, but moved to California during the gold rush, later returning to the Northwest—eventually to Baker County.

The farmers raised wheat and oats, which, by 1859, they were transporting to markets in Portland and the Willa-

In 1851 Tualatin Academy's classes moved from the Congregational Church's log cabin into this new building, Old College Hall, which remains standing today. Sidney Harper Marsh served as the first president from 1854 to 1879. Courtesy of Pacific University.

mette Valley. Hogs left behind by the HBC were bred for local consumption and market.

Cedar Mill, Beaverton, Farmington, Scholls, Tualatin, and Sherwood

In 1847 Samuel Walters was among the first to settle in Cedar Mill. The densely forested land made it difficult to clear areas for growing wheat and other crops, but the early pioneers persisted. The vast stands of timber in the area prompted John H. Jones to vacate his claim in Columbia County, where he had been working at a sawmill. In 1855 he and his father Justus established a small mill on Cedar Mill Creek.

In 1846 settlers began arriving in the area of Beaverton, originally known as Beaverdam. Lawrence Hall and his brother built a gristmill, and Thomas H. Denney and James McKay built a sawmill on Fanno Creek. Both mills contributed to the early growth of a sizeable farming community. In the early 1850s a group of settlers from Indiana arrived, including the families of Miles Davies, William Robinson, Thomas Stott, and Henry B. Tucker.

Augustus Fanno (1804–?)

Born in Maine; worked as seaman, teacher in Mississippi and subsequently Missouri

Arrived in Oregon in 1846 with pregnant wife and one child; helped build rafts at The Dalles for the transport of settlers' wagons

Settled at Linn City, but following death of his wife and second child during childbirth, took claim on Fanno Creek at Beaverton in 1847

Developed an onion that thrived in Oregon climate

Formed business partnership with sons Augustus J. and Alonzo R.; company became largest onion producer in Oregon in late 1890s

Married Martha Ferguson; one child; 1851 married Rebecca Jane Denney; six children

(The 1857 Augustus Fanno Farmhouse was restored by the Tualatin Hills Park and Recreation District.)

A small community later known as Farmington developed southwest of Beaverton. Philip and Sarah Harris, H. H. Hendrix, and George W. Richardson were among the early arrivals in the 1840s. In 1847 Peter B. Scholl, a relative of Daniel Boone, settled south of Farmington, where he later founded the town of Scholls.

Between 1850 and 1853, more than 25 families settled southeast of Scholls where Tualatin is located today. Samuel Galbreath called the landing where he operated his ferry service Galbreath, but when the citizens built a bridge across the river in 1856, the community became known as Bridgeport. The town's name was changed to Tualatin in the late 1880s. By 1859 there were a number of businesses established to serve passersby and the residents, mostly farmers. Many of the settlers held other jobs in Portland or neighboring communities.

In 1855 John Hedges and John A. Taylor built Tualatin's first school on John and Catherine Hedges' property. Isaac Ball served as the first school teacher and later the school clerk, county commissioner, and justice of the peace. Dr. Nathaniel Robbins was the community's physician.

John Sweek helped establish Tualatin's first schools and worked on the construction of Boones Ferry Road into Portland. Courtesy of the Tualatin Historical Society.

Maria Sweek expanded the log cabin she and John built in 1852 while he was in Idaho during the 1860s gold rush operating a freighting business. The southern colonial style house remains as a private residence today. Courtesy of the Tualatin Historical Society.

Settlement and farming began in the area of Sherwood in 1853. Most of the families there were southerners, as evidenced by the colonial-style homes they built in later years. Early pioneers such as the Hall and Zimmerman families became self-sufficient and would travel to Portland but twice a year to purchase staples.

Sampling of Washington County Family Surnames in 1859

Allen	Cummins	Graham	Hornbuckle	Meek	Scholl	Tucker
Anderson	Davies	Greenwood	Jones	Merrill	Scott	Walker
Arnspiger	Day	Griffin	Kellogg	Mills	Shaver	Wall
Ball	Dean	Hall	Kindt	Painter	Smith	Walters
Barr	Denny	Hare	Lenox	Porter	Stott	Welch
Brown	Eells	Harris	Lousignont	Reed	Sweek	Wilcox
Buxton	Emerick	Hedges	Lyman	Richardson	Taylor	Wilkes
Byrom	Fanno	Henderson	Marsh	Roberts	Tongue	Williams
Clark	Flippin	Hendrix	McKay	Robbins	Trullinger	Zimmerman
Clemmens	Fryer	Hicklin	McKenzie	Robinson		
Cornelius	Galbreath	Hill				

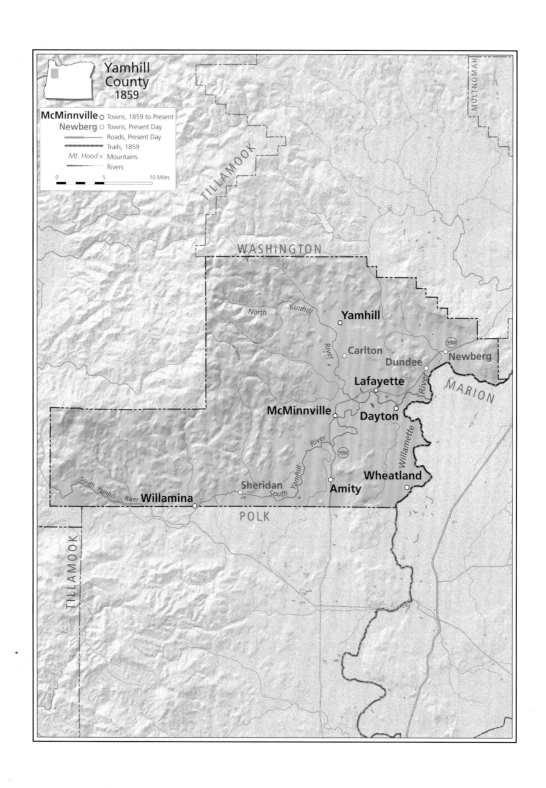

Yamhill
County
1859

McMinnville ○ Towns, 1859 to Present
Newberg ○ Towns, Present Day
━━━ Roads, Present Day
━━━ Trails, 1859
Mt. Hood △ Mountains
━━━ Rivers

0   5   10 Miles

MULTNOMAH

TILLAMOOK

WASHINGTON

North   Yamhill

Yamhill

River

Carlton

Dundee   99W

Newberg

Lafayette

MARION

McMinnville

Dayton

River

99W

Wheatland

Willamette

South Yamhill   River

Sheridan

South

Amity

Willamina

Yamhill   River

POLK

TILLAMOOK

19 1859 YAMHILL COUNTY

Yamhill was one of the four original districts created by the provisional legislature in 1843 and included a much larger area until its boundaries were changed several times during the creation of a dozen new counties. Lafayette became the county seat in 1847 and continued as such until the voters elected to move the seat to McMinnville in 1886. The first courthouse in Lafayette was located in a former store purchased by the county in 1850, but when it was destroyed by fire in 1857, a new brick courthouse was built the following year. According to the 1860 U.S. Census, the county population was 3245.

Yamhill County had two well-traveled roads by 1859. One was the previous Indian trail that paralleled today's Baker Street in McMinnville, and the other was a wagon road connecting the county seat of Lafayette to Dayton and Newberg. In 1851 a bridge had been built across the Yamhill River in Lafayette, with funds partially raised by subscription from local residents. Floods later destroyed the bridge, but C. B. Hawley built another one in 1857 for the county. Ferries also operated across the river.

Around 1851 the first steam-propelled boat began operating between Lafayette and Canemah in Clackamas County by way of the Yamhill and Willamette rivers. In 1859 the *Hoosier*, which had the short run on the Tualatin River the previous year, began making tri-weekly trips from the Willamette up the Yamhill River to Dayton. The Yamhill Steamboat Company was organized that year to transport farm products to Portland and California. The steamers made stops at Dayton and McMinnville—when the waters were high enough.

Early History

The Yamhill band of the Kalapuya Indians had lived along the Yamhill River in present-day Yamhill County for thousands of years. Their culture, lifeways, and fate were similar to those of the other Kalapuya in the Willamette Valley.

Fur company employees were the first Euro-Americans to arrive in Yamhill County in 1814. A flood of settlers arrived in the 1840s and '50s. The *Dictionary of Oregon History*, edited by Howard McKinley Corning, notes that "Yamhill, Mother of Oregon" was a term applied because so many Oregon

Trail emigrants of 1843 and 1844 settled in the Yamhill Valley. The valley soon became the agricultural center of the entire Willamette Valley.

Lafayette, Dayton, and McMinnville

Joel Perkins founded the town of Lafayette in 1846 on the main Indian trail that traversed the Willamette Valley. Sometimes referred to as Falls of Yamhill River or Yamhill Falls because of its location, Lafayette was the site of several firsts, including Oregon's first circuit court session in 1847, the first U.S. court session held in the Pacific Northwest in 1849, and Oregon's first county fair in 1854.

After the discovery of gold in California and southern Oregon, the town became the principal trading center of the western Willamette Valley. Farmers brought their produce to Lafayette to sell or trade to the many wholesalers in the business of shipping supplies to the miners by pack train. Perkins himself made several trips to California, and unfortunately was murdered in 1856 while returning home.

Lafayette also provided goods and services to the departing or returning miners. Many of them chose the town as the place to raise their families. The Methodists built a church and shared it with other denominations.

Joel Palmer and Andrew Smith laid out the town of Dayton in 1849 on half of each of their claims, and donated a portion to the city, which today is known as Courthouse Square Park. The relocated 1856 Fort Yamhill blockhouse dedicated to Palmer is located in this park.

Palmer sold his first house to J. B. Jacobs in 1852, who promptly enlarged it and opened Dayton's first hotel. Palmer established a sawmill on Palmer Creek behind his second residence completed in 1860. This structure, significantly renovated, remains today as a restaurant. The sawmill burned sometime around 1860.

West of Dayton, John G. Baker, Samuel Cozine, and William T. Newby were the first to settle near McMinnville—all three arriving in Oregon in 1843. In the early 1850s Newby built a gristmill and in 1856 he platted the city, which was becoming a prosperous farming community.

General Joel Palmer
(1810–1881)

Born in Ontario, Canada, of American parents; raised in New York; worked in Pennsylvania and Indiana

On trip to Oregon in 1845, helped Barlow's party blaze trail around Mount Hood and locate Barlow Pass for establishment of alternate Barlow Road route to Willamette Valley

Moved his family to Oregon in 1847

Published his 1845 *Journal of Travels Over the Rocky Mountains* in 1847, which served as guide for others who followed

Served in Cayuse War and as peace emissary

Ventured to California gold rush in 1848 before settling in Dayton

Served as superintendent of Indian affairs from 1853 to 1857, receiving criticism for his humanitarian attitude toward Indians

Involved in several business enterprises

Served in both houses of state legislature; lost election for governor in 1870; served as Indian agent at Siletz Agency in 1871

Married Sarah Ann Derbyshire; eight children

Abigail Jane Scott Duniway
(1834–1915)

Born in Illinois; arrived in Lafayette in 1852 with father and siblings; her mother and one brother died on Oregon Trail

Taught school in Eola in Polk County until marrying Benjamin C. Duniway in 1853 and settling on their claim in Lafayette

Wrote *Captain Gray's Company or Crossing the Plains and Living in Oregon* in 1859—first novel to be commercially published in Oregon

Assumed financial and family responsibilities (five sons) following husband's crippling accident in 1862 and loss of the family farm

Taught school, ran boardinghouse, and operated hat shop in Albany

Moved to Portland in 1871

Became nationally-known women's suffrage advocate and editor and publisher of *New Northwest*, a weekly newspaper

Wrote novels published in *New Northwest* and several other books—fiction, her autobiography, and poetry

General Joel Palmer, the Superintendent of Indian affairs, with the difficult task of negotiating nine cessation treaties with Oregon's Indians. Courtesy of the Oregon Historical Society, OrHi 362.

Abigail Scott Duniway in 1871 when she was editor of *New Northwest*. Image courtesy of Special Collections and University Archives, University of Oregon libraries.

Sebastian Cabot Adams
(1825–1898)

Born in Ohio; raised and educated in Illinois

Settled in Carlton in 1850, but under terms of agreement reached with W. T. Newby, moved to McMinnville in 1855 to build houses

Founded and taught at Christian day school, which later became Linfield College

Served as county clerk and state senator

Moved to Salem in 1869 where he served as minister of Christian Church and organized Unitarian church

Wrote *A Chronological Chart of Ancient, Modern and Biblical History* in 1871, which included a 21-panel fold-out chart, and engaged in a successful book tour for six years. (The book sells for up to $2000 today.)

Married three times, became widower twice, and predeceased third wife; four children by first wife, Martha E. McBride

John Gordon Baker house built by him in 1852.
Courtesy of the Oregon Historical Society, OrHi 50507.

Sebastian C. Adams built this house on Baker Street in 1858. The decorative features were added some years later by Ben Hartman. Courtesy of the Oregon Historical Society, OrHi 50504.

Accounts differ about the founding of what eventually became today's Linfield College, but it appears that the Christian Church (Disciples of Christ) established the original school in the late 1840s. Bankruptcy led to the school being deeded to the Baptists around 1849. In 1856 Sebastian C. Adams took charge and a four-room schoolhouse was built on land donated by William and Sarah Newby. In 1858 the school was chartered as the Baptist College in

McMinnville. The name was later changed to McMinnville College and, finally, Linfield College in 1922.

Dundee and Newberg

A number of families, including the Heaters and the extended Shuck family, settled the Chehalem Valley where Dundee is located today. Farmers grew wheat or grazed sheep on the Red Hills in Dundee. John G. Thompson and Peter M. Coffin were among the sheep farmers, raising valuable breeding stock. Seawood Fulquartz settled along the west side of the Willamette River and established Fulquartz Landing at Hess Creek for local farmers to use for transporting their crops on the Willamette.

Ewing Young was one of the earliest settlers on the western side of the Willamette River in the Newberg area, but he died in 1841. By the early 1840s many of the earliest pioneers arriving from the Oregon Trail took donation land claims and established farms in the region.

Yamhill and Carlton

West of Newberg, the town on the North Yamhill River currently known as Yamhill developed as an agricultural and trading center of the Willamette Valley called North Yamhill. It had a sawmill and the first gristmill built in Yamhill County. Sylvanus Moore, George Perkins, and Benjamin Stewart were among the early settlers.

Settlement in the area of present-day Carlton began in 1844 with the arrival of the Peter Smith family. He was instrumental in the organization of the Methodist Episcopal Church and occasionally conducted the services and taught in the school connected with the church.

The Dr. James McBride family was prominent in the area. He traveled throughout the Willamette Valley on horseback tending to the sick.

Grand Ronde Reservation

In 1856 the Grand Ronde Reservation was established on around 60,000 acres of timberland on the eastern side of the Coast Range between southwestern Yamhill County

Dr. William Lysander Adams
(1821–1906)

- Born in Ohio; educated at Bethany College in Virginia
- Arrived at Yamhill in 1848 with his family
- Farmed and taught school; went to California gold fields two times and returned with herd of cattle
- Under a pen name, wrote political satire tract published in 1852 in *The Oregonian* called "Treason, Stratagems, and Spoils"
- Bought his brother Sebastian's donation land claim in Carlton
- Purchased *Oregon Spectator* in 1855 and renamed it *Oregon Argus*; moved his family to Oregon City until 1859 when they returned to their farm
- Credited with moving Oregon public opinion into the anti-slavery camp through his newspaper
- Appointed collector of U.S. Customs in Astoria in 1861; served until 1867
- Studied medicine and law in Philadelphia and received his M.D. and law degrees; practiced medicine in Portland from 1874 to 1877
- Published *A History of Medicine and Surgery from the Earliest Times*, which exposed medical frauds
- Spent final days residing in Hood River
- Married twice; eight children with Frances O. Goodell and two with Mary Susan Mosier

Grand Ronde Reservation drawing in early days. Courtesy of the Salem Public Library, Ben Maxwell Collection, #6076.

Chief Sam, signer of the Rogue Indian treaties of 1853 and 1854. Sketch by Eugène de Girardin at the Grand Ronde Reservation in 1856. Courtesy of the National Archives of Canada, C114436.

and northwestern Polk County. The reservation originally was intended to serve only as a temporary camp until conditions could be stabilized on the nearby Coast Reservation. However, in 1857 President James Buchanan signed an executive order making the temporary encampment a permanent reservation.

In the meantime, in January of 1856, Kalapuya, Molalla, Rogue, Shasta, and Umpqua Indians had been removed to the reservation. Robert Kentta, the Cultural Resource Director for the Confederated Tribes of Siletz, in Part VIII of his series of articles about the history of the Siletz on the tribe's Web site, vividly describes one of the journeys: In the summer of that year, hundreds of additional Indians from southern Oregon were loaded on the deck of the steamship *Columbia* at Port Orford and taken up the coast to the Columbia River. (Two such voyages were made.) From there the ship traveled up the river to Portland. The rest of the trip up the Willamette and Yamhill rivers to the temporary camp at Grand Ronde was made on other boats and barges, and also on foot.

Chief Sam and his band of Rogue Indians included people from both the Shasta and Takelma; they were removed to the Grand Ronde Reservation. The remainder of Upper Rogue Indians were first removed to Grand Ronde and then to the Coast Reservation.

Removed from their ancestral lands where they knew how to subsist on the available natural resources, the reservation Indians at Grand Ronde were largely dependent on the U.S. government for provision of the means to eke out a living. The early conditions on the reservation mirrored those of the Coast Reservation: starvation, disease, violence, hard labor, and restricted movement enforced by the U.S. Army stationed at Fort Yamhill. Many escaped, trying to return to their homelands, but most were tracked down and returned.

The Indians relegated to the Grand Ronde Reservation were largely unaffected by the ongoing settlement and growth of Oregon until the early 20th century when they agreed to the allotment and sale of unallotted lands. In 1954 the federal government terminated recognition of the Grand Ronde and did not reinstate it until 1983 with enactment of the Grand Ronde Restoration Act. In 1988 the U.S. Congress re-established a 9811-acre reservation in the mountains northwest of Grand Ronde in Yamhill County. The headquarters of the Confederated Tribes of the Grand Ronde and their Spirit Mountain Casino, which includes an historical exhibit in the lobby, are located in Grand Ronde in Polk County.

Willamina, Sheridan, Amity, and Wheatland

The first settlers arrived in the area of present-day Willamina and Sheridan in the late 1840s, and included J. N. Branson, James Brown, Charles E. Fendall, and Jeremiah Lamson. A number of the earliest arrivals had moved by the time of the 1860 census, likely due to the proximity of the community to the reservation or perhaps, like the Absalom B. Faulconers, they moved away temporarily so their children could attend school. The Faulconers moved to Spring Valley near Bethel in Polk County, where their children attended the Bethel Institute, returning to Willamina in 1861.

The first post office and precinct district for both communities of Willamina and Sheridan originally used the Willamina name, but changed to Sheridan in the 1860s. A church was organized in 1850 near Sheridan.

Joseph Watt (1817–1890)

- Born in Ohio; first came to Oregon in 1844; returned to Missouri in 1847 to accompany his family to Yamhill County
- Transported sheep and carding machine across the plains, becoming Oregon's first woolen manufacturer by establishing plant on Rickreall Creek in Polk County in 1849
- Financed establishment of Willamette Woolen Company in 1856–58—first woolen mill on Pacific Coast on Mill Creek in Salem
- Made first shipment of wool from Oregon to foreign port and first shipment of Oregon wheat to New York and Liverpool markets—both in 1868
- Married L. A. Lyon; five children

Settlement of Amity started in the late 1840s. Brothers Ahio S. and Joseph Watt, along with Enos C. Williams, were the founders of Amity. Other early settlers included Eugene Breyman, Cyrus Smith, and Jerome B. Walling.

Ahio Watt taught at the log schoolhouse built in 1849 called Amity. The Amity Church of Christ formed in 1846, meeting in members' homes until the schoolhouse was built.

In southeastern Yamhill County, where Wheatland later developed and then waned after the flood of 1861, Daniel Matheny established Matheny's Ferry in 1844. It was the first ferryboat on the Willamette River large enough to carry a wagon and team of oxen or horses. Matheny and his sons operated the ferry for many years before selling it. The ferry still operating today is called the *Daniel Matheny* and is one of the few remaining on the river.

First platted as Atchison, the community of stores, mills, hotels, two warehouses, and a landing later became known as Wheatland—wheat was the main export crop of the area and it was raised on both sides of the river. Albert Zieber was one of the last merchants to vacate the town after the 1861 flood.

George Kirby Gay (1797–1882)

- Born in England; began work as mess boy on ships at age ten
- Arrived in Oregon for first time in 1812 with Wilson Price Hunt Expedition
- Resumed work on sailing ships; returned to Oregon on two separate trips—in 1835 with John Turner party and one with Ewing Young and Willamette Cattle Company in 1837
- Bred herds of Spanish cattle that roamed Yamhill and Polk counties
- Built first brick house west of Rockies in 1841–42 from bricks made from local clay; miniature replica stands on Newell House grounds at Champoeg in Marion County
- Hosted travelers and several of Wolf Meetings which led to 1843 Champoeg meeting and formation of provisional government
- Mined for gold in California in 1848 and once was wealthiest man in Willamette Valley, but died a pauper
- Married three times; eight children

Sampling of Yamhill County Family Surnames in 1859

Chehalem Valley

Adams	Chaplin	Everest	Heater	Kinney	Palmer	Simmons
Agee	Coffin	Ewing	Hembree	Lippincott	Payne	Smith
Baker	Cook	Ferguson	Hendrix	Martin	Perkins	Stagg
Ball	Cooper	Fletcher	Henry	McBride	Perry	Stewart
Baxter	Cowles	Fouts	Hess	Merchant	Ramsey	Stillwell
Bean	Cozine	Fulquartz	Hibbard	Millican	Rogers	Stout
Bird	Crawford	Goodrich	Hubbard	Moore	Rowland	Thompson
Brisbane	Deskins	Graham	Jacobs	Morris	Scott	Walker
Brutscher	Duniway	Green	Johnson	Newby	Shelton	Williams
Campbell	Edson	Hawley	Jones	Olds	Shuck	Woods
Carey						

Willamina, Sheridan, Amity, and Wheatland

Booth	Buffum	Ewing	Lady	Matheny	Walling	Williams
Breyman	Burch	Fendall	Lamson	Sampson	Watt	Yocum
Brown	Chapman	Gay	Lancefield	Smith	Weil	Zieber
Buell	Eades	Graves	Lynch			

Bibliography

Affiliated Tribes of Northwest Indians. *A Travel Guide to Indian Country*. Oregon ed. 2005–2006.

———. Northwest Indian Country. www.tribaltourism.com.

Archer, Howard. *Gresham: The Friendly City*. Gresham, Oregon: Gresham Historical Society, 1967.

Atwood, Kay. "'As Long As the World Goes On': The Table Rocks and the Takelma." *Oregon Historical Quarterly* (Winter 1994–95): 516–533.

———. *Illahe: The Story of Settlement in the Rogue River Canyon*. Ashland, Oregon: self-published, 1978.

———. *Mill Creek Journal: Ashland Oregon 1850–1860*. Ashland, Oregon: self-published, 1987.

———, interviewer and ed. *Recollections: People and the Forest: Oral History Interviews*, vol. 1. Medford, Oregon: Forest Service USDA, Pacific Northwest Region, Rogue River National Forest, 1980.

Aumsville Historical Society. *The History of Our Community: Aumsville, Oregon*. Aumsville, Oregon: Aumsville Historical Society, 2004.

Bakken, Lavola J. *Lone Rock Free State*. Myrtle Creek, Oregon: The Mail Printers, 1970.

Baltimore Colony Centennial Committee. *The Baltimore Colony and Pioneer Recollections*. 2nd ed. N.p.: Baltimore Colony Centennial Committee, 1959, 1985.

Barrett, Carol. *As It Was: Stories from the History of Southern Oregon and Northern California*. Ashland, Oregon: Jefferson Public Radio, 1998.

———. *Women's Roots in Southern Oregon and Northern California*. Medford, Oregon: Jefferson Public Radio, 1993.

Barrett, Fred. *Sea-Mountain: Cascade Head-Salmon River. Anthology: The Oregon Coast*. Portland, Oregon: Alder Press, 1993.

Barton, Lois. *Spencer Butte Pioneers: 100 Years on the Sunny Side of the Butte 1850–1950*. Eugene, Oregon: Spencer Butte Press, 1982.

Bates, Carol. *Scio in the Forks of the Santiam*. N.p.: self-published, 1989.

Beckham, Curt. *Myrtle Point Beginnings*. Myrtle Point, Oregon: self-published, 1986.

―――. *The Myrtle Point Herald's Kurt's Korners*. Myrtle Point, Oregon: The Myrtle Point Herald, 1980.

Beckham, Dow. *Stars in the Dark: Coal Mines of Southwestern Oregon*. Coos Bay, Oregon: Arago Books, 1995.

―――. *Swift Flows the River: Log Driving in Oregon*. Coos Bay, Oregon: Arago Books, 1990.

Beckham, Stephen Dow. *Identifying and Assessing Historical Cultural Resources: Region 6, U.S.F.S.* Portland, Oregon: Forest Service, USDA, Pacific Northwest Region, 1978.

―――. *The Indians of Western Oregon: This Land Was Theirs*. Coos Bay, Oregon: Arago Books, 1977.

―――. *Land of the Umpqua: A History of Douglas County, Oregon*. Roseburg, Oregon: Douglas County Commissioners, 1986.

―――. *Lonely Outpost: The Army's Fort Umpqua*. Reprinted from *Oregon Historical Quarterly*. Portland, Oregon: Oregon Historical Society, 1969.

―――. *Requiem for a People: The Rogue Indians and the Frontiersmen*. Corvallis, Oregon: Oregon State University Press, 1996.

―――. *The Simpsons of Shore Acres*. N.p.: Arago Books, 1971.

Benton County Historical Society & Museum. *A Pictorial History of Benton County*. Corvallis, Oregon: Corvallis Gazette-Times, 2000.

Benton County Parks Department. *Fort Hoskins Historic Park* (brochure). Corvallis, Oregon: Benton County Parks Department, 2006.

Berg, William. *Gearhart Remembered: An Informal History*. Portland, Oregon: Gearhart Homeowners Association, 2001.

Bettis, Stan. *Market Days: An Informal History of the Eugene Producers' Public Market*. Eugene, Oregon: Lane Pomona Grange Fraternal Society, 1969.

Binder, Ardelle Weaver. *Really, Grandpa!* Eugene, Oregon: self-published, 1990.

Black, John and Marguerite. *Ruch (roosh) and the Upper Applegate Valley: An Oregon Documentary*. Medford, Oregon: Webb Research Group, 1989.

Bondinell, Carl. *The Continuing History of Jackson County*. Central Point, Oregon: The Morning News, 1979.

Booth, Richard A. *The Davidsons of Missouri Flat*. Coos Bay, Oregon: B & B Publishing, 2005.

Boulter, Gladys, and Connie Weide Liles. *The Salt of the Earth: Pioneers of Evans Valley*. N.p., 1992.

Bowen, William A. *The Willamette Valley: Migration and Settlement on Oregon Frontier*. Seattle: University of Washington Press, 1978.

Brown, Carroll E. *History of the Rogue River National Forest, Oregon*, vol. 1.

Medford, Oregon: U.S. Forest Service, Rogue River National Forest, 1960.

Brumback, Marion. *Stories of Old Dundee*. Newberg, Oregon: Impressions by Stram, 1981.

Bulkin, Frances E. *Stories of Old Jacksonville*. Medford, Oregon: Confidential Business Agency, 1959.

California State University, San Marcos. Native American Documents Project. http://www.csusm.edu/nadp/

Calkins, D. Ordell. *Ione and Us: Historical Sketches of Ione, Morrison County, Oregon: The Early Years (1899 to 1932)*. Sacramento, California: self-published, 1982.

Canby Herald. *Canby, Oregon: The Early Years*. Canby, Oregon: Canby Herald, 1997.

Carey, Charles H. *General History of Oregon through Early Statehood*. Portland, Oregon: Binford & Mort, 1971.

Carlson, Jen. *Wagon Trains Lead to Roses in December: City of Drain 1859–1959*. N.p.: self-published, 1960.

Carlton Elementary School Bicentennial Club. *Reflections of Carlton: From Pioneer to Present; the Story of Carlton, Oregon*. Carlton, Oregon: n.p., n.d.

Cary, M. S., and P. H. Hainline. *Brownsville*. Brownsville, Oregon: Calapooia Publications, 1976.

———. *Shedd*. Brownsville, Oregon: Calapooia Publications, 1978.

———. *Sweet Home in the Oregon Cascades*. Brownsville, Oregon: Calapooia Publications, 1979.

Case, Robert Ormand. *The Empire Builders*. Portland, Oregon: Binford & Mort, Publishers, 1947.

Castle, Darlene, Brenda Eddleman, Meg Hughes, Riley Hughes, and Paul Thompson. *Yaquina Bay 1778–1978*. Newport, Oregon: Lincoln County Historical Society, 1979.

Chambers, Anne, interviewer. *Recollections: People and the Forest. Oral History Interviews*, vol. 3. Medford, Oregon: Forest Service USDA, Pacific Northwest Region, Rogue River National Forest, 1990.

Chandler, Stephen L. *Cow Creek Valley: From Mi-wa-leta to New Odessa*. Drain, Oregon: self-published, 1981.

Chase, Don M., and Marjorie Neill Helms. *Pack Saddles and Rolling Wheels: The Story of Travel and Transportation in Southern Oregon and Northwest California from 1852*. Crescent City, California: The Del Norte Triplicate, 1959.

Chenoweth, J. V. *The Making of Oakland*. Oakland, Oregon: self-published, 1970.

Chilton, W. R. *Gresham: Stories of Our Past: Campground to City*. Gresham, Oregon: Gresham Historical Society, 1993.

City of Eugene. *Oregon Cultural Resource Inventory: City of Eugene Final Report*. Eugene, Oregon: City of Eugene, 1985.

City of St. Helens. *Nomination for National Historic District*. St. Helens, Oregon: City of St. Helens, 1984.

Clackamas County Historical Society. *Oregon Centennial 1859–1959*. Oregon City: Clackamas County Historical Society, 1959.

———. *Clackamas County Historical 1962–1963*. Oregon City: Clackamas County Historical Society, 1963.

———. *Clackamas County Historical 1968–1969: The "Firsts" of Clackamas County*. Oregon City: Clackamas County Historical Society, 1975.

Clackamas County Policy and Project Development Division. *Clackamas County Cultural Resource Inventory: November 1984*, Book 6. Oregon City: Clackamas County, 1984.

Clark, Cleon L. *History of the Willamette Valley and Cascade Mountain Wagon Road*. Bend, Oregon: Deschutes County Historical Society, 1987.

Clark Jr., Malcolm. *Eden Seekers: The Settlement of Oregon, 1818–1862*. Boston: Houghton Mifflin Company, 1981.

Clatsop-Nehalem Confederated Tribes. Our History. http://www.clatsop-nehalem.com/history.htm

Cleaver, J. D. *Island Origins: Trappers, Traders & Settlers*. Sauvie Island Heritage Series. Portland, Oregon: Oregon Historical Society, 1986.

———. *Two Island Immigrants: The Bybees & the Howells*. Sauvie Island Heritage Series. Portland, Oregon: Oregon Historical Society, 1986.

Clough, Bess A. *1858–1958 Then to Now: One Hundred Years in Canyonville*. Canyonville, Oregon: self-published, 1958.

Columbia County Historical Society. *Columbia County History*, vols. 1, 3–16 (1961, 1963, 1966–77).

Combs, Welcome Martindale, and Sharon Combs Ross. *God Made A Valley*. Camas Valley, Oregon: n.p., n.d.

Comerford, Jane. *At the Foot of the Mountain*. Portland, Oregon: Dragonfly Press, 2004.

The Confederated Tribes of Grand Ronde. Culture. http://www.grandronde.org/culture/

Confederated Tribes of Siletz. Siletz History, by Robert Kentta. http://ctsi.nsn.us/History_and_Culture.html.

Confederated Tribes of the Coos-Lower Umpqua-Siuslaw. Culture: Culture & History. http://216.128.13.185/CTCLUSINEW/Culture/CultureHistory/tabid/228/Default.aspx.

The Confederated Tribes of the Umatilla Indian Reservation. Our History and Culture. http://www.umatilla.nsn.us/history.html.

The Confederated Tribes of Warm Springs. Tribal Community: History and Culture. http://www.warmsprings.com/warmsprings/Tribal_Community/History__Culture/.

Coquille Indian Tribe. http://www.coquilletribe.org.

Corning, Howard McKinley, ed. *Dictionary of Oregon History*. Portland, Oregon: Binford & Mort Publishing, 2004.

———. *Willamette Landings: Ghost Towns of the River*. Portland, Oregon: Oregon Historical Society, 1973.

Cow Creek Band of Umpqua Tribe of Indians. The Cow Creek / Umpqua Story. http://www.cowcreek.com/story/index.html.

Creswell Area Historical Society. *Creswell's Centennial 1873–1973*. N.p.: Creswell Area Historical Society, 1973.

Crook County Historical Society. *The History of Crook County, Oregon*. Prineville, Oregon: Crook County Historical Society, 1981.

Crutchfield, James A. *It Happened in Oregon*. Guilford, Connecticut: The Globe Pequot Press, 1994.

Culp, Edwin D. *Oregon: The Way It Was*. Caldwell, Idaho: The Caxton Printers, Ltd., 1981.

Daley, Venita. *The Rogue River Valley's Early History*. Medford, Oregon: Mail Tribune, 1948.

Darneille, Dorothy. "Wilderville: A Way of Life." *The Oldtimer*. Kerby, Oregon: The Oldtimer, 1962.

Daughters of the American Revolution, Oregon Society. *Oregon Historic Landmarks: Willamette Valley*. Portland, Oregon: Oregon Society, Daughters of the American Revolution, 1963.

———. *Oregon Historic Landmarks: Willamette Valley*. Portland, Oregon: Oregon Society, Daughters of the American Revolution, 1971.

Decker, Edith. *The Pictorial History of Josephine County*. Portland, Oregon: Pediment Publishers, 1998.

De Marco, Gordon. *A Short History of Portland*. San Francisco: Lexikos, 1990.

Dennon, Jim. "Jennie Michel, Clatsop Celebrity." *Cumtux* 8, no. 4 (Fall 1988).

Dimon, Elizabeth F. *Twas Many Years Since: 100 Years in the Waverly Area 1847–1947*. Milwaukie, Oregon: self-published, 1981.

Dodds, Linda S., and Nancy A. Olson. *Cedar Mill History*. Portland, Oregon: self-published, 1986.

Dodge, Orvil Ovando. *Pioneer History of Coos and Curry Counties, Or.: Heroic Deeds and Thrilling Adventures of the Early Settlers*. 2nd ed. Bandon, Oregon: Coos-Curry Pioneer and Historical Association 1969. (1st ed. 1898)

Douglas County Planning Department. *Historic Resources of the City of Myrtle Creek, Oregon*. Roseburg, Oregon: Douglas County Planning Department, 1984.

Douthit, Nathan. *A Guide to Oregon South Coast History: Traveling the Jedediah Smith Trail*. Corvallis, Oregon: Oregon State University Press, 1999.

———. *Uncertain Encounters: Indians and Whites at Peace and War in Southern Oregon: 1820s to 1860s*. Corvallis, Oregon: Oregon State University Press, 2002.

Down, Robert Horace. *A History of the Silverton Country*. Portland, Oregon: The Berncliff Press, 1926.

Dunn, Joy B., ed. *Land in Common: An Illustrated History of Jackson County, Oregon*. Medford, Oregon: Southern Oregon Historical Society, 1993.

Edwards, Patricia Ann, Nancy Seales O'Hearn, and Marna Lee Hing. *Sawdust & Cider: A History of Lorane, Oregon and the Siuslaw Valley*. N.p.: self-published, 1987.

Elliott, Roy A. *Profiles of Progress: Linn County, Oregon*. Eugene, Oregon: self-published, 1971.

End of the Oregon Trail Interpretive Center. http://www.endoftheoregontrail.org/.

Endres, Maxine. *A View of the Valley: Willamina, Oregon—The Beginning 1843–1881*. Lafayette, Oregon: Yamhill County Historical Society, 2000.

Engeman, Richard H. *The Jacksonville Story*. Jacksonville, Oregon: Southern Oregon Historical Society, Inc., 1980.

Estacada City Hall. *Comments and Analysis of Historic Resources with Historical Background July 1991: Clackamas County Historical Resources Inventory 1989–92*. Estacada, Oregon: City of Estacada.

Fagan, D. D. *The Yaquina Bay Country and Its People: As Recorded by D. D. Fagan in 1885*. Newport, Oregon: Lincoln County Historical Society, 1959.

Flora, Stephanie. The Oregon Territory and its Pioneers. http://www.oregonpioneers.com/ortrail.htm.

Fowler, Connie, and J. B. Roberts. *Buncom: Crossroads Station: An Oregon Ghost Town's Gift from the Past*. Jacksonville, Oregon: Buncom Historical Society, 1995.

The Friends of South Slough. *South Slough Adventures: Life on a Southern Oregon Estuary*. Coos Bay, Oregon: The Friends of South Slough, 1995.

Fulton, Ann. *Banks: A Darn Good Little Town*. Banks, Oregon: self-published, 1995.

———. *Iron, Wood & Water: An Illustrated History of Lake Oswego*. San Antonio, Texas: Historical Publishing Network, 2002.

Gallagher, Mary Kathryn. *City of Lebanon Historic Context Statement*, Part 1. Lebanon, Oregon: City of Lebanon, 1994.

———. *Historic Context Statement: City of Corvallis, Oregon*. Corvallis, Oregon: National Park Service, U.S. Department of Interior, 1993.

Gault, Vera Whitney. *A Brief History of Astoria Oregon 1811–1900*. Astoria, Oregon: Bruce Berney, 1996.

Genaw, Linda Morehouse. *Gold Hill and Its Neighbors Along the River*. Central Point, Oregon: self-published, 1988.

———, and Richard C. Morgan. *At the Crossroads: A History of Central Point 1850–1900*. Central Point, Oregon: self-published, 1989.

Gillette, Preston W. "Stories of Clatsop." *Cumtux* 14, no. 4 (Fall 1994).

Haines, Francis D., and V. S. Smith. *Gold on Sterling Creek, a Century of Placer Mining*. Medford, Oregon: Gandee Print Center, 1964.

Hanson, Inez Stafford. *Life on "Clatsop"*. Seaside, Oregon: self published, n.d.

Harmon, Rick, ed. "Aspects of Southern Oregon History." Special issue, *Oregon Historical Quarterly* (Winter 1994–95).

Harpham, Joseph Evans. *Doorways Into History*. Eugene, Oregon: self-published, 1966.

Hawkins III, William J., and William F. Willingham. *Classic Houses of Portland, Oregon 1850–1950*. Portland, Oregon: Timber Press, 2005.

Hegne, Barbara Morehouse. *A Journey Back: Eagle Point, Lake Creek, Brownsboro, Climax*. Sparks, Nevada: self-published, 1990.

———. *Settling the Rogue Valley: The Tough Times—The Forgotten People*. N.p.: self-published, 1995.

———. *Unforgettable Pioneers*. N.p.: self-published, 1987.

Hill, Edna May. *Josephine County Historical Highlights*. Grants Pass, Oregon: Josephine County Library System and Josephine County Historical Society, 1976.

Hodges, M. Constance. *Lords of Themselves*. N.p.: Delcon Historical Publications, 1978.

Hood River Historical Society. *History of Hood River*. Hood River, Oregon: Hood River Historical Society, 1982.

Horn, Huston, and Editors of Time-Life Books. *The Pioneers*. (Old West Series). Alexandria, Virginia: Time-Life, 1975.

Hussey, J. A. *Champoeg: Place of Transition*. Portland, Oregon: Oregon Historical Society, 1967.

Ingle, Ronald E. *Oasis in the Desert: The Story of Hermiston from Sagebrush to City*. Caldwell, Idaho: self-published, 2002.

Inman, Leroy B. *Early Days…on the McKenzie*. Roseburg, Oregon: self-published, 1992.

John F. Kennedy Middle School T.A.G. Class. *Bailey Hill: Past and Present*. Eugene, Oregon: Eugene School District 4J, 1985.

Johnson, Olga Weydemeyer. *They Settled in Applegate Country: Frontier Days along the Lower Applegate River in Southern Oregon*. Grants Pass, Oregon: self-published, 1978.

Joyner, Janet, interviewer. *Recollections: People and the Forest. Oral History Interviews*, vol. 2. Medford, Oregon: Forest Service USDA, Pacific Northwest Region, Rogue River National Forest, 1990.

Justen-Satterwhite, Betty. "A Walluski Pioneer." *Cumtux* 4, no. 1 (Winter 1986).

Kent, William Eugene. *The Siletz Indian Reservation: 1855–1900*. Portland, Oregon: Portland State University, 1973.

Kittel, Joanne, and Suzanne Curtis. *Early Yachats History: The Yachats Indians, Origins of the Yachats Name, and the Reservation Years*. N.p.: 1996.

The Klamath Tribes. History. http://www.klamathtribes.org/history.html.

Knuth, Priscilla. *"Picturesque" Frontier: The Army's Fort Dalles*. Portland, Oregon: Oregon Historical Society Press, 1967.

Koler/Morrison Planning Consultants. *City of Lake Oswego: Cultural Resources Inventory 1989*. Lake Oswego, Oregon: City of Lake Oswego, 1989.

———. *A Survey and Inventory of Historic Resources: City of Seaside, Oregon*. Oregon City: Koler/Morrison Planning Consultants, 1987.

Krambeal, Gaynell. *A History of Eagle Point and Surrounding Communities*, vol. 1. N.p., 1979.

Kramer, George. *Historic Context Statement for the City of Talent, Oregon*. Ashland, Oregon: City of Talent, June 1994.

Kruse, Anne Applegate. *The Halo Trail*. Yoncalla, Oregon: self-published, 1954.

Lake Oswego Public Library. *In Their Own Words: Reminiscences of Early Lake Oswego*. Lake Oswego, Oregon: City of Lake Oswego, 1976.

Lane County Historical Society. *Yesterday's Adventure: A Photographic History of Lane County, Oregon*. Eugene, Oregon: Lane County Historical Society, 1998.

League of Women Voters of McMinnville, Oregon. *McMinnville: Into the Second 100 Years*. McMinnville, Oregon: League of Women Voters of McMinnville, 1971.

Lebanon Museum Committee. *A Brief Historical Sketch of Lebanon Oregon*. N.p., 1942.

Lee, G. H. *Something about Sutherlin*. Sutherlin, Oregon: self-published, 1990.

Lockley, Fred. "Interview with Mrs. George Flavel." *Cumtux* 7, no. 1 (Winter 1986).

Lossner, Ann. *Looking Back: People and Places in Early Keizer Area*. Keizer, Oregon: self-published, 1990.

Lowenstein, Steven. *The Jews of Oregon 1850–1950*. Portland, Oregon: Jewish Historical Society of Oregon, 1987.

Lower Umpqua Historical Society. *Official Bicentennial Project of the Lower Umpqua Historical Society: Reedsport, Oregon: Pictorial History of the Lower Umpqua*. Reedsport, Oregon: Lower Umpqua Historical Society, 1976.

Loy, William G., Stuart Allan, Aileen R. Buckley, and James E. Meacham. *Atlas of Oregon*. Eugene, Oregon: University of Oregon Press, 2001.

Madison, Leona Spayde. *The Saga of the Kellogg Crescent: A History of the Land and People Along Oregon's Umpqua River 1543–1988*. Oakland, Oregon: Crescent Press, 1989.

Mapes, Virginia. *Chakeipi "The Place of the Beaver": The History of Beaverton, Oregon*. Tigard, Oregon: Community Newspapers, Inc., 1993.

Martinazzi, Loyce, and Karen Lafky Nygaard. *Tualatin: From the Beginning*. Tualatin, Oregon: Tualatin Historic Society, 1994.

McArthur, Scott. *Monmouth, Oregon: The Saga of a Small American Town*. Monmouth, Oregon: self-published, 2004.

McCormick, Gail J. *Our Proud Past*, vol. 1. Mulino, Oregon: Gail J. McCormick Publishing Company, 1992.

McKay, Harvey J. *St. Paul, Oregon 1830–1890*. Portland, Oregon: Binford & Mort, 1980.

McKean, Samuel T. "Memoirs of Samuel T. McKean." *Cumtux* 13, no. 1 (Winter 1992).

McLagan, Elizabeth, and The Oregon Black History Project. *A Peculiar Paradise: A History of Blacks in Oregon, 1788–1940*. Portland, Oregon: Georgian Press Company, 1980.

McLane, Larry L. *First There Was Twogood: A Pictorial History of Northern Josephine County*. Sunny Valley, Oregon: Sexton Enterprises, 1995.

McWade, John. "Lone Ranch Borax Mine" in *Curry County Echoes*, vol. 1 (1973–1974). Bandon, Oregon: The Curry County Historical Society, 1978.

Meinig, D. W. *The Great Columbia Plain: A Historical Geography 1805–1910*. Seattle: University of Washington Press, 1995.

Miles, John, and Richard R. Milligan. *Linn County, Oregon: Pioneer Settlers— Oregon Territory Donation Land Claim Families to 1855*, vols. 1–10. Albany, Oregon: Linn Benton Genealogical Services, 1983.

Minter, Harold A. *Umpqua Valley Oregon and Its Pioneers*. Portland, Oregon: Binford & Mort Publishers, 1967.

MyFamily.com, Inc. http://www.rootsweb.com/~websites/usa/oregon.html.

National Park Service. U.S. Department of the Interior. http://www.nps.gov/state/or/.

News-Times. *The First 100 Years Lincoln County 1893–1993*. Newport, Oregon: News-Times, February, 1992.

Newton, Sidney W. *Early History of Independence, Oregon*. Salem, Oregon: self-published, 1971.

Nichols, Rodger, and Dan Spatz. *A Sesquicentennial History of Wasco County*. The Dalles, Oregon: The Dalles Chronicle, 2004.

Nielson, Carole. *People and Stories of the Rogue River Country: Yesterday and Today*. N.p.: n.d.

Nolan, Edward W. *Coburg Remembered*. Eugene, Oregon: Lane County Historical Society, 1982.

North Lincoln Pioneer and Historical Association. *Pioneer History of North Lincoln County, Oregon*, vol. 1. McMinnville, Oregon: The Telephone Register Publishing Company, 1951.

Northwest College of the Bible. Pioneer History to about 1900. http://ncbible.org/nwh/orhistmenu.html.

O'Donnell, Terence. *That Balance So Rare: The Story of Oregon*. Portland, Oregon: Oregon Historical Society Press, 1988.

———. *An Arrow in the Earth: General Joel Palmer and the Indians of Oregon*. Portland, Oregon: Oregon Historical Society Press, 1991.

———. *Cannon Beach: A Place by the Sea*. Portland, Oregon: Oregon Historical Society Press, 1996.

O'Hara, Marjorie. *Ashland the First 130 Years*. Ashland, Oregon: Northwest Passages Publishing Inc., 1986.

The Old Mill RV Park & Event Center. Garibaldi and the Old Mill History. http://www.oldmill.us/html/history.html.

Olkowski, Virginia S. *Heirloom Homesteads: A Guide to Historic Homes in Eugene, Oregon*. Eugene, Oregon: Heirloom Homesteads, 1993.

Oregon Historical Society. http://www.ohs.org/.

The Oregonian Staff. *The Oregon Story 1850–2000*. Portland, Oregon: Graphic Arts Center Publishing, 2000.

Oregon Parks and Recreation Dept: Heritage Programs: Oregon Heritage Commission. Oregon's Statehood Sesquicentennial. http://www.oregon.gov/OPRD/HCD/OHC/statehood.shtml.

Oregon Secretary of State. Oregon State Archives. Echoes of Oregon History, 1837–1859. http://arcweb.sos.state.or.us/echoes/defaultechoes.html.

Oregon State Archives. Oregon Blue Book. http://bluebook.state.or.us/cultural/history/history.htm.

The Outlook. *A Pictorial History of East Multnomah County*. Portland, Oregon: Pediment Publishing, 1998.

Peters, Vera, ed. *Remembering Our Childhood: A Pictorial History of Gresham, Oregon*, vol. 1. Gresham, Oregon: Gresham Pioneers, 1984.

Peterson Del Mar, David. *Oregon's Promise: An Interpretive History*. Corvallis, Oregon: Oregon State University Press, 2003.

Peterson, Emil R., and Alfred Powers. *A Century of Coos and Curry*. Portland, Oregon: Binford & Mort, Publishers, 1952.

Pfefferle, Ruth. *Golden Days and Pioneer Ways*. Grants Pass, Oregon: Bulletin Publishing Company, 1995.

Polley, Louis E. *A History of the Mohawk Valley and Early Lumbering*. Marcola, Oregon: Polley Publishing, 1984.

Pompey, Sherman Lee. *A History of Boston, the Town that Moved West to Become Shedd in Linn County, Oregon*. Harrisburg, Oregon: Pacific Specialties, 1974.

Port, Ranger Lee. *Notes on Historical Events: Applegate Ranger District*. Medford, Oregon: Rogue River National Forest, 1945.

Potter, Miles F. *Oregon's Golden Years: Bonanza of the West*. Caldwell, Idaho: The Caxton Printers, Ltd., 1982.

Potts, Robert. *Remembering When: A Photo Collection of Historic Albany, Oregon*. Albany, Oregon: Albany Regional Museum, 1992.

Prantl, Mrs. Carl (Annabell). *City of Gervais: One Hundred Years as an Incorporated City 1878–1978*. Gervais, Oregon: City of Gervais, Centennial Committee, 1978.

Pruitt, Claudette Morning. *Come Take a Historic Journey … along the Galice Trail*. Grants Pass, Oregon: Morning Creek Enterprises, 2004.

Pursley, Edward. *Florence: A Diamond Set Among the Pearls*. Florence, Oregon: The Siuslaw News and Oregon Coast Printing and Publishing Company, 1989.

Rees, Helen Guyton. *Fairview: On Duck Lane*. Fairview, Oregon: self-published, 1988.

The Register Guard. *Looking Back Lane County: A Pictorial Retrospect*. Eugene, Oregon: The Register Guard, 2005.

Reynolds, Susan P. *Historical Overview of the Alsea/Lobster Valley Region of Benton County, Oregon*. Philomath, Oregon: Benton County Historical Society, 1993.

Riddle, George W. *History of Early Days in Oregon*. Riddle, Oregon: The Riddle Enterprise, 1920.

Ringhand, Harry E. *Marie Dorian and the Trail of the Pioneers*. Milton Freewater, Oregon: Valley Herald, Inc., 1971.

Robbins, William G. *Hard Times in Paradise: Coos Bay, Oregon 1850–1986*. Seattle: University of Washington Press, 1988.

Ross, George W., Joan Campbell, and Sandra Wilson. *The Blue Valley: A History of Creswell*. Creswell, Oregon: Creswell Area Historical Society, 1993.

Salem Public Library. Salem Online History. http://www.salemhistory.net/.

Satterfield, Archie. *The Tillamook Way: A History of the Tillamook County Creamery Association*. Tillamook, Oregon: Tillamook Creamery, 2000.

Schroeder, Walt. *They Found Gold on the Beach: History of Central Curry County—An Oregon Documentary*. Gold Beach, Oregon: Curry County Historical Society Press, 1999.

Schwantes, Carlos Arnaldo. *Long Day's Journey: The Steamboat & Stagecoach Era in the Northern West*. Seattle: University of Washington Press, 1999.

Shampine, Irene L. *Williams Memories*. Williams, Oregon: self-published, 1978.

Smith, John E. *Bethel, Polk County, Oregon*. Corvallis, Oregon: self-published, 1941.

Smith, Reiba Carter, and Louetta Zumwalt Shaw. *In the Land of Bunch Grass, Gold and Trees*. Long Creek, Oregon: Long Creek Light, n.d.

Smith, R. Gess. A Place Called Oregon. http://gesswhoto.com/

Snyder, Eugene E. *Early Portland: Stump-Town Triumphant: Rival Townsites on the Willamette, 1831–1854*. Portland, Oregon: Binford & Mort, Publishers, 1970.

———. *Skidmore's Portland: His Fountain & Its Sculptor—From Buckboards to Bustles*. Portland, Oregon: Binford & Mort, Publishers, 1973.

———. *We Claimed This Land: Portland's Pioneer Settlers*. Portland, Oregon: Binford & Mort Publishing, 1989.

Southern Oregon Historical Society. http://www.sohs.org/Index.asp.

The South Umpqua Historical Society. *Pioneer Days in the South Umpqua Valley*, vols. 5–13. Canyonville, Oregon: The Society, 1975–1980.

Spencer, Omar C. *The Story of Sauvies Island*. Portland, Oregon: Binfords & Mort for the Oregon Historical Society, 1950.

Statesman Journal. *A Pictorial History of the Willamette Valley*. Portland, Oregon: Pediment Group, 1997.

Steele, Harvey. *Hyas Tyee: The United States Customs Service in Oregon, 1848–1989*. N.p.: Department of the Treasury, U.S. Customs Service Pacific Region, n.d.

Stein, Harry H. *Salem: A Pictorial History of Oregon's Capital*. Norfolk, Virginia: Donning Company/Publishers, 1981.

Steinbacher, Martha. *In the Beginning: East Linn County Echoes*. Sweet Home, Oregon: self-published, 1979.

———. *Images of America: Sweet Home in Linn County: New Life, New Land*. Chicago, Illinois: Arcadia Publishing, 2002.

———. *Yesterday's Memories: East Linn Museum Echoes*. N.p.: East Linn Museum, 2000.

Strain, Patti Boice. *Floras Creek Precinct and the Boice Family of Curry County*. Myrtle Point, Oregon: self-published, 2003.

Street, Willard, and Elsie Street. *Sailors' Diggings*. Wilderville, Oregon: Wilderville Press, 1973.

Suttles, Wayne. ed., *Handbook of North American Indians: Northwest Coast*, vol. 7. Washington, D.C.: Smithsonian Institution, 1992.

Sutton, Jack. *110 Years with Josephine: The History of Josephine County, Oregon 1856–1966*. Grants Pass, Oregon: Josephine County Historical Society, 1967.

Swanson, Rev. Fred L. *Centennial Jubilee History: First Presbyterian Church Brownsville, Oregon, 1857–1957*. Brownsville, Oregon: Order of Session, 1964.

Tartar, Lena Belle. *Chronicles from Pedee, Oregon*. Corvallis, Oregon: Continuing Education Publications, 1974.

Tess, John M. *Uphill Downhill Yamhill: The Evolution of the Yamhill Historic District in Portland, Oregon*. Portland, Oregon: National Trust for Historic Preservation, 1977.

Thompson, Roger Knowles. *John Bonser and His Family*. Issaquah, Washington: Issaquah Historical Society 2001. Issaquah History On-Line. http://www.issaquahhistory.org/.

Tonn, Frances Wilson. *Sams Valley History*. Eugene, Oregon: University of Oregon Extension Monitor, 1925.

Trinklein, Michael. The Oregon Trail. http://www.isu.edu/%7Etrinmich/Oregontrail.html.

Tweedell, Bob. *Millrace History*. Reprint. Eugene, Oregon: The Register-Guard, n.d.

Tweedt, Bess. *Historic Harrisburg: A Little Town on the Willamette River*. Harrisburg, Oregon: self-published, 1994.

Umatilla County Historical Society. *Umatilla County: A Backward Glance*. Pendleton, Oregon: Umatilla County Historical Society, 1981.

U.S. National Archives and Records Administration. The National Archives. http://www.archives.gov/.

Velasco, Dorothy, and Lane County Historical Society. *Lane County: An Illustrated History of Emerald Empire*. Northridge, California: Windsor Publications, Inc., 1985.

————, and Mara Velasco. *Springfield Between Two Rivers: An Illustrated History*. Montgomery, Alabama: Community Communications, Inc., 1999.

Walker Jr., Deward E., ed., *Handbook of North American Indians: Plateau*, vol. 12. Washington, D.C.: Smithsonian Institution, 1998.

Walling, Albert G. *History of Southern Oregon, Comprising Jackson, Josephine, Douglas, Curry and Coos Counties*. Portland, Oregon: self-published, 1884.

Watts, James Loring. *The History of Scappoose*. Scappoose, Oregon: Grant Watts Parent Organization, 1984.

Webber, Bert and Margie. *Jacksonville, Oregon: The Making of a National Historic Landmark*. Fairfield, Washington: Ye Galleon Press, 1982.

Wheeler, L. M. *History of Linn County, Oregon*. N.p.: Linn County Pioneer Memorial Association, 1982.

Wild Rivers History Partners. *Highway to History: 101 Historic Miles along America's Wild Rivers Coast*. Brookings, Oregon: Wild Rivers History Partners, 2003.

Winterbotham, Jerry. *Umpqua: The Lost County of Oregon*. Brownsville, Oregon: self-published, 1994.

Workers of the Writers' Program of the Work Projects Administration in the State of Oregon. *Oregon: End of the Trail*. Portland, Oregon: Binfords & Mort, 1940.

Writers Discussion Group. *Golden Was the Past 1850–1970: Cottage Grove*. Cottage Grove, Oregon: Sentinel Print Shop, 1970.

Wyatt, Steve M. *Taft: Transformation of a Waterfront Community to a Resort Town—Cultural Resource Inventory*. Taft, Oregon: City of Taft, n.d.

Yamhill County Historical Society. *Old Yamhill: The Early History of Its Towns and Cities*. Lafayette, Oregon: Yamhill County Historical Society, 1976.

The Yoncalla Historical Society. *Yoncalla Yesterday*. Yoncalla: The Yoncalla Historical Society, 2001.

Zerzyke, Anna. *The Story of Rainier 1805 to 1925*. Rainier, Oregon: self-published, 1925.

Index

Lovejoy, Asa L. and Elizabeth McGary, 36, 64, 67, 188
Lowe, Thomas, 177
Lowe, Thompson, 100
Lowery, James M., 135
Lownsdale, Daniel H., 185, 189, 191–192
Lucas, Daniel, 154
Lucas, Thomas H., 200
Lucier, Etienne, 176
Luelling, Henderson, 32, 68, 70, 127, 235
Luse, Henry, 97
Lyle, John, 197
Lyman, Horace, 191

MacEwan, Robert S., 83
Mack, William and Louisa, 73
Macksburg, 73
Macy, William, 29, 231, 233
Madras, 236
Malheur County, 239–240
Malo, Fabian, 178
Manifest Destiny, 17
Marcy, Randolph B., 28
Marion County, 74, 170–183
Marion County Family Surnames, 183
Marlan, Henry, 84
Marple, P. B., 36
Marsh, Josiah, 228
Marsh, Sidney Harper, 253
Martin, Charles G., 153
Masterson, William A., 146, 149
Matheny, Daniel, 264
Matthieu, Francois X., 177
McBride, James, 261
McBride, John R., 36
McCarver, Morton Matthew, 60, 64–65, 192
McClosky, John, 67
McCormick, S. J., 36
McCully, Asa A., 167
McCully, David, 167
McCully, J. W., 125
McDaniel, John, 132
McDonald, Finan, 231, 238

McHaley, John, 181
McInnish, E. B., 162
McKay, J. B., 176
McKay, James, 253
McKay, Malcolm, 90
McKay, Thomas, 90, 231, 238
McKenzie, Donald, 61, 146
McKenzie, Isaac, 249
McKinlay, Archibald, 177
McKinney, John, 165
McLeod, Alexander Roderick, 96, 103, 110, 146
McLoughlin, John and Marguerite Wadin McKay, 19–20, 60, 61, 64, 176
McManus, Patrick F., 122, 127
McMinnville, 257, 258, 260–261
McMurry, Fielden, 149
Medford, 121, 122
Meek, Joseph L., 30, 34, 176, 231, 251
Meek, Stephen H. L., 28, 29, 111, 192, 230, 231, 233
Meek, William, 70
Mehl, Gottlieb, 221
Meier, Aaron, 190
Meigs, Charles R., 36
Memaloose Island, 224, 228
Menefee, William R., 229
Merlin, 136, 141
Merrill, Joseph, 92
Merriman, William, 132
Metcalfe, Robert, 210
Metzger, William, 36
Michel, Jennie, 79
Mill City, 158, 162
Miller, Augustus F., 105
Miller, Cincinnatus H. "Joaquin", 150, 151
Miller, George, 151
Miller, Hulin, 151
Miller, James, 219
Miller, Richard, 36
Miller, Samuel S., 182
Miller, Theresa Dyer (Minnie Myrtle), 150
Mills, William, 252

Milton, 87, 88–89
Milton Freewater, 242, 244
Milwaukie, 60, 61, 68–70, 75, 127, 191, 235
Mission Bottom, 20, 172, 175
missions, missionaries, 43, 68, 173, 174
    American Board of Commissioners for Foreign Missions, 22, 226
    Clatsop Mission, 21, 78, 83
    Lee, Daniel (see Lee, Daniel)
    Lee, Jason (see Lee, Jason)
    Saint Anne Mission, 21
    Wascopam Mission, 21, 226, 227, 228
    Whitman, Marcus (see Whitman, Marcus)
    Whitman Mission (Waiilatpu Mission), 22, 226
    Willamette Mission (Mission Bottom and Salem), 16, 20, 171, 175, 176
Molalla, 36, 60, 73, 75
Molalla Prairie, 59, 60
Monmouth, 199, 200, 201
Monroe, 41, 50, 52–53, 55
Monteith, Thomas and Christine M. Dunbar, 158–160
Monteith, Walter, 158–160
Moore, Charles, 201
Moore, Isaac R., 36, 161
Moore, Robert, 66
Moore, Sylvanus, 261
Morgan, Peter, 208
Moro, 241
Morris, A. P., 164
Morrison, John L., 188
Morrow County, 240–241
Mosby, Dave, 153
Mosier, Jonah H., 228–229
"Mother of Oregon" (Brown), 252
"Mother of Oregon" (Yamhill County), 257
Mountain Men, 19, 20, 30, 176, 207, 251

Willamette Cattle Company, 30, 38, 264

Willamette Meridian, 31

Willamette River, 47, 148, 153, 175–176

    Indians, 17, 50, 59, 60, 61, 157, 187, 251

    transportation, 27, 41, 49, 69, 74, 146, 160, 167–168, 171, 176–177, 185 192, 257, 261

Willamina, 258, 263, 265

Williams, former Williamsburg, 140, 143

Williams, Enos C., 264

Williams, George H., 36, 198

Williams, Moses, 129

Williamson, Robert S., 225, 230

Wilson, Henry W. and Veronica Manning, 208

Wilson, John, 167

Wilson, W. H., 219

Wilson Price Hunt Expedition, 19, 229, 239, 241, 242, 245, 264

Wilsonville, 60, 74, 75

Winchester, 49, 109, 113–114, 119, 213

Winchester, F. C., 91

Winship, Nathan, 87

Wolf Meetings, 30, 33, 83, 177, 264

Wood, Sidney, 92

Woodson, former Wood's Landing, 92, 93

Woodward, Luther T., 163

Wool, John E., 223

Wright, Lazarus, 116

Wright, Milton, 182

Wyeth, Nathaniel J., 20, 208, 229, 231, 241

Yachats, 56, 217

Yamhill, former North Yamhill, 261

Yamhill County, 30, 45, 50, 199, 202, 256–265

Yamhill County Family Surnames, 265

Yaudes, George, 127

Yaudes, Mathias, 127

Yoncalla, 214, 218–220

York, Emily J., 173

Young, Charles W., 151

Young, E. G., 115

Young, Ewing, 30, 33, 110, 123, 261, 264

Young, Nicholas A., 132

Zieber, Albert, 264

Zumwalt, Solomon and Nancy, 150

Jeff Marschner

JANICE MARSCHNER was born and raised in the San Francisco Bay area and has lived in Sacramento since 1973. She
and her husband have two grown children. Her parents grew
up in Eugene, Oregon, and Marschner spent many summers visiting her grandmother in Eugene and other relatives
in the Eugene and Portland areas.

She graduated from the University of California, Davis, in
International Relations and earned a Masters in Public Policy and Administration at California State University, Sacramento. Before taking an early retirement to concentrate on
her love of research and writing, she worked for a state senator and as a legislative analyst for the State of California.

Her first book, *California 1850: A Snapshot in Time*, com-
memorated California's sesquicentennial in 2000. Her second book, *California's Arab Americans*, documented for the
first time the contributions of California's early pioneers
from the Arab world.

She and her husband, Jeff Marschner, visit Oregon regularly and spent a year exploring its rich history in the hope
that others could use this book to do the same.